A TREASURY OF FAVORITES

scrapbook
TIPS & TECHNIQUES

Presenting over 700 of the best scrapbooking
ideas from *Creating Keepsakes* publications.

PRODUCED EXCLUSIVELY FOR LEISURE ARTS

CREATING Keepsakes

Founding Editor	Lisa Bearnson
Co-founder	Don Lambson
Editor-in-Chief	Tracy White
Special Projects Editor	Leslie Miller
Copy Editor	Kim Sandoval
Editorial Assistants	Joannie McBride, Fred Brewer
Administrative Assistant	Michelle Bradshaw
Art Director	Brian Tippetts
Designer	Joleen Hughes
Production Designers	Just Scan Me!, Exposure Graphics
Publisher	Mark Seastrand
Media Relations	Alicia Bremer, 801/364-2030
Director of Sales and Marketing	Tara Green
Web Site Manager	Emily Johnson
Assistant Web Site Editor	Sarah Thatcher
Production Manager	Gary Whitehead
Business Sales Assistants	Jacque Jensen, Melanie Cain
Advertising Sales Manager	Becky Lowder
Advertising Sales, West Coast	Debbie Hanni, 801/583-1043
Advertising Sales, West Central	Barbara Tanner, 801/942-6080
Advertising Sales, East Central	Jenny Grothe, 801/377-1428
Advertising Sales, East Coast	RaNay Winter, 801/796-7037
Wholesale Accounts	800/815-3538

Donna Hair, stores A–G,
and outside of U.S., ext. 235

Victoria James, stores H–R, ext. 226

Kristin Schaefer, stores S–Z
(except "Scr"), ext. 250

Sherrie Burt, stores starting with "Scr,"
ext. 244

Kim Robison, distributor accounts, ext. 251

PRIMEDIA
Consumer Magazine & Internet Group

Vice President, Group Publisher	David O'Neil
Circulation Marketing Directors	Dena Spar, Janice Martin
Promotions Director	Dana Smith

PRIMEDIA, Inc.

Chairman	Dean Nelson
President & CEO	Kelly Conlin
Vice-Chairman	Beverly C. Chell

PRIMEDIA Consumer Media and Magazine Group

Chief Operating Officer	Daniel E. Aks
EVP, Consumer Marketing/Circulation	Steve Aster
SVP, Chief Financial Officer	David P. Kirchhoff
SVP, Mfg., Production & Distribution	Kevin Mullan
SVP, Finance	Kevin Neary
SVP, Chief Information Officer	Debra C. Robinson
SVP, Consumer Marketing	Bobbi Gutman
VP, Manufacturing	Gregory Catsaros
VP, Business Development	Jasja de Smedt
VP, Direct Response & Classified Advertising	Carolyn N. Everson
VP, Single Copy Sales	Thomas L. Fogarty
VP, Manufacturing Budgets & Operations	Lilia Golia
VP, Database / e-Commerce	Suti Prakash

PRIMEDIA Outdoor Recreation and Enthusiast Group

SVP, Group Publishing Director	Brent Diamond
VP, Comptroller	Stephen H. Bender
VP, Marketing and Internet Operations	Dave Evans
VP, Human Resources	Kathleen P. Malinowski

SUBSCRIPTIONS

To subscribe to *Creating Keepsakes* magazine or to change the address of your current subscription, call or write:

Phone: 888/247-5282

International: 760/745-2809

Fax: 760/745-7200

Subscriber Services

Creating Keepsakes

P.O. Box 469007

Escondido, CA 92046-9007

Some back issues of *Creating Keepsakes* magazine are available for $5 each, payable in advance.

NOTICE OF LIABILITY

The information in this book is distributed on an "as is" basis, without warranty. While every precaution has been taken in the preparation of this book, neither the author nor PRIMEDIA Inc. nor LEISURE ARTS, Inc. shall have any liability to any person or entity with respect to any liability, loss or damage caused or alleged to be caused directly or indirectly by the instructions contained in this book.

TRADEMARKS

Trademarked names are used throughout this book. Rather than put a trademark symbol in every occurrence of a trademarked name, we state we are using the names only in an editorial fashion and to the benefit of the trademark owner with no intention of infringement of the trademark.

CORPORATE OFFICES

Creating Keepsakes is located at 14901 Heritagecrest Way, Bluffdale, UT 84065. Phone: 801/984-2070. Fax: 801/984-2080. Home page: *www.creatingkeepsakes.com*.

Copyright © 2004 PRIMEDIA Inc. All rights reserved. No part of this book may be reproduced or transmitted in any form or by any means, without the prior written permission of the publisher, excepting brief quotations in connection with reviews written specifically for inclusion in magazines or newspapers, or single copies for strictly personal use.

Scrapbook Tips & Techniques
Hardcover ISBN# 1-57486-406-8
Softcover ISBN# 1-57486-422-X
Library of Congress Control Number 2004102014

Published by Leisure Arts, Inc., 5701 Ranch Drive, Little Rock, Arkansas 72223, 501-868-8800. *www.leisurearts.com*. Printed in the United States of America.
Vice President and Editor-in-Chief: Sandra Graham Case
Executive Director of Publications: Cheryl Nodine Gunnells
Senior Publications Director: Susan White Sullivan
Director of Designer Relations: Debra Nettles
Licensed Product Coordinator: Lisa Truxton Curton
Special Projects Director: Susan Frantz Wiles
Special Projects Designer: Lisa Laney-Hodges
Associate Editors: Steven M. Cooper, Susan McManus Johnson, and Kimberly L. Ross
Senior Art Operations Director: Jeff Curtis
Art Imaging Director: Mark Hawkins
Imaging Technicians: Stephanie Johnson and Mark Potter
Publishing Systems Administrator: Becky Riddle
Publishing Systems Assistants: Clint Hanson, John Rose, and Chris Wertenberger
Senior Director of Public Relations and Retail Marketing: Stephen Wilson

Publisher: Rick Barton
Vice President, Finance: Tom Siebenmorgen
Director of Corporate Planning and Development: Laticia Mull Dittrich
Vice President, Retail Marketing: Bob Humphrey
Vice President, Sales: Ray Shelgosh
Vice President, National Accounts: Pam Stebbins
Director of Sales and Services: Margaret Reinold
Vice President, Operations: Jim Dittrich
Comptroller, Operations: Rob Thieme
Retail Customer Service Manager: Stan Raynor
Print Production Manager: Fred F. Pruss

a resource you can trust

CREATING KEEPSAKES is proud to be the leading magazine in the scrapbooking industry. We work hard to keep you informed about the latest innovations and trends in the world of scrapbooking, sharing the newest techniques and freshest design ideas in every issue. When it comes to preserving your memories, you can rely on *Creating Keepsakes* to teach you how to create beautiful works of art that will be cherished for generations to come.

Scrapbook Tips and Techniques is a compilation of the best articles and columns from *Creating Keepsakes* over the past three years. Inside, you'll learn exciting, innovative ways to use your favorite scrapbooking supplies. You'll be introduced to fun, artistic techniques you can use to enhance your memories. Plus, you'll find invaluable tips for taking better photographs and writing heartfelt, expressive narrations for them.

Your scrapbook is more than just a decorated photo album. It's an illustrated storybook of the things that are important to you. It celebrates the memories that have shaped your life and the lives of your loved ones. It's an expression of your personal style. Let *Scrapbook Tips and Techniques* ignite your creativity and inspire you to craft beautiful and meaningful pages that share what's important to you. This is one resource you're sure to reach for again and again!

Sincerely,

Tracy

Editor-in-Chief
Creating Keepsakes Magazine ♥

71

As Sammy walked along the beach with his cousin Matt, he left behind this precious footprint in the sand for me to capture on film forever.

TAMMY LOMBARDI

249

LYNNE MONTGOMERY

Creating Keepsakes

contents

SCRAPBOOK TIPS AND TECHNIQUES

19

265

116

180

25 ways to trim your scrapbooking time

The Need for Speed

Not long ago, my husband looked over and said, "You're editor-at-large of a scrapbook magazine, yet you're not caught up on your pages. Why's that?" I thought about it for a moment, then pointed to the dinner on the table, the dry cleaning I'd picked up, the kids' homework, my wall calendar and the hundreds of documents on my work desk. "I try," I told him, "but I guess you could say I'm busy."

I'm sure you can relate. Not only are we scrapbookers, we're parents, spouses, employees, friends and more. Like the tortoise in Aesop's fable, we try to be steady—but we could use a hare's speed sometimes on our scrapbook pages. Here are 25 tips to help you reach the finish line in flying colors.   →

BY JANA LILLIE

ILLUSTRATION BY
HISHAN AKGULIAN

Figure 1. If you use the same-size photos often on your scrapbook pages, cut extra photo mats in advance. *Photo by Timmie Aragon.*

Pre-cut Photo Mats

I commonly mat my photos with a thin white mat. To save time and money, I buy white cardstock by the pack. When I have spare time, I cut several white mats to a 4¼" x 6¼" size that's perfect for 4" x 6" photos (Figure 1). I keep the mats within reach so they're ready at a moment's notice when I'm scrapbooking.

Even faster: Purchase paper that's precut to mat size (such as Little Sizzles by Sizzix or Mat Stacks by DieCuts with a View). Or, get your local, full-service copy center to cut stacks of paper for you.

—*Jennifer McGuire, Cincinnati, OH*

Plan, Plan, Plan

My best tip is to plan, plan, plan! While I'm in the doctor's office or waiting for my kids, I jot down ideas for the pictures I need to scrapbook. When I'm ready to begin, I just convert the ideas to my layout. I finish a layout in about a fourth the time it would take otherwise, and I never have to worry about scrapper's block.

—*Kim Johnson, Brodhead, WI*

ONE TECHNIQUE

Use only one technique at a time! It keeps you focused. It keeps your work area cleaner. It keeps you finishing page after page.

I'm not really a chronological scrapper. The layouts I produce in one sitting are not going to appear together in albums. As a result, when I scrapbook I focus on one technique at a sitting. For example, if I want to dry-emboss, I gather enough materials to do the technique on several layouts during the same session.

I find the "single technique" approach so much more efficient than switching techniques for each layout. It makes me more creative because I want my layouts to look unique.

—*Amy Jester, Madison, WI*

Figure 2. Crop a portion of a picture faster with a super-jumbo craft punch. *Page by Mary Larson.* **Supplies** *Photo accent and vellum:* Danelle Johnson, Creative Imaginations; *Brads:* American Tag Co.; *Giga square punch:* Marvy Uchida; *Computer font:* Garamouche, Impress Rubber Stamps.

Crop with a Punch

Rather than trim each side of a photo with an X-acto knife, I crop the sides simultaneously with a super-jumbo square punch (Figure 2). This works particularly well when I want to highlight one section of a photo.

To crop a photo, I simply turn the punch upside-down, then place the photo in the punch and position it by framing the spot I want to punch out. If the section I've targeted is too far into the middle of the picture and the punch can't reach it, I trim a piece off the side of the picture so I can properly center my punch where I want it. I then press down firmly and quickly for a clean punch through the photo.

—*Mary Larson, Chandler, AZ*

Editor's note: You're not limited to square shapes in jumbo or super-jumbo styles. Marvy Uchida, for example, also offers round, rectangular and oval shapes that are great for pictures.

Figure 3. Cut photo mats—and even lettering—with scissors for a quick, casual look. *Sample by Allison Strine.* **Supplies** *Patterned paper:* Karen Foster Design.

Fast Photo Mats

I love shortcuts! One of my favorite tricks is to use scissors—not a paper trimmer—to cut mats for a fun, whimsical look (Figure 3).

—*Allison Strine, Atlanta, GA*

Quicker Ovals

I use ovals often on my scrapbook pages and wanted a faster, more efficient way to cut them out. After purchasing oval-cutting templates from Creative Memories, I used them to help me create a system that would help me choose oval size and the best way to crop my photos.

After cutting scrap cardstock into rectangles, I cut an oval hole in each rectangle. The Creative Memories ovals come in four sizes and the accompanying blades in three colors, so I labeled each sample according to the template size and color of blade used. (For example, I labeled one rectangle "4 x 6 green" and another "3.5 x 5 red.")

Each time I consider cropping a photo into an oval, I get out my rectangles. Since each has an oval cut out of it, I can place the rectangle over the photo and see what the resulting image would look like (Figure 4). I can determine which size looks best and exactly how to position the oval on the photo.

Once I've got the oval where I want it, I position my cutting oval (the plastic template part) in the exact middle of the sample hole. I then remove the rectangle. My template is in place and I'm ready to cut my oval.

—*Helena Jole, Tacoma, WA*

Figure 4. Place your rectangle over a photo to see what the resulting image would look like. *Oval guide by Helena Jole, photo by Kelli Dalley.*

Letter Matting

When I cut out letters for a title, I like to mat them so they "pop" visually. Unfortunately, matting letters the traditional way can be pretty time-consuming. To cut my time in half, I create a faux mat with the WordArt feature in Microsoft Word.

To fake a title mat, select Toolbars on the View menu, then WordArt. Click on the tilted A at left, then select "OK" to bypass the formatting options. Type in your title and select the font and size for your type. Make sure your title is still highlighted so the WordArt menu is activated.

Click on the icon that shows a paint can and brush. You'll see a screen with Fill and Line options. Change your fill color, line color, line type and line weight as desired. The greater the weight, the thicker the line.

When you output the results, you can cut the word out once but it will look like it's been cut out twice (Figure 5). This technique works best when printing on light cardstock and using a darker-colored line.

—*Vivian Smith, Calgary, AB, Canada*

Figure 5. Cut letter-matting time in half with the help of your computer and WordArt. *Idea by Vivian Smith.*

Use Copies

As a traveling soccer mom, I spend a lot of time at practices, games and tournaments. These all include a lot of "down time." I take advantage of this by doing my basic page designs at home. I then make black-and-white copies of the pages and take them to games. During spare moments, I work on journaling or page embellishments for the pages. This has saved me a ton of time!

—*Michele Duffy, Edina, MN*

glass BLOCK

When I think of the one element in my home that I love the most, it's the glass block window in my bathroom. The window is situated just above the garden bathtub in our master bathroom. We keep a honeycomb shade over the window the majority of the year to keep it cool in our bathroom. During the winter months I love to open the shade and see the beautiful glass. John gets to enjoy it the most because he spends a lot of time soaking in the tub reading books and magazines. I have to admit I'm a little jealous of his ability to spend so much time next to my favorite spot. When we first moved into our home, I had big plans to decorate the bathroom – paint the walls sage green or tan, stencil ivy along the window and add a curtain on the smaller window. But as the years go by I really enjoy the simple look in here. The window gives such a nice, natural light. It's a great place to get shots of Tatum splashing in the tub. I think I'll leave the walls as they are and just enjoy the beauty of the glass block window just a little while longer.   — Written August 10, 2002.

Figure 6. Cut four photos the size of a business card for a comfortable fit on the bottom of an 8½" x 11" page. *Page by Kim Heffington.* **Supplies** *Brad:* American Pin & Fastener; *Computer fonts:* Tempus Sans (journaling), Microsoft Word; Bickley Script LET ("glass") and Problem Secretary ("Block"), downloaded from the Internet.

Business Cards

A business card is the perfect size for trimming four photos (vertical orientation) to fit the width of an 8½" x 11" page (Figure 6). You can also use it to trim five photos (horizontal orientation) to fit the depth of an 8½" x 11" page.

—*Kim Heffington, Avondale, AZ*

One Trip

I don't pick up my pictures from the developer unless I also have time to pick up coordinating paper, stickers, die cuts and more. I store the pictures, paper and accents together in a binder until I'm ready to scrapbook them.

—*Leslie Pingley*
Farmington, MN

Custom Backgrounds

I save time by creating custom background papers in advance. (I once did 12 backgrounds in a two-hour block!) I like to use cardstock, and I work with different combinations of my favorite colors in analogous or monochromatic color schemes.

When I'm ready to scrapbook photos, I simply look through my supply of custom background papers, rotating them in different directions to see which format looks best.

—*Cindy Knowles, Milwaukie, OR*

Even faster: Check out the preprinted, color-blocked papers from All My Memories (*www.allmymemories.com*) and SEI, Inc. (*www.sei.com*). Still prefer to create your own backgrounds? Try the color blocking templates from Deluxe Cuts (*www.deluxecuts.com*).

Figure 7. Incorporate your subject's handwriting into the design of your layout. *Page by Shelley Sullivan.* **Supplies** *Pen:* Zig Writer, EK Success; *Inspiration for crooked stripes:* Lisa McGarvey.

5 Speed Tips

I scrapbook faster by following these five practices:

◆ I don't mat every photo. If a photo has a non-distracting background and strong colors, I let it stand on its own.

◆ I rarely scrap a two-page layout. This forces me to choose only my best photos. Twenty years from now, I'll have fewer scrapbooks to move around!

◆ I use my own handwriting for journaling (either on the front of the layout or on a personal note on the back). I'm not very computer savvy, and I often find I can write journaling faster than I can get the computer to print it.

◆ When taking pictures, I try to fill the frame and eliminate the need to crop out cluttered items in the background.

◆ I struggle with journaling, so sometimes I ask my daughter to look at her pictures and tell me what she'd like to say about them. Or, I have her write her own journaling (Figure 7). This makes my daughter feel proud and includes her "voice" in her scrapbooks.

—*Shelley Sullivan, Abbeville, SC*

WORK IN REVERSE

"Reverse scrapbooking" saves me time. When I have multiple pictures on a topic, I don't focus on finding the "right" pictures to scrapbook. Instead, I pull out the papers, stickers and other accents I have for that theme and build pages, leaving space for photos and journaling. I've found that I can do 2–3 pages in the time it normally takes for one!

—*Lana Rickabaugh, Maryville, MO*

Figure 8. For an artistic look in a hurry, highlight your photo with a pre-cut frame. *Page by Lisa Russo.* **Supplies** *Patterned paper:* Anna Griffin; *Ribbon:* C.M. Offray & Son; *Photo frames:* Hobby Lobby; *Inkpad:* Memories; *Fibers:* Rubba Dub Dub, Art Sanctum; On the Surface; *Snap:* Making Memories; *Computer font:* 2Peas Sophisticated, downloaded from *www.twopeasinabucket.com*; *Other:* Trim.

Frame It!

Add dimension and avoid matting with a pre-cut photo frame (Figure 8). You can also add quick flair with ready-made ribbon and trim. Love the look of chalked, torn paper edges? Run a dye inkpad along them instead. It's much faster!

—*Lisa Russo, Woodstock, GA*

PAGE PACKETS

Over the past year, I've worked on two scrapbooks simultaneously: my family album and a vacation album that highlights our trip to Disney World. To save time, I make "page packets." Here's how my process works:

◆ As soon as I get my photos developed, I group them according to how I think I'll scrapbook them.

◆ I look through my supplies and pull out items that will work well with my photos or theme. I also go through my idea books and magazines and gather ideas to store with my pictures.

◆ I put my packets of photos, supplies and ideas into a clear, 12" x 12" keepsake folder and store them until I'm ready to scrapbook them. Everything I need is right at my fingertips, and I save precious scrapbooking time.

—*Andrea Myers, Temperance, MI*

clay tiles, tinted photos, slide holders and more

Figure 1. Use photo-editing software to create the look of a hand-tinted photo. *Page by Heather Uppencamp.* **Supplies** *Patterned paper:* Sonnets, Creative Imaginations; *Vellum:* Autumn Leaves; *Computer font:* Scriptina, downloaded from the Internet; *Mesh:* Magic Mesh, Avant Card; *Nailhead:* Beadazzled, Pebbles in my Pocket; *Ribbon:* C.M. Offray & Son; *Other:* Safety pins, circle tags and eyelets.

Tinted Photos

Did you realize you can control the density of the color in your scanned photos? For the page in Figure 1, I scanned a color photo and manipulated it with my photo-editing software. I electronically removed all but seven percent of the color. The result? You can barely see the pink in my daughter's dress and the yellow, purple and green of the flowers in her hands.

—*Heather Uppencamp, Provo, UT*

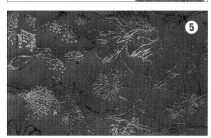

Figure 2. Customize raised-print patterned paper with embossing powder. *Page by Terri Zwicker for Club Scrap.* **Supplies** *Printed cardstock:* Club Scrap; *Embossing powder:* PEARLustre, Stampendous!.

Emboss Raised-print Paper

Transform raised-print patterned paper into heat-embossed images in the color of your choice. Simply follow these easy steps:

❶ Select a small portion of the paper to work with (a 3–4" square is plenty). Heat the raised ink with an embossing gun until the ink becomes dark. Avoid over-heating the paper—this can cause the raised ink to "melt" into the paper.

❷ Generously sprinkle embossing pow-der over the heated area and shake off the excess. You may need to brush off extra particles.

❸ Heat the surface again to melt the powder.

❹ Repeat the process until the desired surface is complete. You can add Radiant Pearls or Perfect Pearls for an even more embellished look (Figure 2).

❺ Enjoy the lovely results.

—*Tricia Morris, Club Scrap*

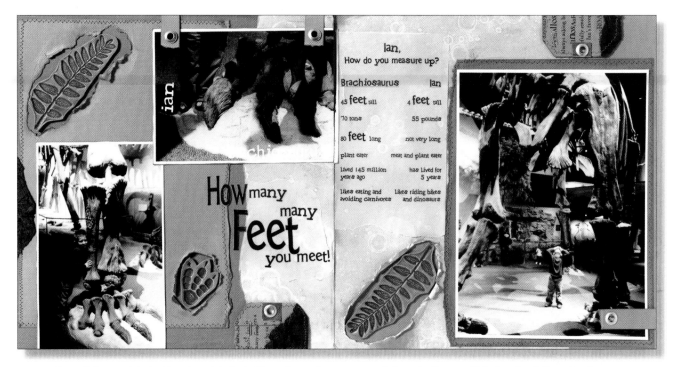

Figure 3. Press an inked rubber stamp into heated foam for a unique page accent. *Pages by Shannon Wolz.* **Supplies** *Patterned and specialty paper:* Provo Craft; *Foam:* Funky Fun Foam, 4Kids Company; *Stamping ink:* Colorbox Fluid Chalk, Clearsnap; *Rubber stamp:* Leaf Impressions, Hero Arts; *Metallic rub-ons:* Craf-T Products; *Computer fonts:* CK Constitution and CK Evolution, "Fresh Fonts" CD, *Creating Keepsakes*; 3 Grammies 5, downloaded from the Internet; *Vellum:* Paper Adventures; *Eyelets:* Creative Impressions; *Metal:* ArtEmboss. *Idea to note:* To create the dinosaur footprints, Shannon inked the foot of her son's dinosaur toy, then "stamped" it into heated fun foam.

Fun Foam Stamping

Cut a piece of Fun Foam to the size of your accent, then heat the foam with an embossing gun until the foam is very soft. Apply permanent or dye-based ink to a rubber stamp, then press it into the warm foam. Hold the stamp in place a few seconds while the foam cools, then remove the stamp. Stamp images, words or letters (see Figures 3 and 4).

—*Maria Pane, Lutherville, MD*

Figure 4. Stamp into a dark color of Fun Foam with white ink. *Samples by Shannon Wolz.* **Supplies** *Foam:* Funky Fun Foam, 4Kids Company; *Rubber stamps:* Art Impressions ("Love" word), Impress Rubber Stamps (daisy), Rubber Stampede (medallion) and Stampabilities (Chinese word for love); *Stamping ink:* Colorbox Fluid Chalk, Clearsnap (gray and black) and Stampabilities (white).

Fun Foam Stamping steps:

Step 1. Heat the foam with an embossing gun.

Step 2. Apply ink to a rubber stamp.

Step 3. Press the rubber stamp into the warm foam.

Figure 5. Stamp into paper clay to create custom letter tiles. *Page and samples by Paula Hogan for Stampin' Up!* **Supplies** *Rubber stamps:* Ferns, Itty Bitty Backgrounds, Alphabet Antiques and Just Journaling II, Stampin' Up!; *Vellum, pen and brass template:* Stampin' Up!; *Stamping ink:* Tsukineko and Stampin' Up!; *Paint:* Lumiere, Jacquard Products; *Pigment powder:* Pearl Ex, Jacquard Products; *Paper clay:* Creative Paperclay Company; *Other:* Embroidery floss.

Paper Clay Tile Title

Create letter tiles for your next page title (Figure 5) by following these steps:

❶ Roll out paper clay to approximately ⅛" thick. Stamp your title letters into the clay, pressing firmly to make a deep impression. Use a craft knife to cut a square around each letter.

❷ Smooth out the rough edges with a water-moistened fingertip, then let the clay dry. You can also bake it according to the manufacturer's directions. After the clay dries, lightly sand it with fine sandpaper.

❸ Mix a small amount of Aztec Gold Pearl Ex with Pearlescent White Lumiere and paint each piece of clay.

❹ Add more Aztec Gold powder to the mixture to get a brighter gold color. Use a fine paintbrush to apply it inside the stamped impressions.

—Paula Hogan, Stampin' Up!

❶

❷

❸

❹

expecting AnnA.

I am 25.
I am expecting my fourth child.
I am excited, nervous, and crazy.

Your brothers and sister will be 7, 5, and 3 when you are born. We will have an even number of boys and girls in our family.

I can't wait to meet you. To kiss your nose and smell your skin. I daydream about what you will look like, how you will cry, what quirky personality traits you will have.

You will have the best baby pictures known to mankind.

I am so thrilled you are a girl.

We love you Anna Banana.

aug. 4 2002

Slide Holders

I love showing off small details of a photo (especially when the rest of the picture isn't very good). Slide holders give me a wonderful way to highlight these images (Figure 6). I just cut my picture small enough to fit behind the slide and adhere it. Voilà—instant accent!

—*Tara Whitney, Valencia, CA*

Figure 6. Frame small photos with slide holders. *Page by Tara Whitney.* **Supplies** *Vellum:* Paper Adventures; *Waxy flax and slide holders:* Scrapworks; *Computer font:* CK Constitution, "Fresh Fonts" CD, *Creating Keepsakes.*

Before You Stamp

If you want to include a stamped image on a page but aren't sure how it will look on your finished layout, try this easy tip. When I include a lot of stamping on my page (like the alphabet stamps), I apply chalk to the rubber stamp, then stamp it wherever I want the image to appear on the layout. If I like the placement, I use my inkpads. If I decide against it, no harm done—I just erase the chalk image. This method saves me from having to start over!

—*Renee Villalobos-Campa, Winnebago, IL*

FITTING PHOTOS IN TEMPLATES

When cropping a photo to fit in a template, place the photo upside-down on your light box, then trace the template design on the back of the photo. The light from the light box lets you see the picture so you can center the template correctly. You don't have to worry about getting ink or pencil marks on the front of your print.

—*Sara Madrigal, Tempe, AZ*

letter tiles, interactive titles and more

Figure 1. Try this technique with photos of buildings, monuments and landscapes. *Page by Teri Anderson.* **Supplies** *Computer fonts:* 2Peas Oatmeal Cookies and 2Peas Beautiful, downloaded from *www.two-peasinabucket.com*; *Vellum:* Provo Craft; *Hemp:* Westrim Crafts; *Fiber:* Stitches, Making Memories; *Netting:* Pulsar Paper. *Idea to note:* Teri hand-stitched the stems and centers of the flowers.

Picture Piecing

While on vacation in Denver, Colorado, I visited the Molly Brown House. The picture in Figure 1 is actually comprised of five pictures I took of the house from the outside. To create this look, I pieced the pictures together, then rubbed a fine piece of sandpaper along the outside edges of the photos. This softened the edges and drew attention to the picture of the house, rather than the seams where the photos overlap. I think it also made the pictures look more like a single picture than five different ones put together.

—*Teri Anderson, Idaho Falls, ID*

Ceramic Tags

Create a variety of unique page accents using ceramic tags. The ceramic surface absorbs color like watercolor paper, making it very easy to watercolor, stamp or color with markers. You can also use colored pencils, pigment powder, chalk and metallic rub-ons to add color. Give the tags a shiny finish with a decoupage or heat-embossed finish.

Here are five techniques to try:

❶ Stamp a flower image on the ceramic tag (Figure 2). After the ink dries, lightly apply a coordinating color of rub-ons. Tie the ceramic tag to a paper tag with fiber or embroidery floss.

❷ Ink the entire front of the tag with pigment ink, then coat it with clear Ultra Thick Embossing Enamel and heat emboss it. Repeat this process twice to create a glazed surface (Figure 3). Before

Figure 2. Embellish ceramic tags with flower stamps for a lovely spring look. *Page by Julie Turner.* **Supplies** *Patterned paper:* K & Company; *Fabric:* Jo-Ann Crafts; *Tags and nail heads:* 7 Gypsies; *Fiber:* DMC; *Ceramic tiles:* Cridge; *Rubber stamps:* Hero Arts; *Stamping ink:* Ranger Industries; *Rub-ons:* Craf-T Products. *Idea to note:* Julie folded up the edges of the mat and chalked them lightly to add dimension.

Figure 3. Braid floss to make a tie for a tag. *Sample by Julie Turner.* **Supplies** *Ceramic tile:* Cridge; *Stamping ink:* Tsukineko; *Embossing enamel:* Suze Weinberg; *Fiber:* Making Memories; *Dried flower:* Nature's Pressed.

Figure 4. Color a charm and add a classy tie for a memorable look. *Sample by Julie Turner.* **Supplies** *Ceramic tag:* Cridge; *Watercolor:* Winsor & Newton; *Silk embroidery ribbon:* Bucilla; *Charms:* Ink It!; *Beads:* Designs by Pamela.

the last layer cools, place the dried flower into the molten enamel. If you have problems making the flower adhere, gently heat the surface again. Be sure to let the ceramic tag cool before picking it up!

❸ Color a ceramic heart charm (Figure 4) with a wash of pink watercolor paint, then glue the lock charm to the front. Fashion a creative tie using silk embroidery ribbon, beads and a key charm.

❹ Cover the entire surface of the ceramic tag with chalk (Figure 5). Tear a piece of patterned tissue paper and adhere it to the lower half of the tag using Perfect Paper Adhesive. Using this same adhesive, decoupage the front of the tag with one or two more layers. When dry, add a photo and tassel.

❺ The thin ceramic circles look great with stamped letters (Figure 6). Apply a little chalk to the tag to complement the colors in your layout.

—Julie Turner, Gilbert, AZ

Figure 5. Do a little decoupage for a dressed-up look. *Sample by Julie Turner.* **Supplies** *Ceramic tag:* Cridge; *Chalk:* Craf-T Products; *Tissue paper:* Hallmark; *Decoupage medium:* Perfect Paper Adhesive, USArtQuest; *Other:* Tassel.

Figure 6. Lend a sophisticated touch to thin ceramic circles with stamping and chalking. *Sample by Julie Turner.* **Supplies** *Ceramic tag:* Cridge; *Rubber stamp:* Hampton Art Stamps; *Stamping ink:* Ranger Industries; *Chalk:* Craf-T Products.

Waiting Out Scrapper's Block

I hate to admit it, but sometimes I get a serious case of "scrapper's block." I have to put a layout away for a while, then come back to it at a later date. I used to simply put my supplies and photos in a sheet protector so they stayed together, but often I returned to my layout only to find I couldn't remember what I'd done the last time I worked on it. Consequently, I had to start all over again.

I've since cured this problem with 3M's Scotch Restickable Glue Stick. Before I put a layout away for a while, I apply the glue to temporarily hold my design in place. Then, when my "scrapper's block" is gone, I can more easily pick up where I left off.

I've also started using this glue while I'm in the middle of designing a layout. I can keep my elements in place while I mull over different options, yet still move pieces easily if I decide to change something. I can even prop up my pages to get a look at them from a distance.

The glue stick works well on most vellum and is nearly invisible. I've also used it to stick down postcards and other items I may want to remove someday.

—Kristen Hess, Peoria, AZ

Figure 7. To create an interactive title, look for words that rhyme or have the same ending. *Pages by Shannon Wolz.* **Supplies** *Square punch:* McGill; *Computer fonts:* CAC Leslie and CAC Logo Alternate, Broderbund; Garamouche, Impress Rubber Stamps; *Rubber stamps:* PSX Design; *Stamping ink:* Brilliance, Tsukineko; *Chalk:* Craft-T Products; *Other:* Apricot seeds.

Fiber and Eyelets

When using eyelets and fibers on a page, first thread the fiber through a wide-eyed needle. "Sew" the fiber through the eyelet holes. If you have trouble getting the fiber to go through the hole, try "pushing" the fiber through with a hole piercer.

—Michelle Spiers, Kittrell, NC

Interactive Titles

Flaps are a fun and creative way to add more space to your page. While creating one, I "discovered" that I could use the flap to make an interactive title. In Figure 7, the first part of the word "Discover" ("Dis") was covered with the flap. On top of the flap, I placed the prefix "Un." This changes the title from "Uncover" to "Discover" when you lift the flap.

With a little creativity, you can come up with your own interactive titles. Here are a few examples to get you started:

- Today and Tomorrow
- Imagine and Imagination
- Moment and Mother
- Cooking and Cookies
- Eat and Treat

The list goes on and on. Any words that rhyme will work. You can also create sentences. For example, if the top flap says "When it's **us,**" the bottom flap can say, "It's a bon**us.**"

If you really want to be creative, use two flaps, placing one on each side. You only need one letter in common. For instance, "**one**" is "w**on**derful" on one of my pages.

Try a sentence, a quote or just a word to create your own interactive title!

—Shannon Wolz, Casper, WY

Figure 8. Create custom background paper and customize stickers with watercolors. *Page and samples by Suzee Gallagher.*
Supplies
Watercolors: Grumbacher; *Watercolor pencils:* Prismacolor, Sanford; *Walnut ink:* All the Extras; *Stickers:* Magenta; *Pen:* Sharpie, Sanford; *Paint:* Lumiere, Jacquard Products; *Title font:* Inspired by the computer font Marmydose, downloaded from the Internet; *Other:* Foam stamp and transparency sheet.

Custom Watercolor Background

To achieve a free-flowing, subtle look for your background paper, try this easy technique. It uses a variety of water-based paints and was inspired by Rhonda Solomon.

❶ Starting in the center of the page, apply the watercolor paint to the cardstock or watercolor paper. Work your way out, moving from light to dark. I like watercolor paint in tubes since it seems more vibrant than the dry palettes.

❷ Using a wide paintbrush, move the colors around to your liking. Remember to keep a misting bottle handy so you can keep the colors flowing on the cardstock as you work.

❸ If time is an issue, use a heat gun to help speed up the drying process. Dry the top of the paper, then flip it over and dry the other side.

❹ To create a watermarked image on your page, brush a thin coat of Lumiere metallic paint on a foam stamp. Stamp the image on your paper (you don't need to worry about sealing or prepping).

❺ Apply a light wash of walnut ink to tint and subdue the colors. You can flick the ink with your paintbrush to get the look of splattered ink. You can also tint your stickers.

To create the title, print out the text in a large font and color it in with watercolor or pencils. Blend the colors together with a damp paintbrush, then outline the letters with a brown Sharpie marker. You can then reduce the image, copy it onto a transparency, and adhere it to your page layout.

—*Suzee Gallagher, Villa Park, CA*

Figure 9. Use small plastic tiles as embellishments. *Page by Nancy Taylor for Hero Arts.* **Supplies** *Plastic tiles:* The Paper Magic Group; *Rubber stamps and stamping ink:* Fanciful Flowers, Ink 'N' Stamp and Hero Arts; *Other:* Handmade paper.

Figure 10. Use crystal lacquer to adhere buttons or charms to tiles. Or, use it over stickers to create a glass-like surface. *Samples by Lori Fairbanks.* **Supplies** *Plastic tiles:* The Paper Magic Group; *Car buttons:* Blumenthal Lansing; *Stickers:* PSX Design (sunflower, butterfly and bee) and Doodlebug Design (stitched accents); *Crystal lacquer:* Stampin' Up!.

Tile Accents

I found charming plastic alphabet tiles in an office sup-ply and educational store and immediately wanted to try them on a scrapbook page (Figure 9). The tiles come in upper and lowercase letters and can be used as-is or embellished. They're fun to use, inexpensive and readily available.

Try placing small stamped pieces of colored cardstock inside the tiles. Stickers will also work. For a more dimensional look, apply crystal lacquer inside the tile.

—*Nancy Taylor for Hero Arts Rubber Stamps*

embossed metal, letter stamps and more

Figure 1. Use a wooden stylus to prevent tearing metal as it's dry embossed. *Pages and samples by Nicole Gartland.* **Supplies** *Computer fonts:* Spring (title) and Sulatko (small title), downloaded from the Internet; CK Newsprint, "Fresh Fonts" CD, *Creating Keepsakes; Stamping ink:* Clearsnap; *Rubber stamp (for background):* All Night Media; *Embossing powder:* Stamp n' Stuff; *Metal:* Once Upon a Scribble; *Bunnies:* Nicole's own design.

Dry Embossing Metal

I love using metals to create accents, but find that simple dry embossing doesn't give me a very clear image. I started experimenting with doubling up my lines, pushing out the hollow spaces, and texturing the metal with a buffing block to create a fun, "stuffed" look.

Here's what you need to get started:

◆ **Metal sheets.** For these samples, I used Scrap Metal by Once Upon a Scribble. It's very flexible and cuts easily with scissors or a craft knife.

◆ **An image to emboss.** I doodled my own pictures, but feel free to use scanned →

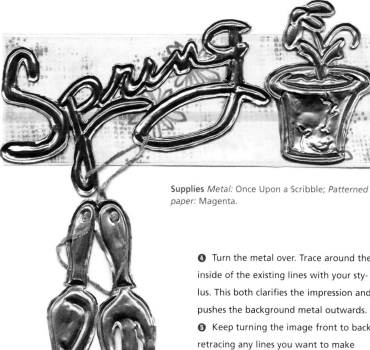

Supplies *Metal:* Once Upon a Scribble; *Patterned paper:* Magenta.

and printed stickers, clip art or die cuts. I recommend generally using images with simple lines for a clearer impression.

◆ **An embossing stylus.** I use wood and steel styluses, which are inexpensive and readily available. While I use both (I like to change pressure width as I work), you can do just as well working with just one. Here's how to use an embossing stylus:

❶ Tape the image over the metal. If the metal is two-sided, place the side you want to show facing up.

❷ Place the metal on a soft surface (such as a mouse pad) and lightly run your stylus over the image. Trace every line you want to see on your finished piece.

❸ Remove the taped image and keep it as a handy reference. Using your stylus, re-trace your indentations, making them deeper. I retrace the same design area with my stylus several times to avoid tearing or puncturing the metal. This lets the image "stretch" slowly, allowing the lines to go deeper without puncturing the image.

❹ Turn the metal over. Trace around the inside of the existing lines with your stylus. This both clarifies the impression and pushes the background metal outwards.

❺ Keep turning the image front to back, retracing any lines you want to make deeper or cleaner. This can be a one-time process, or you may need to go back and forth many times.

❻ With the back side facing you, gently push the "hollow" spaces down for a pushed-out or "stuffed" look. You can use the flatter end of your stylus, a fingertip or even a pen cap for this.

Here are a few variations (see examples on this page):

◆ **Flower pot.** To create a distressed and worn look, I push the inner metal out far. This helps it look slightly soft and stretched. I use my fingertip to push it in again. A couple of "cracks" add to the effect.

◆ **Basket.** This basket shows the back of the design, which is equally fun and usable.

◆ **Words.** I write the title and follow the steps as usual. If you want to use the back of the design (as seen on the basket), simply flip the title. If you want to hand write it, use a black pen on thin paper (standard printer paper works well). Lay the paper upside-down to

trace. You'll be able to see through it enough to trace your original lines.

◆ **Add color.** For the bunnies in Figure 1, I dabbed a white inkpad over the finished design. For the tulips, I buffed the metal's surface and applied purple ink using a cotton swab. Because most inks won't dry on metal, I sprinkle a light coating of embossing powder over the ink and heat it to dry and seal the ink. This adds an almost glassy finish.

—Nicole Gartland, Portland, OR

Supplies *Metal:* Once Upon a Scribble.

Supplies *Metal:* Once Upon a Scribble; *Stamping ink:* Clearsnap; *Embossing powder:* Stamp n' Stuff.

"Frame" Your Subjects

Take pictures in novel settings, and you can create intriguing surroundings for your photo subjects as well. At left, note how Melissa Gould of Redmond, Washington, captured not only a fun picture of two playful kids, but vibrant colors and visually interesting curves.

Debbie Singson of Orem, Utah, wanted to capture her daughter's love of swimming, so she took a picture of her daughter as she floated happily in a pool. Note how the inner-tube and surrounding water frame the girl's face and direct attention to her.

When Michele Ritchie of Norristown, Pennsylvania, took this sweet picture of her son peering out from behind a fence, she knew the strong lines and wooden textures would make a natural frame.

MELISSA GOULD

DEBBIE SINGSON

"Blackmail" Album

Embrace your bad photos! I took a small square template and cut my bad photos (bad hair, weird looks and more). I then arranged them on black cardstock in a black album that's affectionately known as the "blackmail album." Every so often my family looks through it and has a really good laugh!

—*Christine Lally, Waterloo, WI*

MICHELE RITCHIE

Spell It with Stamps

BY KAREN BURNISTON

Has the stamping bug bit you? Are you itchy for inks and silly for stamping? If you're like me, it's hard to resist letter stamps. They come in so many sizes and styles—the bigger ones are perfect for titles, while the smaller ones are great for journaling highlights and subtitles. Plus, they're fun to play with. Here are some fun (and funky) twists for those letter stamps and other scrapbook supplies.

Supplies *Letter stamps:* Wordsworth; *Stamping ink:* Adirondack, Ranger Industries; *Rubber stamps:* Hero Arts.

Mirror Image Letters

Letter stamps can be used to make beautiful reflection lettering. You'll need a solid stamp (such as a shadow or mirror-image stamp), a dye inkpad and letter stamps. Next:

❶ Ink the letter, then stamp it onto the shadow stamp.

❷ Breathe on the shadow stamp to refresh the ink, then stamp it upside-down to make the reflected letter.

❸ Re-ink the letter stamp and line it up over the reflected letter and stamp. Repeat these steps for each letter.

Additional hints: Stamp the reflected letters first since they require a block stamp where you can't see the exact placement of the letter. It's much easier to line up the non-reflected letter above it.

If you're using an unmounted letter stamp set, you can line up the letters by viewing them through an acrylic block. Or, just "eyeball" the positioning or use a stamp positioner for perfect placement.

Shrink Plastic Letters

You can create miniature versions of the letter stamps with shrink plastic. This example shows the stamps at full size and shrunk. I used the same markers on both (shrinking intensifies the colors).

The best ink for shrink plastic is the permanent variety for non-porous surfaces. This stains your stamps, but it dries immediately on most surfaces and won't bleed or run. However, almost any ink can be used effectively on shrink plastic by setting it with heat. (See step 2 below for heating instructions.)

To create the look shown:

❶ Sand white shrink plastic with sandpaper or a sanding block. This gives the plastic a "tooth" to accept colored pencils or markers.

❷ Stamp the letters with permanent black ink. (Use a heat gun to set non-permanent ink. Be sure to wave the heat gun over the plastic for a few seconds. This will set the ink but won't shrink the plastic.)

❸ Color the letters with colored pencils or markers, then cut out the letters. Punch a hole in the letters if you plan to hang them.

❹ Place the letters on a cookie sheet and bake them for 1–3 minutes at 350 degrees. (Keep an eye on the letters!) You can also shrink them with a heat gun, but the letters often curl onto themselves and stick. You can also use a Shrinky Dink oven, available in most toy stores.

Use mini glue dots to adhere the shrunken letters to the page. You can also hang them from wire, fiber or jump rings if you punched holes in the letters before shrinking them.

Supplies *Letter stamps:* Wordsworth; *Shrink plastic and sanding block:* Lucky Squirrel Press; *Non-porous ink:* CoMotion; *Pens:* Tombow.

Supplies *Letter stamps:* PSX Design; *Stamping ink:* Ancient Page, Clearsnap; *Glue dots:* Glue Dots International; *Embossing powder:* Stampendous!; *Tag:* Shotz, Creative Imaginations; *Nailhead:* JewelCraft; *Pen:* Zig Writer, EK Success.

Raised Pebbles

You can create your own raised pebbles with pop-up glue dots and clear embossing powder. Here's how:

❶ Stamp a word with small letter stamps. Cover each letter with a pop-up glue dot.

❷ Pour clear embossing powder over the dots, covering them thoroughly.

❸ Shake off the excess powder and melt it with a heat gun.

Supplies *Letter stamps:* Wordsworth; *Stamping ink:* VersaMark and Kaleidacolor, Tsukineko; *Brayer:* Speedball; *Specialty cardstock:* MatteKote, Judikins.

Resist Letters

The resist technique is a great stamping technique for making serene titles, but it's all about the paper. Choose coated cardstock, as the plain, uncoated variety won't work.

❶ Stamp letters onto coated cardstock using clear embossing ink or VersaMark ink.

❷ Ink up a brayer on a rainbow inkpad and roll repeatedly over the letters. Watch the letters "resist" the ink and appear as ghost images.

Fillable Letters

Outline letter stamps are perfect for filling. To create this look with a border sticker:

❶ Ink outline letters in black ink, then stamp them onto a border sticker that's still on its backing sheet. If desired, emboss with black powder to intensify the lines.

❷ Cut out each letter. You now have patterned letter stickers!

Variation: Try this technique on patterned paper or a photograph.

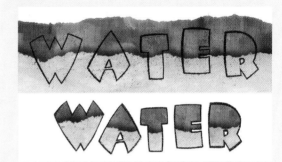

Supplies *Letter stamps:* Paper Candy; *Stamping ink:* Ancient Page, Clearsnap; *Embossing powder:* Stubby Stampers; *Border sticker:* Karen Foster Design.

Supplies *Letter stamps:* Wordsworth; *Stamping ink:* Adirondack, Ranger Industries; *Mesh:* Magic Mesh, Avant Card.

Mesh-Textured Letters

Here's an easy way to add a mesh-textured look to your letters:

❶ Lay a piece of mesh on your cardstock.

❷ Ink the letter with dye ink, then stamp over the mesh, using firm pressure to work the ink through the mesh. Avoid rocking the stamp.

❸ Remove the mesh to reveal the patterned letter. Repeat the process with the remaining letters.

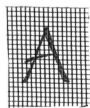

Are you ready to give your letter stamps a workout? Try these ideas or come up with your own variations. Creating unique looks with letter stamps is as easy as, well, A-B-C!

Figure 2. For more font effects in Microsoft Word, click on "Format," then select the "Font" option. *Pages by Donna Downey.* **Supplies** *Football accent:* Jolee's Boutique, Stickopotamus; *Square punch:* Marvy Uchida; *Computer font:* Baskerville Old Face, Publisher 2000, Microsoft.

Tip for Font Unity

A great way to get a cohesive look on your layouts is to use the same font in different ways. For the layout in Figure 2, I used the Baskerville Old Face font for my journaling and italicized key words. I used a shadow effect for the title. For the quote, I italicized the font and added the shadow effect. I stretched the date by adding a space between each letter. I bolded the font for the subtitle.

—*Donna Downey, Huntersville, NC*

Another Way to Adhere Brads

If you want to use large brad shapes (such as stars and hearts) but don't want to poke holes in your paper, bend the tips back and forth until they snap off. It's easy—you won't need wire cutters. Use glue dots to attach the brads to your page or accent.

—*Sheila Bloedow, Seattle, WA*

HEAT EMBOSSING ON VELLUM

It's difficult to see embossing ink on vellum, but I found a great way to line up my stamped images (especially letters) without making mistakes. Using black ink, I stamp my letters on a light-colored paper, then place it under my vellum. I use this as a guide when I stamp on the vellum. I get great results!

—*Bonnie Lotz, West Jordan, UT*

embellished stickers and faux torn photos

Figure 1. Embellish your letter stickers for added interest. *Page and samples by Karen Burniston.* **Supplies** *Patterned paper:* Carolee's Creations (rust) and Karen Foster Design (floral); *Rose accents:* Polly & Friends, Leeco Industries; *Beads and nailheads:* JewelCraft; *Letter stickers:* Sonnets ("grown" and "Emma") and Squigglebets ("E" in "Emma"), Creative Imaginations; Stampendous! ("how"); *Alphabet stamps:* Just for Fun; *Rubber stamps for script:* Rubber Baby Buggy Bumpers; *Lettering template:* Wordsworth ("you've"); *Embossing enamel:* Suze Weinberg; *Stamping ink:* Adirondack, Ranger Industries; *Flower accents:* Bits and Baubles, Creative Imaginations; *Shrink plastic for hearts:* Lucky Squirrel Press; *Computer font:* Roman Fixed Width, downloaded from the Internet; *Other:* Micro beads and gold pen. *Idea to note:* Karen used song lyrics from "How You've Grown" by 10,000 Maniacs.

Paper Corners and Embellished Stickers

You can create photo corners from any paper using just a few folds (Figure 1). Follow these easy steps:

→

Tips & Tricks

Paper Corners

To create folded corners:

1 Punch or cut a square from colored paper, patterned paper or a photograph.

2 Fold the paper diagonally from corner to corner.

3 Open it back up to a square, then fold the other opposing corners the same way.

4 Cut out one of the triangles created by the folds.

5 Fold the two lower flaps to the back and secure them with adhesive.

6 Slide the photo into the pocket.

EASY FOLDED CORNERS

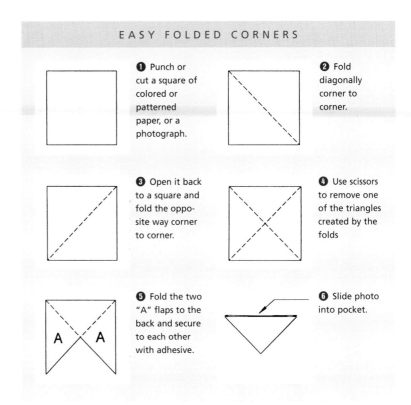

1 Punch or cut a square of colored or patterned paper, or a photograph.

2 Fold diagonally corner to corner.

3 Open it back to a square and fold the opposite way corner to corner.

4 Use scissors to remove one of the triangles created by the folds

5 Fold the two "A" flaps to the back and secure to each other with adhesive.

6 Slide photo into pocket.

Letter Stickers

EMBELLISHED LETTER STICKERS

Love the look of the embellished letter stickers in Figure 1? Here's what you'll need to create the same look:

- Letter stickers
- Waxed paper
- Tacky Tape (or Wonder Tape)
- Micro beads, foil, embossing powder or gold leaf
- Paper plate, craft knife and cutting mat

Follow these three steps:

1 On waxed paper, spell out the word with letter stickers. Run strips of tacky tape across the areas you want to embellish.

2 Trim the portions of the tape not on the letters. (It's OK to cut through the waxed paper.)

3 Remove the protective sheet to expose the sticky tape. Turn the word over and press it firmly into a plate filled with micro beads or other embellishments. A brayer can help set the embellishment. Shake away the excess.

To transfer the stickers to your project, carefully fold the waxed paper back until the tops of the letters are exposed. Press the letters onto your project and gently pull off the rest of the waxed paper.

—*Karen Burniston, Littleton, CO*

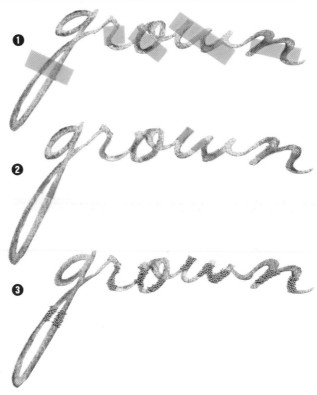

Figure 2. Use a roll and whip stitch on rustic mats and borders. *Pages by Lee Anne Russell.* **Supplies** *Patterned paper:* Lasting Impressions for Paper; *Computer fonts:* 2Peas Jack Frost (title) and 2Peas Chestnuts, downloaded from *www.twopeasinabucket.com*; *Rubber stamp:* Junque; *Stamping ink:* Adirondack, Ranger Industries; *Chalk:* Craf-T Products; *Pewter plaque and eyelets:* Making Memories; *Embroidery floss:* DMC; *Other:* Jute.

Roll and Whip Stitches

When I make a dress for my daughter, I use a roll and whip stitch to bind the raw edge of the fabric. It's a great look for cardstock, which is easier to work with since the roll stays in place (Figure 2). Here's how to stitch it:

❶ Curl the edge of your paper to hide the edge. (A tight curl reduces the bulk of the paper.)

❷ Thread your needle, then knot the end of the thread. Leave a tail that's sufficiently long to tie a bow like the one on the mat for the barn photo. Insert your needle at the base of the curled cardstock (right side up) and pull the thread through the paper. If desired, tuck your knot beneath the curl.

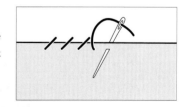

❸ Poke through the paper from the back, about ⅜" from the original insertion point. Continue this process until you've reached the end of the paper. Knot your thread and cut off the remaining tail.

Variation: Glue the back side of two different pieces of patterned paper together. When you make the curl, both papers will show and look like you've piped the paper's edge.

—*Lee Anne Russell, Brownsville, TN*

HEAT EMBOSSING TIP

I loved Rebecca Sower's "Emboss It!" article in the February 2003 issue and wanted to share a tip my Stampin' Up! demonstrator shared with me. To create a safe, effective area to heat emboss on, wrap a magazine with aluminum foil and place it in a clipboard.

You can use the clip to hold down the item you're embossing, and the foil will heat the back of your paper to speed up the melting of the powder. It helps keep your paper from warping as well.

—*Becky Kent, Hilliard, OH*

Figure 3. Tear an opening in your background paper and mount your photo from behind. *Pages by Lana Rickabaugh.* **Supplies** *Patterned paper:* Frances Meyer; *Computer font:* Garamouche, P22 Type Foundry; *Pens:* Zig Millennium, EK Success; *Chalk:* Craf-T Products; *Other:* Frame nailheads and round nailheads. *Ideas to note:* Lana used frame nailheads to accentuate her subtitle. She took photos of information plaques to supplement her journaling.

Faux Torn Photo

Do you love the look of torn photos but hesitate at the thought of tearing them, even if they're duplicates? Tear a hole in your background paper and mount the photo behind the hole. Use patterned paper or cardstock with a white core to mimic the photo paper. Fold or curl the torn edges, then chalk them for added texture (Figure 3).

—*Lana Rickabaugh, Maryville, MO*

SAVE TIME WITH SKETCHES

I'm currently working on three scrapbooks. The "One Sketch, Many Looks" concept saves me a lot of time. When I find or create a sketch, I apply it to each album. I simply change the paper and embellishments to fit each set of pictures. This helps me finish three layouts for three different books in a fraction of the time!

—*Marlene Kinikini, Sandy, UT*

herbs, mosaics and more

Figure 1. Stamp with parsley for a soft look. *Page by Denise Pauley.* **Supplies** *Patterned paper and translucent snaps:* Chatterbox; *Computer font:* Bickley Script, Microsoft Word; *Letter stamps:* Hero Arts; *Stamping ink:* Ancient Page, Clearsnap; *Other:* Parsley.

Herbal Stamping

I love cooking with fresh herbs for the extra layer of flavor they add. And, because I've always got herbs on hand, I was delighted to discover I can use them like rubber stamps. Here's how:

❶ Pick off a single "leaf" or small cluster, then flatten it.

❷ Generously apply ink to the back of the herb, since the "veins" will leave more interesting impressions. To do this, place the herb on a piece of scrap paper, then "stamp" the inkpad onto the leaf until the surface and stem are covered. Any type of ink will work, but if you use a "juicy" pig-

→

ment pad, you may need to heat emboss the ink to set the image or it will smear.

❸ Carefully turn the leaf over and position it where you'd like the image to appear.

❹ Place a scrap of cardstock on top of the herb, then press firmly to transfer the ink. (Using just your fingers to press the herb may create an incomplete or mottled impression.)

Try different herbs to achieve a variety of looks: parsley for a soft, feminine effect (Figure 1), rosemary for a rustic impression (Figure 2), oregano for its resemblance to small skeleton leaves (Figure 3), or basil for a large, feather-like image (Figure 4). Experiment with dainty thyme, wispy dill, funky tarragon, fragrant cilantro and elegant sage to uncover even more artistic effects!

—Denise Pauley, La Palma, CA

Figure 2. Add a rustic touch by stamping with rosemary. *Sample by Denise Pauley.* **Supplies** *Patterned paper:* Club Scrap; *Stamping ink:* Adirondack, Ranger Industries; *Letter tiles:* Making Memories; *Other:* Rosemary.

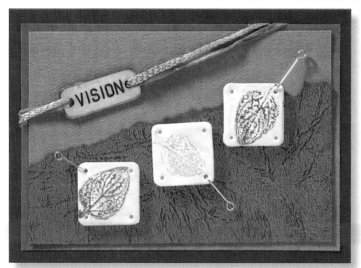

Figure 3. Like a skeletal look? Stamp with oregano. *Sample by Denise Pauley.* **Supplies** *Patterned paper:* Legacy, Design Originals; *Metallic paper:* Bravissimo, Emagination Crafts; *Stamping ink:* Brilliance, Tsukineko; *Embossing powder:* Ranger Industries; *Chalk:* Craf-T Products; *Fibers:* Rubba Dub Dub, Art Sanctum; *Other:* Jeweler's pins, word charm and oregano.

Figure 4. Create a feather-like look by stamping with basil. *Sample by Denise Pauley.* **Supplies** *Corrugated paper:* DMD, Inc.; *Stamping ink:* Ancient Page, Clearsnap; *Mini brads:* GoneScrappin.com; *Jump rings:* Darice; *Other:* Fishing line, beads and basil.

Figure 5. Design unique page accents and tags with acrylic shapes. *Sample by Lori Fairbanks.* **Supplies** *Acrylic tag, markers and black stamping ink:* KrystalKraft, Sunday International; *Rubber stamps:* Club Scrap; *Stamping ink:* Close To My Heart; *Tag:* DMD, Inc.; *Other:* Jute.

Awesome Acrylic Accents

Embellish your pages and cards with customized acrylic accents (available in a variety of shapes). Just follow these easy steps to create unique accents with stamps, inks and even glitter:

❶ Prepare the treated side of your acrylic shape by wiping it with KrystalKraft Cleaner. Let it dry.

❷ Stamp images on the acrylic shape using KrystalKraft ink (a solvent-based stamping ink) and rubber stamps. Dry the ink with a heat gun, as shown in 2a. As shown in 2b, you can also use KrystalKraft Markers to randomly color the entire shape if desired. (The alcohol-based markers won't smear the stamped images.)

❸ Lightly spray the shape with Krystal-Kraft Décor Spray. Use a heat gun to dry it. Repeat this step until you like the look.

❹ Remove the paper liner to reveal your design. Next, attach the shape to your layout by hanging it with jute or fiber. You can also adhere it to your page with crystal lacquer or clear-drying KrystalKraft Glue.

Variations: You can add extra sparkle after step 3 by applying a light, even coat of KrystalKraft glue over the entire shape. Pour glitter over the piece, shake off the excess, and allow the glue to dry for 30 minutes. Seal it with acrylic spray.

Another option? Use Sunday International's 3-D Glass-like embellishments, a variety of shapes that can be customized with patterned paper or gold leaf.

—Harry Ostiz, Sunday International

Supplies *Acrylic tag, markers and black stamping ink:* KrystalKraft, Sunday International; *Rubber stamp:* Rubber Stampede.

Figure 6. Customize papermaking squares for easy mosaic accents. *Page and samples by Darcee Thompson.* **Supplies** *Stamping ink:* Stampin' Up!; *Pen:* Tombow; *Crystal lacquer:* Sakura Hobby Craft; *Computer font:* CK Wanted, "Fresh Fonts" CD, *Creating Keepsakes*; *Chalk:* Craf-T Products; *Papermaking squares:* Arnold Grummer; *Jeweler's thread:* Better Beads.

Easy Mosaic Squares

I love the look of mosaics and tiles but don't like the bulk. My solution? Using Arnold Grummer's papermaking squares. You can customize these lightweight squares with chalks, rub-ons, stamping ink, embossing powder, markers and more. Simply cover them with a glaze, such as crystal lacquer, for a glossy finish. To create the tile pattern in Figure 6 (see "How to Create Mosaic Squares" on the facing page):

❶ Cut off one square and set it diagonally across four squares. Trace around it. Cut along the tracings, then clean up the corners if necessary. The squares are thin enough to cut with scissors.

❷ Apply color to all the pieces. (I used stamping ink here.)

❸ Apply a thin layer of crystal lacquer with a paintbrush. Pop as many bubbles as you can, then let the lacquer dry.

❹ Apply 2–3 more coats of lacquer, popping bubbles each time. Let each coat dry completely between layers.

❺ Arrange the pieces and adhere the squares to your layout.

Variation 1: Adhere a sticker to the square and apply crystal lacquer.

Variation 2: After you apply color to the square, apply a layer of lacquer. While the lacquer's still wet, add a small piece of mesh. Apply two more layers of lacquer.

—*Darcee Thompson, Preston, ID*

How to Create Mosaic Squares

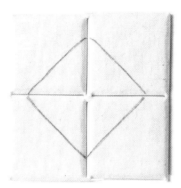

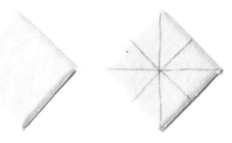

1 Set one square (see lower left) diagonally across four squares. Trace around it, then cut out the square. *Note:* To create accents like those along the bottom of Figure 6, divide the cut-out square into eight sections as shown at bottom right. Cut the triangles to your preferred size and decorate as desired.

Variations

2 Apply color with stamping ink or markers.

Adhere a sticker, then apply crystal lacquer.

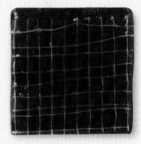

3 Apply crystal lacquer with a paintbrush.

Apply crystal lacquer, add mesh, then apply two more layers of lacquer.

PERFECT EYELETS

Do you ever have problems with distorted eyelets? You know what I mean—you pound away on the back of an eyelet, then turn the project over only to discover that your eyelet is warped.

Try placing an old mouse pad on top of your self-healing mat. The extra layer is just what you need to "cushion the blow." You'll get perfectly pounded eyelets every time!

—KLynne Dunham, Cleburne, TX

TRIMMER TIP

I used to have trouble getting a straight cut on small pieces of cardstock (like those used for photo captions). This was especially troublesome when the paper was too small for the trimmer to hold.

My solution? If I use removable tape to adhere the cardstock to the trimmer, I always get a straight edge. I keep a piece of removable tape stuck to my trimmer so it's always handy.

—Amy Keen, Redford, MI

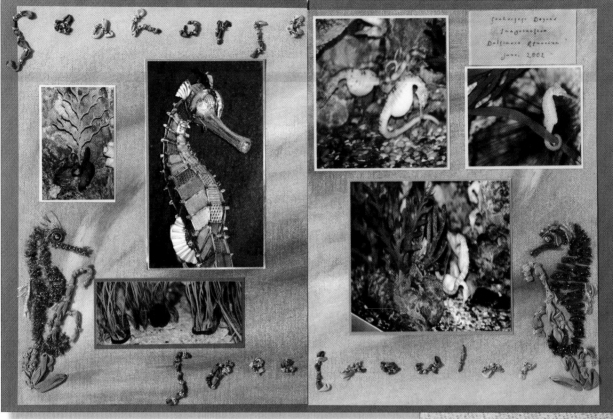

Figure 7. Fill a stencil design with fibers. *Pages by Susan Bascom.* **Supplies** *Seahorse stencil: Big Book of Nature Stencil Designs*, Dover Publications; *Computer font:* 2Peas Crumbly Gingerbread, downloaded from *www.twopeasinabucket.com; Fibers:* Fibers By The Yard and Rainbow Gallery; *Vellum:* PaperCuts; *Embossing powder:* Stampa Barbara; *Patterned paper:* Karen Foster Design; *Other:* Eyelets and ribbon. *Idea to note:* Susan resized the seahorse image on her scanner, then printed out the image.

Fast Fiber Designs

For the layout in Figure 7, I added fibers in the shape of a seahorse template (the technique also works with other template shapes). To do this:

❶ Lightly trace the stencil onto your background paper.

❷ Draw glue lines inside the traced lines. (I like the Zig Squeeze & Roll pen.) Gently tap pieces of fiber into the glue.

❸ Make sure the glue binds the fiber to your paper and that you cover the traced lines with fiber.

To complete the accent, I embroidered a French knot inside an eyelet to represent the seahorse's eye. I printed my title, glued it, then stitched ribbon on top.

—*Susan Bascom, Birmingham, AL*

watercolored accents, cool frames and more

Figure 1. Apply gray chalk to help accents coordinate with tinted black-and-white photos. *Pages by Nancy Rogers.* **Supplies** *Square punches:* Family Treasures (decorative) and Punch It; *Flower punch:* Paper Shapers, EK Success; *Liquid appliqué:* Marvy Uchida; *Computer fonts:* Arial (journaling) and Matisse ITC (title), Microsoft Word; *Photo tinting oils:* Marshall's; *Chalk:* Craf-T Products; *Foam mounting dots:* Ranger Industries; *Other:* Eyelets.

Tinting Accents

I love to pick an object from my black-and-white photos to tint. I then "tint" my accents to match the hand-tinted photos by embellishing them with black or gray chalk or metallic rub-ons (Figure 1).

—*Nancy Rogers, Baton Rouge, LA*

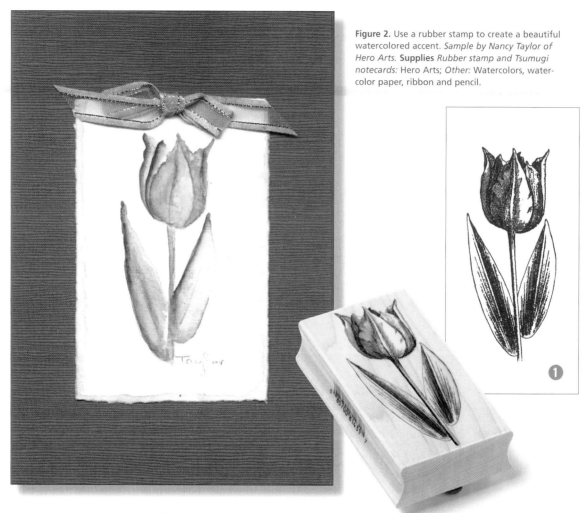

Figure 2. Use a rubber stamp to create a beautiful watercolored accent. *Sample by Nancy Taylor of Hero Arts.* **Supplies** *Rubber stamp and Tsumugi notecards:* Hero Arts; *Other:* Watercolors, watercolor paper, ribbon and pencil.

Watercolor Stamped Images

Create delightful watercolored images with rubber stamps. Next, add a simple mat to create an elegant page accent, or mount the image on a card and give it to a friend (Figure 2). Follow these easy steps:

❶ Stamp the desired image on a piece of scratch paper. Cover the back of the stamped paper with graphite pencil marks, making sure you cover the entire area under your image.

❷ Tear a piece of watercolor paper (available at art supply and craft stores) to the desired size. For this project I used 140 lb. cold press paper. Next, place the stamped image on a piece of watercolor paper (graphite side down) and trace along the lines (2a).

This will transfer the design to your paper (2b).

❸ Create a soft wash frame around your design by dipping your brush in water and running it along the paper's edges. While the paper is still wet, dip your brush in the paint and lightly touch the paper with the brush. Watch the color bleed into the wet border.

❹ Paint the image as desired, using the pencil lines as a guide.

Here are some additional watercolor tips:

◆ Use the stamp label as a guide for using lighter or darker colors.

◆ Start painting with the lighter colors first, then add darker colors.

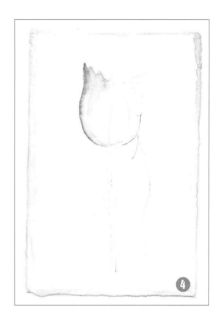

◆ Allow a bit of the white paper to show through the design to give your image the look of a watercolor painting.

◆ To create a hard edge on your painting, be sure the paper is dry before adding colors next to each other. For a soft, blended look, add colors while the paper is still wet.

◆ If you're not familiar with watercolors, experiment with color mixing on a separate piece of paper.

◆ As with any reproduced design, verify the company's angel policy.

Shortcut: Stamp the image with VersaMark ink to create a subtle watermark. Follow steps three and four as directed, or use watercolor pencils to color the image.

—*Nancy Taylor, Hero Arts*

Editor's note: Want more great ideas on using watercolors? Check out Erin Terrell's "Wow Watercolors" feature in our September 2000 issue. The article is also available on our web site at *http://www.creatingkeepsakes.com/magazine/article.ihtml?index_field=516.*

More Looks for Letter Stickers

The article "New Looks with Letter Stickers" (November 2002) didn't include my favorite way to adapt them. Use Slick Writers, Permapaque markers and Brilliance stamping ink to enhance the letters with these techniques:

◆ Stamp small images on larger letter stickers.

◆ Use the pens to add detail or designs to the letters.

◆ Sponge ink on the letters, or stamp them with a texture stamp. This can also tone down or brighten the color of the letters, making them match your layout better.

—*Patti Coombs, Mapleton, UT*

STICKER PLACEMENT HELP

If I'm not sure where I want to place my stickers when I'm working on a layout, I place them on wax paper first. The paper is transparent enough to see through to visualize how the stickers will look on the page. It's easy to remove the stickers and place them on my layout.

Wax paper is also helpful for lining up letter stickers. I place my letters on the wax paper with the top half of the letter hanging off the edge. I move the letters around until I like the placement.

Next, I stick the top half of the letters to my page and peel away the wax paper from the bottom half. You can also cut the wax paper into an oval or circle to position your letters into an oval or circle shape.

—*Betsy Sammarco, New Canaan, CT*

Figure 3. Embellish embossed paper and embossed vellum for an elegant touch. *Pages by Darcee Thompson.* **Supplies** *Embossed paper:* K & Company; *Velvet paper:* SEI; *Silver embroidery floss:* DMC; *Chalk:* Craf-T Products; *Pen:* Gelly Roll, Sakura.

Embellishing Embossed Paper

I found a new way to enhance mono-chromatic embossed paper and vellum (Figure 3):

❶ Cut the embossed paper to the size desired, centering the paper on the embossed image you want to enhance. Cut a piece of cardstock the same size.

❷ Send the cardstock through a Xyron adhesive applicator, then adhere the cardstock to the back of the embossed paper. This strengthens the stitching area so it won't tear. (Other adhesives also work, but the adhesive needs to cover the entire cardstock area.)

❸ Using a needle, pierce holes around the image you want to enhance. Stitch around the design.

❹ Chalk inside the stitched area and adhere the accent to your layout.

To stitch your title, simply write or print your title, pierce holes along the lines and stitch!

—*Darcee Thompson, Preston, ID*

PUNCH STORAGE

For an inexpensive way to store my paper punches, I purchased a double-sided, plastic carrying case for the Hot Wheels Matchbox cars. The case fits approximately 25 average-sized punches (like the Paper Shapers by EK Success) on each side. I've cut out some of the dividers with a craft knife to make larger sections for larger or longer punches. The case is transparent, has a handle for carrying, and often costs less than $5 at a discount store.

—Katie Haymore, Virginia Beach, VA

Quotable Kids

As the mother of two busy boys, ages seven and ten, we're constantly on the go. I carry a small journal with me to note the hilarious and sometimes sentimental things they say not only to me, but also to one another, their friends and family members. While I'm scrapbooking, I refer to this journal to jog my memory. I often find the perfect quote for a particular picture or layout.

I create a "Quotable Quotes" page of unused quotes and use it as a title page for that year's scrapbook. I've also included these quotes in my annual Christmas letter. This allows me to share my children's personalities with loved ones who don't get to see my boys very often.

—Jennifer Morris, Plymouth, MI

Stitched Metal Frame

I asked my mom, a retired seamstress, if I could use my sewing machine to stitch on a lightweight sheet of metal. She looked it over and said I could as long as I used a heavy-duty needle like those made for denim. I bought some needles and gave it a try. Follow these steps to create a stitched, dry-embossed photo frame like that in Figure 4:

❶ Using removable adhesive, adhere a duplicate photo to a sheet of ScrapMetal. This will help hold the photo in place as you sew.

❷ Stitch the picture to the metal with white thread. Tie off the excess thread on the back and tape it down to secure it.

❸ Dry emboss the frame around the photo and trim around the edges. Adhere the frame to your layout with glue dots.

Variation: Weather the metal with sandpaper to make it look older and more rustic. Here are some additional tips I found helpful:

◆ If you'll be turning a corner, leave the needle through the project. Lift the sewing machine foot, then turn the corner. This guarantees a smooth transition around square corners or circles and shapes.

◆ Roll the dial by hand when you get down to only needing one stitch to reach your next meeting point. This assures you won't pass up your mark.

◆ When embossing on thin metal, be careful not to press too hard or you'll tear right through the metal. I like to use a wooden stylus.

◆ Use a rolling pin to smooth out rough edges after punching, cutting or stitching on metal.

—Laura Stewart, Fort Wayne, IN

Figure 4. Create unique page enhancements by stitching and dry embossing thin metal sheets. *Sample by Laura Stewart.* **Supplies** *Metal sheet:* ScrapMetal, Once Upon a Scribble; *Frame template:* Darice.

For-get Me Not

Figure 5. Create an elegant photo mat with punches and embossing enamel. *Page by Erin Lincoln.* **Supplies** *Specialty paper:* ArtisticScrapper.com; *Punch and pop dots:* All Night Media; *Fiber:* On the Surface; *Stamping ink:* VersaMark, Tsukineko; Fresco, Stampa Rosa; *Embossing enamel:* Cloisonné, Stampa Rosa; *Rubber stamp:* Impress Rubber Stamps; *Computer font:* 2Peas Dragonfly, downloaded from *www.twopeasinabucket.com; Other:* Beads and bookplate.

Embossed Frame

When I saw the new decorative punches from All Night Media, I couldn't wait to get hold of them. Once I did, however, I wondered what I was going to do with them. I began experimenting and discovered I could make embossed-metal designs that looked like charms. Even better, once assembled into a frame, these little metal punches created an elegant, sophisticated design that resembled a metal filigree frame like those used to display formal photos. All this from a simple little punch! Here's how to create an embossed frame like that in Figure 5:

❶ Punch 22 decorative punches from white cardstock.

❷ While the punch I used is designed to work as a silhouette punch, go ahead and cut the design from the cardstock. Round the corners for a more elegant look.

Press the punched image into an embossing inkpad, coating the entire surface of one side.

❸ Before the ink dries, coat it with Cloisonné granules. Pour off the excess and melt the ink with a heat gun. While the coating is still molten, pour on a second coat of granules and heat again.

Two coats will give you a more three-dimensional look. Emboss all 22 punches.

❹ Once you're finished embossing, assemble the punches in a frame on a piece of metallic specialty paper, keeping your edges straight. To create a frame for a 4" x 6" photo, I used seven punches for the width and six punches for the height. I used a Xyron machine to apply adhesive evenly and easily to the backs of the punches.

❺ Cut out the inside of the frame, trimming right along the edge of your punches. If desired, line the interior edge with a piece of colored cardstock for

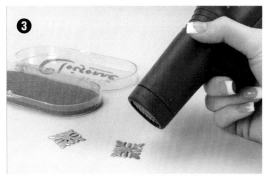

contrast against the photo.

6 Place your photo on your scrapbook page, then adhere your frame on top of the photo. I added depth with pop dots.

Some ideas to note? I assemble my frame separately from my photo so I have more freedom with the dimensions. If I tried to make the frame around my photo, the number of whole punches per side wouldn't equal the length of the photo. By placing the frame on top of the photo, you don't have to crop the photo to fit inside. Instead, you're just covering up what doesn't fit inside the frame.

The small flower accent tucked into the bookplate can be removed (the title stays behind). The journaling appears on the back.

—*Erin Lincoln, Frederick, MD*

Adding Sketches

I wanted to keep track of the sketches featured monthly in "One Sketch, Many Looks," but sticky notes and loose pieces of paper just weren't cutting it. I decided to figure out a way to include Becky Higgins' sketches within her *My Creative Companion* book. Here's the solution I found:

1 Cut your cardstock to 8½" x 5½". Draw, photocopy or print the sketches onto your cardstock, then punch one side with the Rollabind punch. (Rollabind punch systems are available in a variety of styles and price ranges.)

2 Slide the page up and center the existing holes between the punch indicators. Punch again.

3 Now, just add these pages where they fit best in your copy of *My Creative Companion* and "be like Becky" (Figure 6). If you don't have a Rollabind punch or access to one, check binding options at your local copy shop or office supply store. Take your *My Creative Companion* to show them the binding—they should be able to help you.

—*Sharon Bissett O'Neal, Lee's Summit, MO*

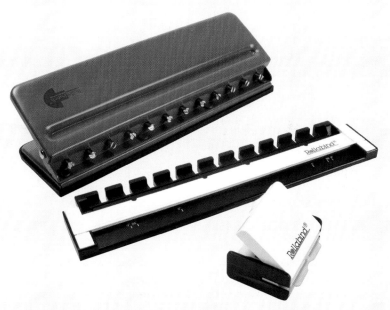

Figure 6. Use a Rollabind punch to customize your copy of *My Creative Companion*.

Editor's note: Find Becky's upcoming sketches on our web site at *www.creatingkeepsakes.com*. Click on "Magazine," "Submit Your Ideas" and "One Sketch, Many Looks." Position your mouse over the sketch images, right-click and select "Copy." Open a Word document and paste the images in. Print them on the paper of your choice, trim and punch.

faux walnut ink and resized frames

Figure 1. Get the look of walnut ink with acrylic paint and water. *Page by Erin Lincoln.* **Supplies** *Acrylic paint:* Plaid Enterprises; *Leaf punch:* The Punch Bunch; *Tag and definition sticker:* Making Memories; *Alphabet stamps:* PSX Design; *Stamping ink:* Ancient Page, Clearsnap; *Pen:* Zig Writer, EK Success; *Computer fonts:* Both 2Peas Rustic and 2Peas Champagne, downloaded from *www.twopeasinabucket.com;* *Other:* Watercolors, fibers and silk leaf.

Faux Walnut Ink

Recently I've become infatuated with the aged look of walnut ink (Figures 1 and 2). With a little experimentation, I've discovered a way to re-create this look with acrylic paint, water and finger painting. Since acrylic paints come in a rainbow of colors, you aren't limited

ARTICLE BY LORI FAIRBANKS

to just the brown antique look. You can also use white paint on dark cardstock for a muted look. Let's finger paint!

❶ Station yourself at the kitchen sink. Squirt two tablespoons of brown acrylic paint onto your fingers, then work the paint into a sheet of white cardstock until it's fully covered. Vary your paint coverage to add depth to your finished product.

❷ Rinse the paint from your hands and the cardstock. Most of the paint will wash away, leaving a washed-out tint to your paper. For a darker color, rinse briefly. Hold the sheet under water longer for just a hint of color.

❸ Let your cardstock dry. After a few hours, place it under a heavy object, such as a box or book, to reduce warping. You're done when the paper is completely dry.

—*Erin Lincoln, Fredrick, MD*

Editor's note: Wondering how to use real walnut ink? See Julie Turner's tips and tags on page 144 of the October 2003 issue.

Figure 2. Experiment with various colors and shades to get the aged look you want. Here, various shades of brown, yellow and pink were used on white cardstock, with white acrylic paint used on brown cardstock for the last one. *Samples by Erin Lincoln.*

Resizing Frames

Is your picture too large or small for your premade frame? Would your photo look better framed as a square instead of a rectangle? You can still use your premade frame with a few adjustments (Figure 3).

Here's how to enlarge your frame:

❶ Cut out a section from the middle of the small sides of *two* frames. Make sure you leave the corners intact.

❷ Overlap the four sides until the frame fits your photo. (I place the frame pieces at 90-degree angles around my photo to get the exact size.) Apply removable adhesive to the overlapping edges. This holds the frame in place so you can remove the photo.

❸ Using a ruler and craft knife, miter the corners by cutting a 45-degree angle through the overlapped layers of the frame. (A quilting ruler shows a 45-degree angle.)

❹ Remove the extra frame pieces. Mount your photo to the layout, then attach the frame to your layout with the corners fitted together. No one can tell your frame is pieced!

Here's how to reduce your frame:

❶ Cut two diagonal corners at 45-degree angles. Adjust the pieces to get the size you want.

❷ Use a removable adhesive to hold the frame in place, then miter the corners with a craft knife. (See step 3 for

→

Leaving the corners intact, cut a small section from the short sides of the frame.

Place the frame pieces around your photo. Apply removable adhesive to the overlapping edges.

Figure 3. Resize premade frames to fit your photos. *Page and samples by Debbie Hill for Polly & Friends, Leeco Industries. Photo by Jennifer Frank.* **Supplies** *Frames:* Polly & Friends, Leeco Industries; *Patterned paper:* 7 Gypsies; *Rubber stamp, stamping ink and chalk:* Stampin' Up!; *Computer fonts:* Apple Chancery, Macintosh (journaling); Aristocrat LET, downloaded from the Internet; *Tags:* Debbie's own design; *Other:* Eyelets.

enlarging the frame.) Adhere the picture and frame to your layout.

Variation: For additional frame accents, cut mini-frames into four pieces and use them as photo or page corners. Cut the straight side for four L-shaped corners, or cut along the diagonal corners for a different look.

—Debbie Hill,
Polly & Friends, Leeco Industries

After removing the photo, use a ruler and craft knife to miter the frame corners.

To reduce the frame, cut two diagonal corners and adjust the pieces to fit your photo.

ALPHABET STAMP HOLDERS

I love my alphabet stamps but hate how they get mixed up whenever I pull one out. To create individually positioned stamp holders, I purchased a block of floral foam from my local craft store. Using the wooden side of each stamp, I pressed a square into the foam block, which is the perfect size to hold each stamp. Now it's easy to keep my stamps organized.

—*Kiersten Schiffer, New Hartford, CT*

Figure 4. Photograph foods associated with traditional family gatherings. *Pages by Sara Tumpane.* **Supplies** *Patterned paper:* Scrap-Ease; *Computer fonts:* Dragonwick (title) and Schlimeyer Book (journaling), downloaded from the Internet; *Chalk:* Craf-T Products; *Pigment powder:* Pearl-Ex, Jacquard Products; *Other:* Aida cloth, fibers, metal buttons and liquid Gum Arabic. *Idea to note:* Sara gilded the edge of her journaling block with a mixture of liquid Gum Arabic and pigment powder.

Food Photography

Thanksgiving just wouldn't be Thanksgiving without my mom's cranberry-orange relish and sweet potato casserole, my sister's made-from-scratch rolls, the golden turkey and my four-layer, pumpkin cheesecake torte. We're passionate about our feast!

Since this meal is so important, why not photograph it? To complete the layout in Figure 4, I created my journaling in the style of a menu, listing the items on the left and describing them and who prepared them on the right.

—*Sara Tumpane, Grayslake, IL*

EYELET TIP

When I create a vellum journaling block that's anchored with eyelets, I don't hammer them directly into the layout because I've made too many costly errors. I make sure I have an extra piece of background paper to attach the journaling block to, and after I've successfully hammered in the eyelets, I then add my block to the layout.

If my background paper is patterned, I'm careful to line up the extra paper behind the journaling block evenly with the background paper so the extra paper is unnoticeable. This prevents colors from neighboring layouts from peeking through. Another benefit is that the rough metal eyelet edges are sandwiched between sheets of paper.

—*Victoria Jimenez, Harrah, OK*

Add Style with Serendipity Squares

Dimension with Paper Roll-ups

After reading "Playful Paper Roll-ups" in the February 2001 issue, I had fun adding them to a few of my layouts. Recently I came up with another use—to add dimension. By varying the width of the cardstock, I can "pop" an element off the page to any degree I choose. I simply cut a piece of cardstock the desired width, roll it up, attach a mounting square to each side of the roll-up, and use it between my background paper and the page element to be "popped" up.

—Joann Pettigrew
Regina, SK, Canada

Punch-out Help

Punch-outs help quick-and-easy layouts come together in a snap. My only complaint is those pesky perforated tags left over after punching out the image. To avoid having to trim them all off, I cut through each perforation with an X-acto knife instead of pushing the image out. I'm not left with any hanging tags, and the resulting punch-out has clean edges.

—Alison Beachem, San Diego, CA

Serendipity squares are small collage pieces that can be used on virtually any layout (see Figure 5). The variety of colors helps pull out the colors in your photos, and the squares serve as visual "bridges" when you're combining two different-colored photo mats.

I make a full sheet of serendipity squares at a time, mat them, then attach them to layouts as needed. Depending on your personal tastes, you can add as much torn paper or rubber stamping as desired.

◆ **SUPPLIES.** To create serendipity squares, you'll need: solid-colored cardstock, patterned paper that includes colors from your photos that you want to emphasize, adhesive, archival pigment inks (pinwheel pads and rainbow pads that pull apart work the best), rubber stamps, embossing powder and a tool for heat embossing (optional).

◆ **STEPS.** Once you've got the supplies needed, follow these steps:

❶ Choose the solid cardstock that will serve as the background for your squares.
❷ If you plan to emboss any of your stamped images, stamp randomly on your solid paper with pigment ink. (If you don't plan to emboss your images, skip to Step 8.) Sprinkle the stamped images with embossing powder, then melt it with a tool for heat embossing.
❸ Starting with the lightest color of ink, daub randomly onto the paper to make small, irregular shapes of color. This type of application is called "direct-to-paper." Don't worry if you cover an embossed image—the ink will wipe off. Cover 10–20% of the page with your first color.
❹ With the next lightest color of ink, use the direct-to-paper technique again, making small irregular, color shapes. Partially overlap your second color of ink over your first to make a third color.
❺ Use this technique with as many colors as you'd like to add. Work from light to dark and add metallic inks last. Leave some areas of your background paper uncolored.
❻ If you embossed, use a tissue to wipe off excess pigment ink from those areas.
❼ Blot your paper and set it aside to dry. Give it adequate time to dry to avoid smearing.
❽ Select your rubber stamps. Good choices include large background stamps that can cover several squares and small images that can fit easily into a single square. I like to choose 4–5 stamps that fit a theme, plus a large background stamp of script.
❾ Using permanent black ink, stamp your larger images randomly on your background paper.
❿ Rip your patterned paper into strips that are approximately ½" to 1" wide and 6–8" long. Adhere strips randomly all over your background.
⓫ Restamp if necessary. With black ink, stamp smaller images in any unfilled space. Don't worry about overall composition of the full sheet, but try to have at least one element (ink, stamp, paper) on every square inch of the paper.
⓬ Use a paper trimmer to cut your large sheet into uniform-sized squares. I like them in 1¼" or 1½" sizes. You'll end up with dozens of delightfully unique squares.
⓭ Mat each square onto a metallic- or solid-colored background layer that's ¼" larger than the square.

—Nancy Korf, Portland, OR

Figure 5. Create a collage of accents to spice up your pages. *Page by Nancy Korf.* **Supplies** *Background rubber stamp:* Asian Poetry, Stampin' Up!; *Chinese seals rubber stamps:* Quatro Elementes, Hero Arts; *Rubber stamps:* Magenta; *Stamping ink:* Clearsnap and Tsukineko; *Computer font:* Viner Hand, ITC Fonts; *Pearl Ex:* USArt Quest; *Embossing powder:* Stampin' Up!; *Other:* Mizuhiki paper cord and Japanese paper treated with Archival Mist deacidification spray.

paper flowers

Figure 1. Use your punches to create dimensional flowers for your layouts. *Sample by Teresa Lewis.* **Supplies** *Patterned paper and letter stickers:* Provo Craft; *Punches:* All Night Media (jumbo flower), EK Success (simple flower and sunburst), Emagination Crafts (small leaf and Christmas star), Family Treasures (large flower) and McGill (small sun and alpine trees); *Chalk:* Craf-T Products; *Craft wire:* Crown Fox; *Ribbon:* Klein Ribbon Corp.; *Eyelets:* Doodlebug Design; *Other:* Teresa used text-weight paper from Kinko's to create the flowers.

Become a Paper Florist

I love punches, and over the last few years, I've collected over 200 of them! Not wanting them to become the latest additions to my "has-been" craft closet, I pulled them out and started looking for new uses for them.

After making dozens of tissue-paper flowers with my daughter last winter, I thought, "I bet I could use this same idea with punches, wire and stationery-weight paper. I could probably make flowers small enough to use as page accents."

Since I love adding dimension to my projects, I quickly began adding these little blossoms to everything I could. Here's how you can create paper flowers with your punches (Figure 1):

❶ First, decide what kind of flower you want, then choose your punches. I find that simple, sym-

CK
technique ★ technique

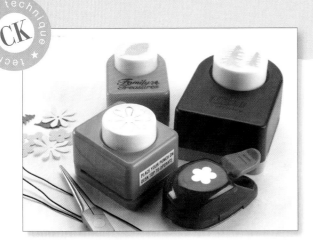

metrical shapes work best. Each flower will need between 3–6 layers, depending on the size of the punch and the desired dimension.

2 Punch out the desired shapes. To save time, I use the Power Punch tool by Tapestry in Time to punch several pieces at once and create flowers in an "assembly line" fashion. Pile shapes on top of one another, then punch holes in the center of the shapes with a ⅛" circle punch.

3 Using small, needle-nose pliers, bend a 6" piece of craft wire at the top. You want it to form a little nub to keep the punches from falling off when you add them. Beginning with the first punched shape, slide it onto the wire and scrunch it around the nub. Continue layering the punches in this fashion, one at a time, until the desired flower size is achieved. Twist the pieces around to stagger the flower petals.

4 Using your pliers, twist the same piece of wire tightly on the underside of the flower, forming a tiny spiral to keep the petals from slipping down. (*Note:* You can use small beads to form both the nub and the spiral if desired.) The tighter you cluster your

blossoms on the wire, the more crush-resistant the flower becomes. You can clip the wire off or use it as a stem.

5 I like to use Delta Archival Glue when attaching the flowers to my page. The adhesive dries clear and will hold dimensional pieces permanently. I also use glue dots as temporary anchors until the craft glue dries.

Here are a few additional tips:

◆ For variety, use a different shape to create the flower's center. A small sun punch works well for a spiky center. You can also use a bead at the end of the wire to make your center.

◆ Don't forget to use your leaf and tree punches to add greenery to your flowers. You can crease the leaves to add dimension.

◆ Use chalk or pigment inks to highlight and shadow the petals and leaves.

You can make any kind of flower with this technique, from funky and exotic to simple and elegant. The real fun comes from experimenting with your punches and seeing all the interesting flowers you can make!

—*Teresa Lewis, Sandy, UT*

paper quilting and exposed brick backgrounds

Figure 1. Add a homemade, quilted look to your pages with stitched and stuffed frames and accents. *Pages and samples by Cindy Cragun.* **Supplies** *Patterned paper:* Patchwork Paper Design; *Cotton batting:* Mountain Mist; *Pearl cotton:* DMC; *Buttons:* Hillcreek Designs; *Computer fonts:* Chicken Shack and Stained Glass, downloaded from *www.twopeasinabucket.com*; CK Fresh, "Fresh Fonts" CD, *Creating Keepsakes.*

Paper Quilting

I've always been drawn to hand stitching and the look and feel of quilts. I wished that I had more time for quilting until I realized that I could "quilt" on my scrapbook pages. Here's how I did it:

❶ Spritz a piece of patterned paper with water. Crinkle it, then iron the wrinkles into the paper to give it a worn look.

❷ Select a template or cookie-cutter shape—you can even create your own design. Cut the shape from the crinkled paper.

❸ Choose a background paper. I like using a color that contrasts with the color of the patterned paper. Use a small amount of adhesive to attach a few corners of the shape to the background paper.

❹ With the help of a self-healing mat,

mouse pad or foam core, pre-poke the stitching holes using a needle, awl or paper-piercer.

⑤ Thread your embroidery needle with embroidery floss or pearl cotton, then tie a knot in
one end. I use anywhere from 2–6 strands of embroidery floss.

⑥ Begin your stitching by going up and down through the holes. This is called a running stitch.

⑦ Before finishing the stitching, leave an opening large enough for a small amount of cotton batting to be stuffed into the stitched shape. Tear small pieces of batting and use an awl to "push" the batting into the shape. You may also use a small dowel or even a toothpick, depending on the size of your shape. Once the batting is in, finish stitching the shape and tie a knot in the back.

⑧ Trim your background paper ⅛" to ¼" from your stitched shape.

⑨ Embellish as you wish.

   —*Cindy Cragun, Patchwork Paper Design*

Eyelet Threader

I had trouble threading fibers through ⅛" eyelets on my layouts, so I made an eyelet "threader" with copper wire. To make a threader, cut a 2½" piece of wire and bend ¼" like a hook until the end almost touches itself. On the other end, make a little curl for the handle.

To use the threader, all you have to do is stick the tiny hook through the eyelet, loop your fibers over the wire, then slide them into the hook. Pull it through the eyelet and slide the fibers off. This works like a charm!

   —*Veronica Johnson, Albion, IN*

Patterned Paper Binders

I own so many patterned papers that I often forget what I have. For quicker paper selection, I store my patterned papers in 8½" x 11" and 12" x 12" page protectors, then sort them into binders by theme (such as floral, checks and plaids, baby or heritage). Any papers I buy are immediately filed into the appropriate category.

When I need to select paper, I just flip through the pages in my binder. I lay my photos and accents on top of each page protector to see if they coordinate with the paper. This may take more time to sort and file, but when I need my entire collection, it's at my fingertips!

   —*Catherine Porterfield, Chesapeake Beach, MD*

Figure 2. Create a worn and weathered look on your layout by adding an exposed brick background. *Pages by Erin Lincoln.* **Supplies** *Patterned paper:* Wübie Prints; *Metallic paper:* Paper Adventures; *Paper crimper:* Fiskars; *Pen:* The Ultimate Gel Pen, American Crafts; *Filmstrip punch:* The Punch Bunch; *Eyelets:* Making Memories; *Chalk:* Craf-T Products; *Computer fonts:* Comet and Marker Fine Point, downloaded from the Internet. *Ideas to note:* Erin used a punch negative and the Empressor by Chatterbox to emboss her page borders. She printed the text in gray and traced over it with a white gel pen to create the look of white text

Exposed Brick Background

While looking for a creative way to scrapbook these pictures of my husband and sister playing around, I turned to my photos for inspiration. I was fascinated by the texture of the blue paint wearing away and revealing the brick underneath, so I followed these steps to re-create the look for my layout in Figure 2:

❶ As you can see, the ripped sections on my layout include tearing away part of a journaling box, so construct your page fully with the exception of adding your photos. I recommend having a good idea where you plan to place your pictures, so you can plan the ripped sections of your background accordingly.

❷ Using a sharp object like the tips of your scissors, pierce the background paper in the center of where you plan to have a tear. You need to use a sharp object because in some cases you're trying to pierce through several layers of cardstock. If you're careful, you can do this without unnecessarily bending the paper.

❸ With your fingers, start tearing away the edges of the hole until the desired diameter is reached. Again, you're work-ing with various layers of cardstock, so work with one layer at a time. I wanted the edges of the bottom piece of paper (blue) to fold up over the edges of the ripped section, so I didn't tear the blue rip as wide as the white rip at upper left. I was able to fold it up and over, leaving no white edges showing.

❹ Place patterned paper (the brick paper in the example) behind the ripped holes and adhere it.

❺ Chalk the edges of your tear to lessen the harsh edges and add a worn look.

—*Erin Lincoln, Frederick, MD*

Transparent Paint Accents

Last summer, my children transformed our patio door into a stained-glass work of art with water-based "Paint, Peel and Stick-on Transparent Paint." It looked like so much fun that I joined in. While working with the paint, I had a wonderful idea—why not use it to paint accents and titles for my scrapbook layouts?

The transparent paint offers almost unlimited options because you can use virtually any printed design as a pattern. You can even create special effects by blending colors and using different tools like toothpicks or brushes.

Because the product is designed for glass and mirrors, I wondered how it would respond to cardstock, photos and page protectors. The only difficulty I've run into is having painted accents stick to each other (sometimes they're impossible to separate without tearing). The painted accents are lightweight, flat, and easy to trim and adhere.

To create painted accents, you'll need tubes of "paint, peel and stick-on transparent paint" (I used Liquid Rainbow).

Figure 3. Create unique accents for your pages using peel 'n' stick transparent paint. *Page by Twyla Koop.* **Supplies** *Patterned paper:* O'Scrap!, Imaginations!; *Hole punch:* McGill; *Photo corners:* Running Rhino & Co.; *Paint:* Liquid Rainbox, DecoArt; *Computer fonts:* Alleycat ICG, Bradley Hand ITC, Bickley Script LET, Apple Chancery and Bertram LET, AppleWorks 6; CK Fun and CK Pretty, "The Art of Creative Lettering" CD, *Creating Keepsakes; Other:* Mini brads and craft wire.

You'll also need a styrene painting blank (I used a Plexiglas board). Have more than one so your children can join you. In our home, three is sometimes not enough!

Simply follow these easy steps:

❶ Place your pattern beneath the Plexiglas.

❷ Squeeze the paint directly from the bottle to outline the design. If you want to fill in the design, gently squeeze the paint and move the tip from side to side.

❸ Let the paint dry for 24 hours (or until the paint is transparent—the paint will appear cloudy until it dries). Gently peel the shapes from the Plexiglas and adhere them to your layout (see Figure 3) with double-sided tape.

—*Twyla Koop, Surrey, BC, Canada*

MORE USES FOR STYLUS

Instead of using a pen or pencil with my Magic Matter by Puzzle Mates, I use a small dry embossing stylus. It makes a nice impression that doesn't have to be erased. I can then easily follow the impression with my scissors.

I also use the stylus for tearing mulberry paper. With the help of a ruler, I score the paper with the stylus. It makes the tearing precise and easy—and I don't need any water. This technique also works great with the Magic Matter when I want to tear the mulberry paper into shapes and circles.

—*Deanna Doyle, Coopersburg, PA*

Supplies *Stickers:* Karen Foster Design; *Foam sheet:* Fibre-Craft; *Circle punch:* Marvy Uchida; *Craft wire:* Artistic Wire Ltd.; *Beads and nailhead:* Jewelcraft; *Jingle bells:* Westrim Crafts; *Other:* Jute.

Supplies *Stickers:* Karen Foster Design; *Foam sheet:* Fibre-Craft; *Button:* Dress It Up; *Foam squares:* Therm O Web.

Figure 4. Use pre-made die cuts to create shadow-box embellishments. *Page and samples by Shannon Landen.* **Supplies** *Patterned paper and die cuts:* All About Me, Pebbles in my Pocket; *Foam sheets:* Fibre-Craft; *Craft wire:* Artistic Wire Ltd.; *Beads, eyelets and washers:* Jewelcraft; *Vellum:* The Paper Company; *Clear film:* Pockets on a Roll, F & M Enterprises; *Star sequins:* Mark Enterprises; *Pen:* Slick Writer, American Crafts; *Foam squares:* Therm O Web; *Computer fonts:* Butterbropapier (journaling) and Problem Secretary (title), downloaded from the Internet; *Stamping ink:* Clearsnap.

Supplies *Punch-outs:* Two Busy Moms; *Clear film:* Pockets on a Roll, F & M Enterprises; *Foam sheet:* Fibre-Craft; *Beads:* Create A Craft.

Shadow-box Accents

Did you know you can create shadow-box accents with preprinted accents and sheets of craft foam? Die cuts, cutouts and stickers work well. When using stickers, first adhere them to cardstock and cut them out. Follow these steps:

❶ Begin by punching or cutting a hole in the accent. Save the punched piece.

❷ Trace the accent twice on the foam sheet and cut the foam ⅛" inside the traced line.

❸ Punch or cut a hole in the top layer of foam (or both layers if the contents of your shadow box are bulky). If desired, place the punched-out piece of your die cut inside the hole. Another option is to offset this piece on top of your finished accent with a pop dot.

❹ Adhere the accent and both layers of foam together.

❺ To create a shadow box with buttons, poke a small hole in the center of the bottom layer of foam. Affix the button shank inside the hole with a small amount of liquid glue.

Variation: To create a shaker-box accent, fill the hole with beads, then adhere a piece of clear plastic film over the top of the accent.

—*Shannon Landen, San Antonio, TX*

Supplies *Cut-out:* We R Memory Keepers; *Foam sheet:* Fibre-Craft; *Button:* Dress It Up.

antique embossing, printing on twill tape and ribbon, and more

Figure 1. Add an elegant finish to your layout with an antique embossed border. *Pages by Tracy Kyle.*
Supplies *Rubber stamps:* Stampendous!; *Stamping ink:* VersaMark, Tsukineko; *Embossing powder:* Hero Arts; *Metallic rub-ons:* Craf-T Products; *Acrylic paint:* Folk Art; *Other:* Mat board.

Antique Embossing

Love the look of embossed ceiling tiles so popular in home décor right now? Try this look on your pages with mat board, watercolor paper or metal accents. Here's how:

❶ Choose a stamp design (mosaic, floral, fleur de lis, toile and antique designs work well).

Stamp your design with clear embossing ink, then sprinkle it with clear embossing powder. Melt the powder with a heat gun. (See steps on page 62.)

❷ Apply a layer of acrylic paint over the entire piece and let it dry. →

Tips & Tricks

❸ Gently scrub the paint from the embossed areas using a damp terry cloth.
❹ Add metallic rub-ons for extra dimension.

Variation: If you're working with metal, apply a layer of paint first and let it dry before stamping your design (Figure 2).
—*Fran Seiford, Stampendous!*

Step 1. Stamp on mat board with embossing ink, then heat emboss.
Samples by Tracy Kyle.

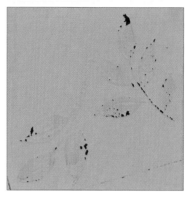

Step 2. Paint a medium-thick layer of acrylic paint over the entire area.

Step 3. Take a damp terry cloth and rub over painted area to reveal the stamped image.

Step 4. Apply metallic rub-ons to add dimension.

Get more innovative stamping ideas in Fran's book, *Embellishments for Rubber Stamp Art*, published by Design Originals.

Hint: Want to ensure an evenly stamped image? Use acrylic stamps and handles. You can see the ink through the handles so you know if the ink has transferred to your surface.

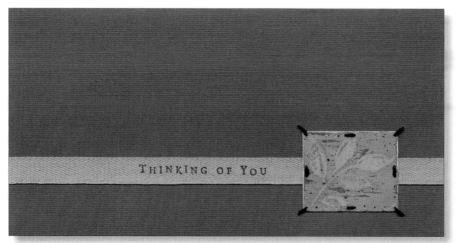

Figure 2. Before stamping the tin, Tracy painted it green so the color would show through. For additional texture, she lightly spattered black paint over the finished tin. *Card by Tracy Kyle.* **Supplies** *Stitched metal tin:* Making Memories; *Embroidery floss:* DMC; *Rubber stamps:* Hero Arts ("Thinking of You") and Stampendous! (leaves); *Stamping ink:* StazOn, Tsukineko; *Acrylic paint:* Folk Art; *Other:* Twill tape.

Figure 3. Soft, muted chalks help form a cozy setting for pictures of tiny kittens. *Page by Kim Morgan.* **Supplies** *Stamping ink:* ColorBox, Clearsnap; Marvy Matchables, Marvy Uchida; VersaMark, Tsukineko; *Letter stamps:* Hero Arts (small) and PSX Design; *Metal letter and eyelets:* Making Memories; *Chalk:* Stampendous!; *Fiber:* On The Surface.

Chalking with VersaMark

Chalk and VersaMark (a watermark stamp pad) have been pairing up on layouts for some time now. It's no wonder—they make a great team! Here's a technique that's sure to add punch to your pages.

To create blocks of mottled color like those in Figure 3:

❶ Choose several colors of chalk that coordinate with your layout. Generously rub a cotton ball in each color of ink and set the cotton balls aside. *Tip:* Chalks change color when applied to VersaMark ink. You may want to experiment on scraps of cardstock.

❷ Painter's tape is less sticky than regular masking tape. Use it to mask off the outside perimeter of the area you wish to color.

❸ Holding the VersaMark pad upside-down, rub inside the masked area until it's completely covered with ink.

❹ Choose a chalked cotton ball and dab color sparsely over the area. Repeat with the remaining colors of chalk until the area is colored.

❺ For a more blended look, rub a clean cotton ball over the entire area. Carefully peel away the tape.

WANT A MORE SPONTANEOUS LOOK?

Try this variation (Figure 4):

❶ Instead of masking off an area, lightly draw its perimeter with a pencil.

❷ Press one corner of the VersaMark pad firmly on the paper and pull it across the area, slowly lifting the pad as you go. Repeat as needed for the design. VersaMark ink tints the paper a shade darker than its original color, so it's easy to see where you've applied the ink.

→

Figure 4. Using textured cardstock creates a different feel. *Pages by Kim Morgan.* **Supplies** *Chalk:* Stampendous!; *Stamping ink:* Hero Arts, Ranger Industries and Tsukineko; *Letter stamps:* Hero Arts (small) and All Night Media; *Embroidery floss:* DMC.

❸ Chalk as instructed in steps 4 and 5. If any chalk ends up in an unwanted area, you can easily erase it.

This look is versatile enough to use almost anywhere on a page. Give it a try and see what you can do with this dynamic duo!

—*Kim Morgan, Pleasant Grove, UT*

PERFECT PUNCH PLACEMENT

I like making cards with a simple square window on the front. The trick is centering and aligning the square punch. To get your punch perfectly aligned every time, follow these easy steps:

❶ Punch a square from scrap paper. Use this piece as your template.

❷ Use temporary adhesive to mount the template square where you want your opening.

❸ Center the punch over the template square. Punch the template out. You now have a perfectly aligned square window.

Try this technique with all your shape punches!

—*Alison Beachem, San Diego, CA*

Figure 5. Print on twill tape or ribbon to create customized word accents. *Page and samples by Faye Morrow Bell.* **Supplies** *Patterned paper:* Design Originals; *Textured card-stock:* Bazzill Basics; *Twill tape:* Wrights; *Computer fonts:* Graverplate (layout) and Mom's Typewriter (twill tape), downloaded from the Internet; CK Tipsy (ribbon), "Fresh Fonts" CD, *Creating Keepsakes; Diamond, star and playing card symbols:* Microsoft Word; *Rubber stamp:* Limited Edition Rubber Stamps (compass); *Ribbon:* C.M. Offray & Son.

Printed Twill Tape

I love using words and lettering as design elements on my layouts. Printing my own words on twill tape and ribbon is a fun and easy way to add a customized textual element. Follow these easy steps to create your own customized ribbon and twill tape:

❶ Type your text into a word-processing program, then print it on a plain sheet of paper. Consider including small dingbats and symbols as part of your text.

❷ Center your ribbon or twill tape over the text. (Work in strong light or use a light box so you can see the text through the ribbon or twill tape.)

❸ Adhere the edges of the ribbon or twill tape securely to your paper with masking tape, then send the paper through your printer again.

In Figure 5, I used my customized twill tape as my layout title. A fun variation?

Try printing a favorite nursery rhyme or children's song lyrics on grosgrain ribbon and tie it around a photo of a sleeping child to create a charming embellishment.

—*Faye Morrow Bell, Charlotte, NC*

Tips & Tricks

Hot Glue Embellishments

Use pH-neutral colored hot glue sticks to add dimensional embellishments to your pages. Try the following fresh ideas:

◆ Use the glue with molds to create raised designs (Figure 6). Coat the mold evenly with pigment ink, then disperse warm glue into the mold. After the glue cools, insert a knife tip in the edge of the mold to pop out the design. Wipe off excess pigment ink and add powdered pigments, foil or metallic leaf. Because of the cling effect, these products will stick to the cool glue.

Hint: For larger molds, use multiple glue guns. This prevents the glue from hardening and cracking.

◆ Create faux wax seals with rubber stamps (Figure 7). Dispense the warm glue onto your work surface (flexible silicon and Teflon surfaces work best). Coat your stamp with clear pigment (or embossing) ink and set it on the glue. Don't press it in—the stamp will sink on its own. When the glue completely cools, remove the stamp and embellish as desired.

◆ Write words or create random, squiggled accents (Figure 8). Remember to write on your non-stick work surface so you can easily transfer the accent to your page.

Try embedding metal or plastic charms and embellishments in the warm glue.

—*DeAnne Velasco Musiel*
Rubba Dub Dub, Art Sanctum

Figure 6. *Tag by DeAnne Velasco Musiel.* **Supplies** *Colored glue sticks, fibers, natural elements and grass mat:* Rubba Dub Dub, Art Sanctum; *Face mold:* Amaco; *Metallic rub-ons:* Craf-T Products.

Figure 7. *Tag by DeAnne Velasco Musiel.* **Supplies** *Colored glue sticks, netting, fibers and rubber stamp:* Rubba Dub Dub, Art Sanctum; *Metallic rub-ons:* Craf-T Products; *Pigment powder:* Pearl Ex, Jacquard Products; *Walnut ink:* Postmodern Design; *Foil:* Sunday International.

Figure 8. *Tag by DeAnne Velasco Musiel.* **Supplies** *Colored glue sticks and fibers:* Rubba Dub Dub, Art Sanctum; *Flower mold:* Amaco; *Metallic rub-ons:* Craf-T Products; *Pigment powder:* Pearl Ex, Jacquard Products; *Metallic leaf flakes:* Amy's Magic Flakes.

Temporary Photo Storage

For two years I organized my photos by separating them in plastic bags and filing them by album category. As my photo collection grew, I had an insurmountable pile of bags, but very few pages to look at. I felt like I was no better off than when I stored the photos in shoeboxes.

I wanted my family to enjoy our photos, so I used temporary adhesive and placed the photos on cardstock and then put them in page protectors in their respective albums. With this process, it took me one day to do more than 10 albums. On the title page of each of these albums, a note says, "Pardon the mess, this book is currently under construction." I no longer feel guilty for "hiding" my photos. When I'm ready to do a "real" page, I can browse through my albums to choose my photos.

—*Cheryl Laubacher, Brecksville, OH*

LETTER STAMPS TIP

Have a set of bold alphabet stamps? Here's how you can add a bit of texture for a completely different look for your stamps. After you've inked each alphabet letter, stamp it once onto a piece of bubble wrap, a scrunched-up paper towel or piece of foil, a washcloth or anything with texture. (You can even draw squiggly lines on your stamps with a toothpick—your imagination is the limit!) Stamp on your paper. You'll notice that the stamps have taken on a new look—they'll have a unique design every time.

—*Kim Demory, Eagle Grove, IA*

ways to include
MORE
PHOTOS

Do a lot more in a little space · by Jana Lillie

Each day, 55 million photos are taken in America. That's 20 billion a year! And guess where those photos end up? Too often, anywhere but on a scrapbook page. Look closely, and you'll find loose pictures lurking in drawers, envelopes and boxes.

Not every picture needs to be scrapbooked, of course. You can toss those "not so great" shots or include extras in divided protectors behind corresponding scrapbook pages. But what about those times when you want to show several strong photos in a limited space? It can be done! Consider the fresh tips and approaches by the following scrapbookers.

Supplies *Rubber stamps:* Hero Arts; *Metal studs:* Dritz; *Eyelets:* Making Memories; *Ink pad:* Clearsnap; *Chalk:* Craf-T Products; *Other:* Jute.

"Matt"
by Charla Campbell
Rogersville, MO

- Display small photos artistically on decorative tags.
- Create a flap to hold additional items by adhering a second piece of paper off-center behind the original page. Fold the paper back over the original page.

17

photos on two pages

"Days of Awe"
by Marcy Schwarz
Syosset, NY

• Scan photos, then create a photo montage with photo-editing software.
• Choose one tint (such as sepia) for the photos to create a simple visual harmony.

15 photos on two pages

Supplies *Patterned and solid papers:* Anna Griffin; *Gold vellum:* Source unknown; *Star of David rubber stamp:* PSX; *Computer fonts:* Hippopotamus (title), downloaded from the Internet; Papyrus (journaling), Microsoft Word; *Snaps and metal tags:* Making Memories; *Letter stickers:* Provo Craft; *Fibers:* Adornaments, EK Success; *Photo montage:* Created with PrintShop Deluxe, Broderbund; *Other:* Paper fasteners. *Ideas to note:* To add a more Jewish feel to her page, Marcy stamped the Star of David lightly in gold on the coordinating solid paper.

"Footprints"
by Tammy Lombardi
Valrico, FL

• Square punch not big enough? Try Tammy's solution: Cut a cardstock square to use as a template. Holding a photo up to the light, position the square behind the photo and adjust it so the subjects appear where you want them. Flip the photo over, trace around the template, then cut out your photo.

5 photos on one page

Supplies *Foot punch:* EK Success; *Vellum tag:* Making Memories; *Computer font:* Century Gothic, Microsoft Word; *Embroidery floss:* DMC; *Brads:* Magic Scraps.

Supplies *Patterned paper:* Scrap-Ease; *Computer font:* CAC Shishoni Brush, downloaded from the Internet; *Fiber:* On the Surface; *Embroidery floss:* DMC; *Fasteners:* Spartan Products; *Clip art:* Edelweiss, MS Design Gallery Live (on Internet); *Embossing powders:* Stampa Rosa (gold) and Top Boss (white); *Chalk:* Stampin' Up!.

"So Long, Farewell"
by Kristen Stittsworth
Ft. Huachuca, AZ

• Create one or more mini-albums to hold extra photos and journaling on a layout.
• To protect your mini-album, cut a hole its same size out of a page protector. People can view the album without removing any pages from the protector.
• Protect your album cover by cutting a square the same size from the lower corner of a page protector. Slide the piece of protector over your mini-album cover, then secure it with a small piece of transparent tape.

9
photos on two pages

Make a Mini-Album for Your Photos

by Kristen Stittsworth

Interested in making a mini-album to hold more photos? I'll show you how. First, select three pieces of square paper (cardstock or a lighter weight of paper). The squares can be any size—just be sure they're true squares. For the mini-album on my "So Long, Farewell" layout, I used 8½" x 8½" squares to create a 4½" square album. Follow these steps to create a similar album:

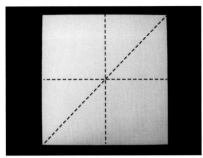

❶ Fold a square piece of paper or cardstock in half (may be scored first), then in half again. Make *one* diagonal fold. Fold the diagonal fold forwards, then back on itself again.

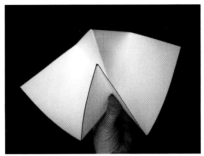

❷ With your fingers, squeeze the diagonal fold together until its two halves meet. When pressed flat, this will comprise one page of your album. Make two more pages using this folding technique.

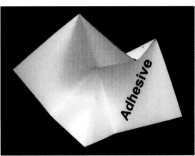

❸ Apply an adhesive to *one* inside square of *one* of your pages. A combination of photo-safe glue and photo mounts works well. Be sure the adhesive stays within the folds of the square.

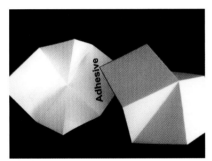

❹ Carefully attach a square on a second page to the adhesive on the square of the first page. You may want to practice this before applying your adhesive so you know exactly how they fit together.

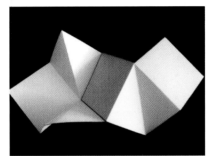

❺ Be sure your two pages are adhered well.

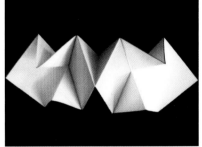

❻ Apply adhesive to *one* inside square of your third page. Adhere it to the free inside square of your second page. All three pages should now be attached.

❼ When pressed flat, the mini-album is complete. Decorate the cover any way you'd like. To keep the album closed, adhere the center of a long piece of ribbon or cord to the place you'll attach your album to your layout. Adhere your mini-album over the center of the ribbon or cord (again, glue and photo mounts work well), then bring the ends of the ribbon or cord around to tie over your album.

❽ Attach photos to the six full squares of your album. Use the opposite divided squares for journaling. Be sure to use photo-safe ink, since your photos will touch your journaling when the album is closed. (If this is still a concern, use duplicate photos.) Be creative and decorate the album any way you choose.

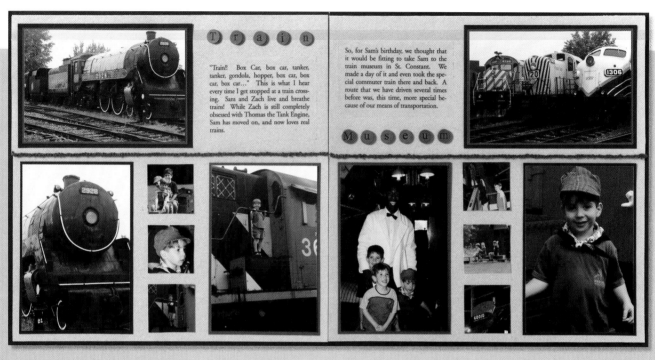

"Train Museum"
by Nicole Cholet
Beaconsfield, QC, Canada

- Run a vertical series of small photos between two larger photos.
- Create flaps that open at the top of the pages to reveal more photos and journaling.

photos on two pages

Supplies *Vellum:* It Takes Two; *Letter snaps:* Making Memories; *Fiber:* Adornaments, EK Success.

This was such a fun together day. Jeff had just returned from a week-long business trip, and we felt the need to have some quality family time. The kids enjoyed the open petting pools the most because they could reach in and touch stingrays, sharks, and starfish. They were taught to use their first two fingers and to be extremely gentle. I was bribed into going into the bird tent, and Drew and Jeff had birds all over them drinking the sugar water we were provided. Kenna was the bravest of us all in touching the sea creatures. She just went for it. And Nate ran around like usual wrecking havoc. Drew seemed very into learning about the different animals, and kept practicing how to say "aquarium". At the end of the day they each picked something out from the gift shop, and we ended our evening eating out and seeing Spy Kids.

AQUARIUM OF THE PACIFIC

august 2002

"Aquarium of the Pacific"
by Tara Whitney
Valencia, CA

• Choose which photos to keep full size, then randomly cut and punch more favorites into square or rectangular shapes. Place them on the layout, then cut additional pictures and journaling blocks to fill in the empty spots.

(12)

photos on two pages

"Snowden Family Album 2001"
by Lynda Snowden
Tocumwal, NSW, Australia

• Create a title page with small sections of photos. Include close-ups of faces for a compelling, personal touch.

36 photos on one page

Supplies *White vellum:* Paper Adventures; *Colored vellum:* Source unknown; *Pens:* Pigma Micron (title), Sakura; Zig Calligraphy (black border), EK Success; *Computer fonts:* CK Classic ("Family"), "The Art of Creative Lettering" CD; CK Cursive ("Snowden Album 2001"), "The Best of Creative Lettering" CD Combo, *Creating Keepsakes; Other:* Eyelets. *Ideas to note:* Lynda's layout is based on a Julie Turner layout in the *2001 CK Scrapbook Hall of Fame* book. To create her title, Lynda typed the words on her computer, output them, then traced them onto vellum.

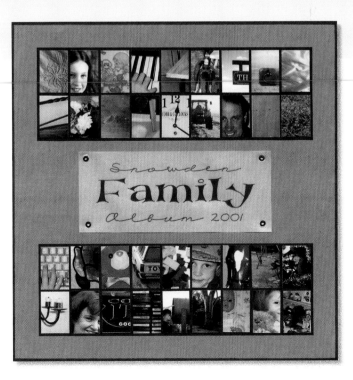

"Diamond Head"
by Jennifer Miller
Humble, TX

- Offset multiple photos in a checker-board format. Keep photo subjects roughly the same size for continuity.

9

photos on two pages

Supplies *Fibers:* On the Surface; *Square punch:* Emagination Crafts; *Buttons:* Making Memories; *Embroidery floss:* DMC; *Computer fonts:* Girls Are Weird (title) and P22 Garamouche (journaling), downloaded from the Internet.

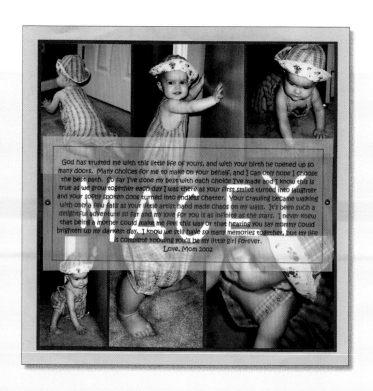

"Macey"
by Jennifer Lamb
Rolesville, NC

- Position photos side by side on a page, then use a vellum overlay for a journaling block. This is a great disguise for less-than-perfect photos as well.

6

6 photos on one page

Supplies *Vellum:* From www.patchworkmemories.com; *Eyelets:* From www.dscrapbooking.com; *Computer fonts:* Envisions ("Macey") and Kristen ITC (journaling), downloaded from the Internet. *Idea to note:* Jennifer used reverse lettering on her "Macey" title.

"It'll Make Your Head Spin"
by Lee Anne Russell
Brownsville, TN

- Include a large photo as your focal point.
- Position nine equal-sized photos on the facing page, leaving enough space between to create visual "lines." Place buttons at the points of intersection.

Supplies *Square punch:* Family Treasures; *Computer fonts:* BethsCuteHmk Bold and TwizotHmk, Hallmark; *Buttons:* Hillcreek Designs; *Embroidery floss:* DMC. *Ideas to note:* Lee Anne created a "splashy" background by cutting swirls from a lighter shade of cardstock and adhering them to a darker shade. Note how she grouped her buttons on the left-hand page for artistic effect.

10

photos on two pages

"Christmas Eve"
by Kim Heffington
Avondale, AZ

- Devote one half of your page to a large photo and journaling block, then use the other half to showcase related pictures.

9

photos on one page

Supplies *Letter stamps:* Hero Arts; *Stamping ink:* Tsukineko; *Pen:* Zig Writer, EK Success.

Supplies *Page extension:* Page Flipper, Paper Adventures; *Vellum:* The Paper Company; *Computer font:* Yippy Skippy, downloaded from the Internet; *Other:* Brads.

"A Week at the Beach"
by Lisa Simon
Roanoke, VA

- Use a page extension for journaling and to free up more page space.
- Place vellum journaling blocks over photos and affix with brads or adhesive.

(13)

photos on two pages

Products to Help You Fit More Photos

Manufacturers know it's tough to keep up with all those photos. Following are some of the solutions they've created to help you scrapbook more photos with style.

Take the worry out of wondering where to position your photos and accents.
The Deluxe Color Blocking Templates by Deluxe Cuts (*www.deluxecuts.com*) are designed to help you present numerous page elements in an aesthetically pleasing way. What if a photo doesn't fit the reserved space? "No problem," says scrapbooker Jennifer Bester. "Simply resize your photo on a scanner or mat it creatively." Check out the new Deluxe Cuts idea book to see how scrapbookers are using the templates.

Puzzle Mates (*www.puzzlemates.com*) has just released an All in One package that comes complete with four 12" x 12" templates, 10 layout ideas, tips and instructions. Discover new ways to include up to 14 photos on a page!
Or, consider using one of the company's puzzle templates to creatively arrange photos in a custom shape.

Close To My Heart (*www.closetomyheart.com*) offers five distinctive, 12" x 12" templates as part of its ABC Scrapbook Program II. Choose from collage, calendar, Granny's Quilt and more.

MARTHA CROWTHER

CLOSE TO MY HEART

ALISON BERGQUIST

Make lots of little pictures.
Want to crop your pictures smaller so you can fit more on a page? Consider the jumbo punches available from Emagination Crafts (*www.emaginationcrafts.com*), Family Treasures (*www.familytreasures.com*), Marvy Uchida (*www.uchida.com*) and McGill (*www.mcgill.com*).

Give your photos a "lift" without lifting a finger.
The Time Savers color-blocked papers by All My Memories (*www.allmymemories.com*) include embossed squares and rectangles that look like photo mats when you place pictures on them.

Other companies with color-blocked paper that lends itself to effortless photo matting include American Crafts (*www.americancrafts.com*), Memories Complete (*www.memoriescomplete.com*) and SEI, Inc. (*www.shopsei.com*).

LYNETTE SOUTHWICK

water play

See how three scrapbookers handle sprinkler fun

Nothing beats a hot summer day like a romp through the sprinklers, especially for four-year-old John Michael Thornton. His mother, Melisa Thornton of Munford, Tennessee, snapped these refreshing photos as he played in the yard last summer.

Melisa sent four pictures to the editors of *Creating Keepsakes* and asked us to help find creative ways to scrapbook them. We gave them to Heather Uppencamp, Tracy Robinson and Lee Anne Russell with the assignment to create a splashy two-page, 12" x 12" layout. Here's what they did. ❤

"Drink in Life"
by Heather Uppencamp
Provo, UT

SUPPLIES

Vellum: Provo Craft

Watch faces: Scrapworks

Clear beads: Magic Scraps

Picture pebble and metal alphabet tags: Making Memories

Alphabet stickers: Fancy Pants, Doodlebug Designs; Sonnets, Creative Imaginations

Computer font: Problem Secretary Regular, downloaded from the Internet

Adhesive: Scrappy Glue, Magic Scraps

HEATHER'S APPROACH

To keep the focus on the photos of John Michael, Heather opted for just cardstock and a simple design. "I chose the rust and orange colors to complement the green background and the warm tones of the photos," she says.

Heather double-matted her focal point and positioned another photo of John Michael (bottom left) looking to the right. "This helps lead the eye to the focal photo," she comments. She encased a smaller picture of John Michael and journaling information in watch faces, which also lend a wet touch to the layout.

Heather's water droplets—clear beads adhered with clear-drying glue—add the perfect touch for a dewy finish.

ARTICLE BY JEANNIE O'BRIEN

"Simple Pleasures"

by Tracy Robinson
Glen Waverly, Victoria, Australia

SUPPLIES

Patterned paper: Source unknown.
Computer fonts: Title: Petra Script (title), downloaded from the Internet; CK Jot (journaling), "The Art of Creative Lettering" CD, *Creating Keepsakes*
Rubber stamps: Dancing Block Alphabet set and Poetic Prints Season, Hero Arts
Silver brads and washers: Source unknown.
Stamping ink: Encore, Tsukineko
Tags: Making Memories

TRACY'S APPROACH

These photos couldn't have arrived at a better time for Tracy. "It was another warm day at the end of an extremely hot Australian summer," she says. Her daughter longed for a similar frolic in the sprinklers, an activity curtailed by drought and water restrictions. "To me, these pictures are just a happy reminder of carefree summer days filled with 'simple pleasures,' " says Tracy.

With photos this strong, Tracy didn't need anything else to tell the story. "They're a great reminder to get in close with your camera and capture the truly joyful moments of childhood," she says. To highlight that joy, Tracy chose a fresh and cool color palette of soft blues and greens.

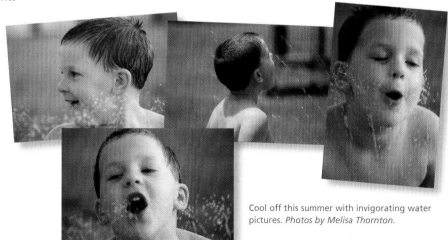

Cool off this summer with invigorating water pictures. *Photos by Melisa Thornton.*

"Water Boy"
by Lee Anne Russell
Brownsville, TN

SUPPLIES

Computer fonts: 2Peas Evergreen (title), downloaded from *www.twopeasinabucket.com*; CK Constitution (journaling), "Fresh Fonts" CD, *Creating Keepsakes*
Punches: Family Treasures and Emagination Crafts
Embossing powder: Amazing Glaze, JudiKins
Pewter sun sticker: Atelier de Paris
Eyelet letters: Making Memories
Concho: Scrapworks
Rubble: Magic Scraps
Other: Fiber

LEE ANNE'S APPROACH

Lee Anne couldn't help creating a wet look for these playful water pictures. "The scene looked so cool and inviting, I wanted to convey that in the pages," she says.

Lee Anne started by coating the title and journaling blocks with several layers of clear embossing powder. "I heated the layers enough to let the embossing powder drip off the paper's edge," notes Lee Anne. "This gave it the look of dripping water." A touch of rubble in various places creates the look of water droplets in the air.

By choosing monochromatic colors, Lee Anne's focus remains on the photos, especially the main one she enlarged. A subtle punched border adds a touch of design without overwhelming the photos. Lee Anne's title was inspired by "Water Boy," a movie starring Adam Sandler.

Paint a Backdrop

PHOTOGRAPHY

MICHELLE COLEMAN

Love the artistic backdrops used in studios? Paint your own! To create this backdrop, Michelle Coleman of Kaysville, Utah, strung wire between two plant hooks in her ceiling. She hung an old, white, king-sized sheet from the wire with clothespins.

Next, Michelle squirted several shades of tan and white Delta acrylic craft paint on a sturdy paper plate, crossing the lines of color. She applied the paint with a sea sponge for a marbled effect. *Note:* The paint will soak through; watch what the sheet touches as it dries. While painting, Michelle pressed a piece of cardboard on the other side of the sheet.

Stitch It!

JOURNALING

Want a homey, handcrafted look for your journaling? Stitch it! For the example here, Melanie Pontius of Ogden, Utah, sewed together squares of fabric. Next, she wrote her journaling with a white sewing pencil (available at most fabric stores) and stitched over the letters with embroidery floss.

Supplies *Craft wire:* Artistic Wire Ltd.; *Fiber:* On the Surface; *Buttons:* Dress It Up, Jesse James & Co.; *Embroidery floss:* DMC; *Circle punch:* McGill; *Pen:* Zig Writer, EK Success.

Repeat a Color Pattern

DESIGN

For a fun design touch, repeat a color pattern on your page. Here, Jordan Stone of Columbia, Missouri, repeats her blue, red and green pattern in three places: the rhinestones above her black-and-white photo, the slide holders framing her color photos, and the three rhinestones at bottom right on the page. Note how the order remains the same.

Supplies *Letter stickers:* Sonnets, Creative Imaginations; *Alphabet beads and craft wire:* Westrim Crafts; *Slide holders:* From www.scraps-ahoy.com; *Computer font:* 2Peas Sleigh Ride, downloaded from www.two-peasinabucket.com; *Other:* Rhinestones, beads and photo corners.

Ready, Set, Shoot!

TIME-SAVER

Bored with typical page titles? Not enough time to cut out all those intricate letters? Do what Jennifer Howland of North Adams, Massachusetts, does—let your camera take care of your title (or even your journaling).

Some ideas? Consider the following:

◆ At a beach, write a title in the sand (see below) and snap a picture.

◆ At a wedding, take a picture of a wedding program that tells about the bride and groom.

Use your imagination and your camera to save time!

BRIAN TIPPETTS

butterfly kisses

See how three scrapbookers captured the memory

FIVE-YEAR-OLD KAYCIE loves butterflies. Her mother, Debbie Landis of Goleta, California, says Kaycie was so excited to share everything she knew about butterflies with Lynn, a family friend. Imagine Kaycie's surprise when she learned Lynn raises monarch butterflies! Lynn gave the girl a chrysalis and a caterpillar and told her to watch as it evolved into a butterfly.

Debbie couldn't help taking pictures of

Kaycie as her daughter learned how to handle the new butterfly. She sent these five photos to *Creating Keepsakes* and asked us to find scrapbookers who could capture the beauty of Kaycie with her butterfly in a layout. We asked three talented scrapbookers—Patti Tschaen, Heidi Gnadke and Jodi Heinen—to give their interpretations of these cute pictures. Here are their versions of this memorable moment. ❤

"Butterfly Kisses"
by Patti Tschaen
Holmdel, NJ

SUPPLIES

Patterned paper: Making Memories
Butterfly die cut: Patti's own design
Butterfly rubber stamp: PSX Design
Computer font: Bradley Hand ITC, downloaded from the Internet

PATTI'S APPROACH

Patti just couldn't disregard the "Butterfly Kisses" title. Why? Because "even though the photos inspired it, the journaling and Kaycie's own words required it!" While sorting through her supplies, Patti came across a butterfly stamp that supplied the unique, graphic look she wanted.

With five eye-catching photos to use in this layout, Patti opted to feature the photo that best illustrates butterfly kisses. Notes Patti, "I kept the focus on this photo by using it on the first page and using the other photos as accents." Note how she cut out the butterfly for the top left accent.

Patti used purple mat accents to highlight the focal points and help balance the two pages.

ARTICLE BY JEANNIE O'BRIEN

"Little Girl Giggles and Butterfly Kisses"

by Heidi Gnadke
Centerville, MN

SUPPLIES

Patterned papers: Sonburn (multi-colored) and
Karen Foster Design (purple)

Fiber, eyelets and metal-rimmed tags:
Making Memories

Vellum and metallic paper: Paper Adventures

Flathead eyelets: Dotlets, Doodlebug Design

Computer fonts: Brock Script ("Butterfly") and
Echelon (journaling), downloaded from the
Internet

Metal: Art Emboss, AMACO

Clip art: Picture It!, Microsoft

Embossing powder: JudiKins

Ribbon: C.M. Offray & Son

Silk flowers: Silk Vision

Tag: Heidi's own design

Ideas to note: After printing part of her title
block and tags on vellum, Heidi immediately
heat-embossed them with silver embossing
powder. To create the metal accents, she
printed clip-art images, then dry-embossed
the patterns onto lightweight metal.

HEIDI'S APPROACH

Heidi was thrilled to see Debbie's expressive pictures. Even better, she was delighted to find Sonburn paper that included her layout's featured colors (lavender, green and blonde) and a nature theme. The centers of the flowers even pick up the orange of the butterfly.

"The patterned paper is visually complex, so I used a smaller amount," says Heidi. She added femininity with soft vellum tags, ribbon and silk flower accents. To soften the bright pink flower, Heidi mounted her journaling (printed on vellum) over the photo. As an elegant finale, Heidi hand-cut "Butterfly" in the metallic and purple patterned papers.

Capture a child's joy as she discovers the mysteries of nature.
Photos by Debbie Landis.

"Because"

by Jodi Heinen
Sartell, MN

SUPPLIES

Vellum: it takes two
Fiber: Adornaments, EK Success
Rubber stamp: Magenta Rubber Stamps
Stamping ink: ColorBox, Clearsnap
Embossing powder: Commotion
Computer fonts: Freestyle (journaling) and
Scriptina (quote), downloaded from the
Internet
Other: Ribbon

JODI'S APPROACH

Before Jodi began her layout, she read several articles about monarch butterflies. "I stumbled across a quote and included it to help pull everything together," she says.

Like Heidi and Patti, Jodi kept her main focus on the photo that shows the butterfly on Kaycie's nose. "I tried to stay away from strong embellishments that would detract from the photographs," she notes. Because the butterflies are so vivid, Jodi opted to let them stand on their own as accents.

Jodi admits that it was difficult to work with five dynamic photographs. "Debbie did a great job filling the lens with her subject," she says. "There was nothing to crop out!"

The Unexpected Angle

Look at most photos, and you'll find people in everyday stances. Pull a switch and photograph someone hanging upside-down! It's a surefire way to grab attention (see page by Cindy Knowles of Milwaukie, Oregon).

Scrapbook the photo in a playful yet memorable way. Position some (but not all) text upside-down. Include arrows to help determine direction. Then, sit back and watch people view the page from every angle!

Page by Cindy Knowles. **Supplies** *Patterned papers:* Carolee's Creations (green) and Provo Craft (antique); *Computer font:* Sister Europe (Mac font), downloaded from the Internet; *Craft wire:* Artistic Wire Ltd.; *Embroidery floss:* DMC; *Pop dots:* Stampa Rosa; *Sun design:* From thank-you card; *Other:* Burlap and slide holder.

Interviewing Mom

May's the month for mothers, so kidnap yours for lunch and a heart-to-heart talk. Ask her these questions and record her answers:

- How would you describe your personality?
- What are your interests?
- What do you value most in life and why?
- What's the dumbest/silliest thing you've ever done?
- How did you meet Dad? What was your first impression?
- What was it like dating Dad? How did he ask you to marry him?
- If you could change anything in your past or present, what would it be and why?
- How would you like to be remembered after you're gone?

It's in the Cards

Next time you're staring at leftover paper and accents from a scrapbooking session, do what Heidi Gnadke of Centerville, Minnesota, does: make a card or two. "Once I've figured out which items work well together," says Heidi, "the rest is easy. I just whip up a beautiful card that can be sent to someone at a moment's notice."

Note: Heidi's original layout appears on page 85.

Card by Heidi Gnadke. **Supplies** *Patterned papers:* Karen Foster Design (light purple) and Sonburn (multi-colored); *Metallic and vellum papers:* Paper Adventures; *Metal-rimmed tags:* Making Memories; *Letter stamps:* Hero Arts; *Embossing powder:* JudiKins; *Dotlets:* Doodlebug Design; *Silk flowers:* Silk Vision; *Metal:* Art Emboss, AMACO; *Butterfly clip art:* Picture It!, Microsoft.

Reflect the Weather

While wind, sun, rain and snow can wreak havoc on a picture-taking session, they can also add visual energy and charm. Note how Stephanie Ford of Sumter, South Carolina, captured the gentle breeze sifting through her cousin's hair. Next time the weather contributes with anything from drenched skin to a dusting with snow, pull out your camera!

STEPHANIE FORD

love in postwar europe

Three memorable treatments of vintage photos

RALPH WARD'S INFECTIOUS SMILE was enough to win any girl's heart, and when this handsome Army officer married Pearl Morrison during World War II, she wasn't about to leave him. The couple was almost inseparable as they traveled throughout postwar Europe attending to Ralph's military duties. Their daughter, Carroll Carter of American Fork, Utah, found these photos of her parents after both had died.

Vintage photos can be challenging to scrapbook, so Carroll asked CK's editors to find talented scrapbookers who could handle them well. We gave the photos to Carol Wingert, Kelly Anderson and Renee Camacho and asked them to capture the couple's relationship and postwar travels in a memorable way.

"Ralph & Pearl"

by Carol Wingert
Gilbert, AZ

SUPPLIES

Patterned paper: Ever After Scrapbook Co (stripe) and Karen Foster Design (newspaper)

Rubber stamps: Postmodern Design and DeNami Design

Computer fonts: Typist and Wendy, Microsoft Word

Metal letter and brads: Making Memories

Hat pin and star studs: Memory Lane

Paint: Lumiere, Jacquard Products

Stamping ink: Ranger Industries

Stencil: Ma Vinci Reliquary

Punch: Family Treasures

Slide mount: Manto Fev

Metal plate: 7 Gypsies

Ribbon: Ink It

CAROL'S APPROACH

Before scrapbooking a heritage page, Carol studies the era when the photos were taken. "I look for the mood of the people and popular colors and major events from that time period," she says. Since World War II was a somber time, Carol chose a subdued tone and monochromatic colors.

"I wanted to bring in masculine and feminine characteristics," notes Carol. She featured Ralph's photo with aged metal accents and newsprint paper. She framed the photo of Pearl with lace, ribbon, a hat pin and antique paper.

"Ralph & Pearl Ward"

by Kelly Anderson

Tempe, AZ

SUPPLIES

Fibers: Special Effects

Gold buckle and clock studs: 7 Gypsies

Transparency image: ARTchix Studio

Embossing ink and powder: PSX Design

Gold numbers and wood letter: Walnut Hollow

Stamping inks: Fresco, Stampa Rosa; Brilliance and
VersaColor, Tsukineko

Other: Walnut ink, vintage postcard, aged glassine envelope,
ruler, clock hands, calendar charm, hemp, star studs, skeleton leaf,
buttons and trim

Ideas to note: Kelly used the eyelets from the packaging of the
7 Gypsies product. She used an interactive portrait portfolio to
showcase the journaling and single photo of Ralph.

KELLY'S APPROACH

Says Kelly, "When I saw these wartime photos, I knew this layout
called for walnut ink and other aging and distressing techniques."
Note how she aged the ruler, journaling block, tags and photo mat.

Along with her embellishments, Kelly added a vintage touch by
handwriting the journaling to reflect what Pearl's journaling may
have looked like in her diary. A stamp and old postcard reinforce the
Wards' overseas travels, since "they must have written bundles of letters to friends and family in the United States," says Kelly.

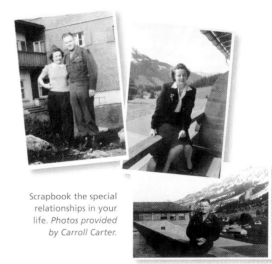

Scrapbook the special
relationships in your
life. *Photos provided
by Carroll Carter.*

"Adventure of a Lifetime"

by Renee Camacho
Nashville, TN

SUPPLIES

Patterned paper: Design Originals (map and dictionary), 7 Gypsies (black and crème script), K & Company (green floral)

Computer font: CK Constitution, "Fresh Fonts" CD, *Creating Keepsakes*

Alphabet letters, small tag, and definitions: FoofaLa

Letter stickers: Sticko by EK Success

Stamping ink: Ranger Industries

Nailheads: Findings, 7 Gypsies

Photo corners: Canson

Brads: Lost Treasure

Other: Pop dots, safety pin, corrugated paper and twine

RENEE'S APPROACH

What an adventure Ralph and Pearl must have had! As soon as Renee read the journaling, she knew map paper would complement the couple's travels throughout Western Europe. "I also wanted to reinforce the photos' vintage feel by using vintage patterned papers," she says. With so many products on the market, Renee says she had difficulty narrowing the choices down to just a few.

To incorporate Carroll's extra journaling, Renee created a pocket behind the left-hand picture. She included a journaling tag in the pocket. ♥

A Study in Contrast

Look around, and you'll find contrast everywhere. Photograph the differences! Notes Allison Landy of Phoenix, Arizona, "Find two things that are seemingly different—like new versus old, dark versus light, or smooth versus rough—and shoot them next to each other. Have fun celebrating the differences!"

ALLISON LANDY

Surface Beauty

Next time you're taking pictures of sights with intriguing textures, snap extra pictures to use in your page design. Cheryl Sumner of Nevada City, California, loved the bricks and paving stones at Mission San Juan Capistrano, so she took extra photos of the interesting surfaces. Cheryl punched squares from the photos, then used them to create a mosaic border.

CHERYL SUMNER

Supplies *Square punch:* Family Treasures.

The #1 Rule

Rules. While some are followed religiously, others take on a life of their own. Scrapbook the results! Here, Lisa Russo of Oswego, Illinois, shares the "number-one" rule her son Aidan received from his preschool teacher. She tells how he has applied it in welcome—and not-so-welcome—ways.

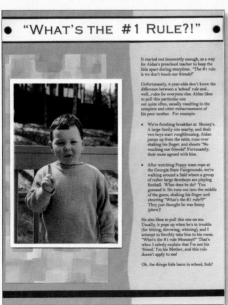

LISA RUSSO

Supplies *Patterned paper:* Magenta; *Computer fonts:* Copperplate Gothic Light and Goudy, Microsoft Word.

Pick up a Screw Post

Tired of wrestling with small screws as your scrapbook grows in size? Susan Piepol of Rockville, Maryland, offers a great solution.

Visit the screws aisle at your local home improvement store and pick up aluminum screw posts that are 1–2" long. The posts have two ends, fit an album's existing screw holes, make it easy to add page protectors, and can easily support the weight of page layouts.

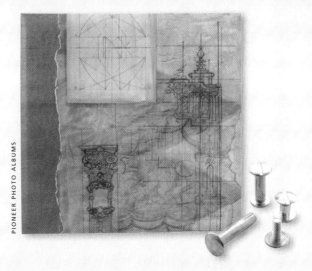

PIONEER PHOTO ALBUMS

jay and lucy

See how three scrapbookers handled two huskies

ONLY A YEAR APART, Siberian huskies Jay and Lucy balance each other out, says owner Liana Suwandi of Dallas, Texas. While Jay, the older of the two at eight, is frisky and loves to play, Lucy is more demure. They've been with Liana almost since birth, and she considers them very much a part of the family.

Liana wanted to see how top scrapbookers would scrapbook her pictures, so *Creating Keepsakes* asked dog lovers Pam Talluto, Sara Tumpane and Amy Grendell to put their creative skills to the test. Check out the resulting layouts that follow, along with the scrapbookers' explanations of why they chose the approaches they did! ❤

"Jay and Lucy"

by Pam Talluto
Rochester Hills, MI

SUPPLIES

Vellum: Colorbök

Wire mesh: Wireform, Paragona

Fiber: Rubba Dub Dub, Art Sanctum

Computer fonts: PC Newsprint and Scriptina, downloaded from the Internet

Tags: American Tag Company

Stamping ink: Tsukineko

Embossing powder: PSX Design

Ribbon: Jo-Ann Stores

Beads: Magic Scraps

Lace: Carolace

Other: Chain, paper clip and thread

Idea to note: Pam cut a thick piece of cardboard into a frame for Jay's picture. Next, she wrapped the frame with paper she'd moistened, crumpled it, then heated the paper with an embossing gun.

PAM'S APPROACH

A dog lover herself, Pam looked at the big picture of Jay and commented, "Those eyes—aren't they the first thing you see?" She could tell that Jay and Lucy are a big part of their owners' family.

While scrapbooking the pictures, Pam tried to keep equal focus on the dogs but maintain their individuality. To accomplish this, she chose a wire mesh and beaded chain for Jay's frame to emphasize his playfulness. She used lace edging and a ribbon-tied tag to bring out Lucy's sweetness.

Pam placed the enlarged photo on the right to visually balance the pages. "With subjects this beautiful," she says, "the bigger, the better!"

ARTICLE BY JEANNIE O'BRIEN

Layout text:

THE TRUEST OF COMRADES, DOGS SHARE OUR HOMES, OUR FORTUNES AND OUR HEARTS

APRIL 2001

LUCY JAY

They're Like Family To Us

we got our first AKC-registered Siberian Husky, Jay, when he was only a six-week old pup. We added Lucy a year later to keep him company. In these photos Jay is 8 years old, and Lucy is 7. While Jay is playful, active and friendly, Lucy is sweet and a bit shy. Both enjoy long walks and naps. On this day, we took pictures of them outside our apartment. The weather was beautiful and we enjoyed capturing our pets on film.

We feel like something's missing if they're not around. Jay and Lucy are two of a kind!

"They're Like Family"

by Sara Tumpane
Grayslake, IL

SUPPLIES

Vellum: The Paper Company

Textured paper: Red Lead Arts

Watercolor paint: Angora

Letter stamps: Hero Arts

Watercolor paper: Strathmore

Metal tags: Making Memories

Clay for collar: Creative Paperclay Company

Embossing powders: Stampendous! (black) and source unknown (copper kettle)

Metal sheeting: ArtEmboss, AMACO

Glue dots: Glue Dots International

Craft paint: DecoArt

Jump rings: Westrim Crafts

Other: Crystal Lacquer by Aleene's (title letters and tags), brass brads and magnetic poetry

Ideas to note: Sara coated the title with Crystal Lacquer for a shiny appearance. For the collar, she rolled the clay into a long strip, straightened the edges, then used the edge of a plastic ruler to create small channels.

SARA'S APPROACH

Sara "just melted" when she saw the photos. Says Sara, "My family swears I was a dog in a former life!" To accentuate the photos on her pages but keep from overpowering them, Sara chose to repeat the dark brown and black colors in her design, as well as the blue from the dogs' eyes.

Sara likes to create embellishments that help "tie" the photos together visually. She crafted a dog collar from clay and a buckle from pounded and embossed metal sheeting. "I used the collar as a graphic line element to move the viewer's eye from left to right," notes Sara.

Shortcut: Use grosgrain ribbon or a canvas strip for the collar.

Capture the canine charm of your dogs on film.

Journaling on layout: We got our first AKC registered Siberian husky, Jay, when he was only six weeks old we got a second Siberian husky, Lucy, a year later to help keep him company.

Jay is eight years old here and Lucy is seven while Jay is playful, active and friendly with everyone, Lucy is sweet and a bit shy, both dogs enjoy long walks and naps.

On this particular day in April 2001 we took pictures of Jay and Lucy outside our apartment in Houston Texas, the weather was beautiful, and we enjoyed capturing our pets on film, they're like family to us, and we feel like something's missing if they're not around Jay and Lucy are "two of a kind"

"Jay and Lucy"

by Amy Grendell
Silverdale, WA

SUPPLIES

Patterned paper: Colorbök

Vellum: Keeping Memories Alive

Circle punch: Carl Mfg.

Tags: American Tag Company and the Heartland Paper Company

Computer fonts: Nevermind and Falling Leaves, downloaded from *www.twopeasinabucket.com*

Nailheads: The Stamp Doctor

Other: Paw prints, traced from a McGill punch

AMY'S APPROACH

Amy chose to keep her layout simple "so I wouldn't draw attention away from the beautiful pictures of Jay and Lucy." She introduced more color to the layout and chose soft, blue stripes to feature the dogs' icy-blue eyes. The stripes also repeat the vertical pattern of the fence in the photo of both dogs.

Amy added two paw prints next to the journaling to reinforce the dog theme. "I also wanted to draw the viewer's eye across the layout," she says.

Better Snow Pictures

Take your best snow pictures yet with these four tips:

◆ Brighten your subject by turning on your camera's fill flash. This will compensate for poor light metering caused by the bright snow.

◆ Get closer to your subject. You'll reduce the amount of white background in your picture, and your camera's light metering will be more accurate.

◆ Center your view on a darker object, such as your subject. Press the shutter down halfway so it meters the dark object instead of the snow.

Without lifting your trigger finger, re-frame your photo, then depress the shutter button com-pletely to take your picture.

◆ To avoid subjects that look too dark in photos, have the subjects face the sun while they're being photographed.

KERRI BRADFORD

All in One

Streamline photo matting and page creation with Kristi Barnes' approach:

❶ Type, then format, your title and journaling on computer.

❷ Output the page, then add a picture to it (no separate mat required).

❸ Do a decorative tear on the top and bottom of the paper.

❹ Cut a "seam" beneath the photo.

❺ Add embellishments to the bottom section.

Perspectives: A Big Plus

Boost your pages' impact by including others' perspectives:

◆ Create journaling blocks with light pencil guidelines. Ask loved ones to write their memories on the blocks.

◆ Interview family members, then scrapbook their perspectives along with yours.

◆ While vacationing, jot notes and memories on postcards and mail them home.

◆ Ask a child to draw a picture for your layout.

◆ Schedule time for family members to record their memories together.

Design Checklist

To help your layout look its best, put it to the test. Ask:

☐ What do I notice first, the photos or the embellishments?

☐ Do the design and colors enhance my pictures?

☐ Does the layout feel balanced and harmonious?

☐ Have I left too little or too much empty space in certain areas?

☐ Do I have a focal point? Have I emphasized the most important items?

☐ Have I tried to include too many fonts, products or techniques?

fields of buttercups

See how three scrapbookers captured the blossoms

WHAT CAN BE MORE PRECIOUS than watching your baby toddle around a field of buttercups? For Lisa Turley of Chesapeake, Virginia, it's watching her daughter Danielle blossom into a lovely young lady who still loves buttercups and wants to save each one she picks.

Lisa treasures these sweet photos of Danielle and asked CK editors for help in scrapbooking them. We gave them to Margaret Scarbrough, Teresa Lewis and Shannon Taylor and asked them to create two-page layouts as beautiful as these three pictures. ♥

And of course, we always have to take turns putting a buttercup under each other's chin to see if we "love butter." This was the first time I took Danielle out to play in her great-uncle Eugene's field and she was in heaven because she had never seen so many buttercups in one place before.

These are some of my favorite photos of my daughter. Even now, I look at the blooming field of buttercups and think about the beautiful little lady my daughter is blooming into.

May 2001

my buttercup

Danielle has loved buttercups ever since she was big enough to toddle around and pick flowers. She picks me a handful every time she sees them and makes sure I save them all in a jar of dried flowers, pressed in books, or placed in keepsake pockets in our albums.

"My Buttercup"
by Margaret Scarbrough
S. Lancaster, MA

SUPPLIES

Textured paper: Creative Imaginations
Mulberry paper: Bazzill Basics
Computer font: 2Peas Glitter Girl, downloaded from www.twopeasinabucket.com
Vellum flower accents: Jolee's by You, Stickopotamus

Letter stamps: Artistic Lowercase, Hero Arts
Stamping ink: VersaColor, Tsukineko
Craft wire: Making Memories
Pop dots: All Night Media
Ribbon: Carolace

MARGARET'S APPROACH

With pictures this vivid, Margaret decided to downplay her background paper and chose clean white cardstock and textured papers. "The pictures had such great yellows and greens that I decided to use them as the focus colors of the layout," she says.

Margaret used pop dots to add extra dimension and interest to the buttercup vellum and button accents along the bottom of the left-hand page. The green craft wire fits in nicely with the green shoots in the bottom right photo. Note how the green title, journaling and ribbon balance the abundance of yellow in the photos.

ARTICLE BY JEANNIE O'BRIEN

"Buttercup Bliss"

by Teresa Lewis
Draper, UT

SUPPLIES

Patterned papers: All My Memories and Carolee's Creations

Flower punches: All Night Media (small), Family Treasures (large), Marvy Uchida (medium)

Computer fonts: A Yummy Apology, Sedona and Broderbund, downloaded from the Internet

Doggie treats clips: Boxer Scrapbook Productions

Brads and paper yarn: Making Memories

Tag template: Coluzzle, Provo Craft

Stamping ink: ColorBox, Clearsnap

Chalk: Craf-T Products

Rubber stamp: DreamWorks

Fun flock: Stampendous!

Other: Butterfly charm and onionskin paper

TERESA'S APPROACH

Teresa had two goals for this layout: keep the focus on the photos and include embellishments to complement the journaling without overwhelming the photos. "I chose to work with colors that were already in the photos so Danielle and her personality would really stand out," she said.

Teresa made the buttercups using her paper florist technique on page 54. She embellished the centers with Fun Flock. She also used onionskin paper, a rubber stamp and chalks to create a "rubbing" on the background of the flower tag.

Let your layout blossom with bright floral photos. *Photos by Lisa Turley.*

"Buttercup Love"

by Shannon Taylor
Bristol, TN

SUPPLIES

Patterned papers: Renae Lindgren (orange),
Creative Imaginations; unknown (yellow stripe)

Dried flowers: Arnold Grummer's Hand Papermaking
Supplies

Metal heart and bookplate: Animadesigns.com

Lettering template: Wacky, EK Success

Glue dots: Glue Dots International

Pop dots: Making Memories

Eyelets: Doodlebug Design

Metal stamps: Foofala

Ribbon: Wal-mart

Idea to note: Shannon stamped the bookplate
with metal stamps.

SHANNON'S APPROACH

After studying the photos, Shannon decided to go with a natural-style layout. She enlarged her focal-point photo to 10" on the left-hand page, then used two strips of ribbon along the right-hand page to help draw the viewer through the layout.

To make her floral title, Shannon used a template to trace her title on an adhesive sheet. After cutting the letters out, she mounted them on cardstock for a firmer backing, then matted them with orange paper. She finished by placing the small pieces of dried flowers on each adhesive letter. Shannon used the same technique for her circle accents. It gave the exact look she wanted. ♥

Get a "Worm's Eye" View

From experience, Charlotte Dymock of the United Kingdom knows the most stunning, artistic shots can come from "getting down and looking up." Notes Charlotte, "This is especially useful when it's tricky to get everything in the same frame."

For this picture, Charlotte crouched so she could capture both the statue and the cathedral in the same shot. "An added bonus was that I could visually crop some scaffolding work right out of the picture" says Charlotte.

CHARLOTTE DYMOCK

Go Graphic with a Grid

Add a sense of drama and sophistication with a decorative grid. Here, Erin Lincoln of Frederick, Maryland, drew, then wove, a grid with embroidery floss. Note the compelling backdrop it makes for her flower accents. Short on time? Draw a grid with your favorite markers!

Supplies *Patterned paper:* Mustard Moon; *Punches:* EK Success (pom pom) and Emagination Crafts (flowers); *Chalk:* Craf-T Products; *Pen:* Zig Writer, EK Success.

Let a Letter Do the Talking

Love personal journaling but short on time and/or talent? Do what Suzy Blankenship of Wittmann, Arizona, does: Scrapbook a page with a loved one's picture and a letter from or about him or her. All you have to do is embellish the page!

Ask family and friends to write you letters about holidays, memories, people and more. Include the letters (or copies) on pages—they're sure to be some of your most treasured.

Supplies
Patterned paper: K & Company; *Metal frame, circle tag and star:* Making Memories; *Brads:* Lost Treasure Arts; *Mesh:* Natural Netting, Scrappin' Fools. *Idea to note:* This page includes two messages— one in a prominent spot, the other (Grannie's heartfelt words to family) hidden in the enclosed journaling block at top left.

Keep Tools Handy

Ever misplaced the scrapbooking tools you use most? Keep them handy with a work apron! With three young children and a busy schedule, Dana Selzer of Alva, Oklahoma, needed to keep closer tabs on her adhesives, scissors, favorite pen and more.

Her big "find"? An apron (99 cents) in the hardware section at Wal-Mart. "I added a custom touch with craft paint," says Dana, "and gave my daughter—who likes to scrapbook with me—her own apron as well." Check your local discount or hardware store.

LUV TO SCRAP

the non-scary scarecrow

Dress up a layout for Halloween

Three-year-old Andy wasn't excited about being a scarecrow for Halloween—in fact, he found the idea quite upsetting. Still, with a little coaxing from his dad, Andy donned the floppy hat, face paint, straw wig, scarf, patched jeans and makeshift suspenders and headed off to playschool.

Carrie Leggett of Macon, Georgia, snapped photos of her little scarecrow and shared them with CK's editors. We asked Nichol Magouirk, Alison Beachem and Angelia Wigginton to create their best scarecrow layouts in 12" x 12" format. See what they each chose to highlight in their layouts. ❤

"Andy"
by Nichol Magouirk
Dodge City, KS

SUPPLIES

Patterned paper: Wordsworth and K & Company

Bookplate: Two Peas in a Bucket

Flat-head eyelets: Stamp Doctor

Measuring tape: 7 Gypsies

Letter stamps: PSX Design

Tags: Anima Designs

Definition: FoofaLa

Thread: Coats & Clark

Skeleton leaf: Black Ink

Circle punch: EK Success

Mesh: Magic Mesh, Avant Card

Sunflower postcards: Stampington and Company

Nailheads: Scrapworks (squares) and Jest Charming (buttons)

Stamping ink: ColorBox, Clearsnap; VersaMark, Tsukineko

Computer font: Maszyna Plus, downloaded from the Internet

Other: Canvas, hemp, buttons and ribbon

NICHOL'S APPROACH

Nichol can relate to last-minute sewing projects (like Carrie's rush to finish this adorable scarecrow costume). "I wanted to emphasize that fact," says Nichol, "so I chose measuring tape paper, canvas and button accents." She used her sewing machine to attach pockets and photos.

To age the pocket accents, Nichol sanded, then inked, sunflower postcards with a stippling brush. She used a circle punch to create the notch in each pocket, then printed the journaling on tags she hid in the pockets.

ARTICLE BY JEANNIE O'BRIEN

Halloween 2001

Andy was the cutest
'scarecrow that
almost never was'
for Halloween this year.
Halloween was fast approaching,
and I knew Andy needed a
costume. I finally decided that
he would be a scarecrow,
and I stayed up late the night
before sewing his costume.

The next morning, Andy cried when I tried
to put the costume on him for playschool.
Luckily, his daddy coaxed him into wearing the
costume that morning and for Halloween night.
Andy looked absolutely adorable, from his
floppy hat down to his gardening boots.
I'll always remember how precious
he was as a scarecrow that Halloween.

andy

scarecrows, corn rows, pumpkins on the vine, leaves curl, winds swirl, fall is right on time   scarecrows, corn rows, pumpkins on the vine, leaves curl, winds swirl, fall is right on time

"Scarecrow That Almost Never Was"

by Alison Beachem
San Diego, CA

SUPPLIES

Corrugated paper: DMD, Inc.

Mesh: Magic Scraps

Heart punch: EK Success

Ribbon: C.M. Offray & Son

Poem: From *www.twopeasinabucket.com*

Metal letters, plaque, square brads and heart:
Making Memories

Computer font: 2Peas Sleigh Ride, downloaded
from *www.twopeasinabucket.com*

Scarecrows, corn rows,
pumpkins on the vine,
Leaves curl, winds swirl,
fall is right on time.

—Unknown

ALISON'S APPROACH

A lison noticed the colors almost immediately. "I wanted to capture the colors that make the photographs so successful—the green rake tines, the yellow flowers and, of course, the orange scarf," she says.

To keep the focus on the pictures and journaling, Alison chose simple embellishments. Note the poem strip that runs along the lower length of the layout.

Alison also wanted to make sure Andy's dad played a prominent part in the layout. After all, she says, "He was so much a part of the story of getting Andy to wear his costume."

Scare up some Halloween
cheer with costume pictures.
Photos by Carrie Leggett.

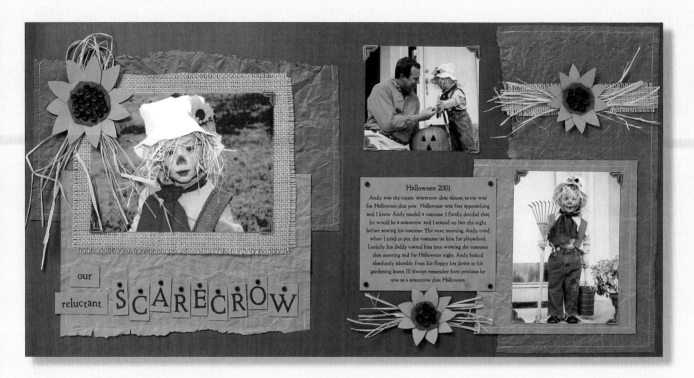

"Our Reluctant Scarecrow"

by Angelia Wigginton
Belmont, MS

SUPPLIES

Textured cardstock: Monochromatics, Bazzill Basics

Computer font: 2Peas Chestnuts, downloaded from *www.twopeasinabucket.com*

Mini brads: American Pin & Fastener

Buttons: Hobby Lobby, Crafts Etc.

Pencils: Prismacolor, Sanford

Chalk: Craf-T Products

Photo corners: Canson

Other: Burlap and raffia

ANGELIA'S APPROACH

Andy's face is so cute that Angelia decided to use the close-up photo as her focal point. "I chose the title after learning that Andy was not happy about being a scarecrow for Halloween," she says.

Two of the photos have a white background, so Angelia chose orange and green paper to help the pictures stand out. She crumpled, flattened and stitched the brown sunflower centers, then added three shades of brown buttons.

Angelia colored the tan photo corners so they would blend in with the rest of the layout. The burlap and raffia accents add a touch of texture. ♥

Words in Place of Photos

Not every layout needs a picture. Here, Wendi Speciale of Round Rock, Texas, created a fun horizontal page titled "I Don't Always Need a Camera." The journaling spotlights tender moments like "the way you rest your head upon my shoulder at the end of a hard day."

While Wendi enjoys taking photographs, she focused here on journaling "best moments" instead. "I didn't want a camera to interrupt our memories," says Wendi.

WENDI SPECIALE

Supplies *Computer software:* Adobe Photoshop; *Computer font:* Century.

The Balky Subject

Your camera's all set, and you've got everything you need—minus a cooperative subject. Despite your pleas, he or she continues to dodge the camera. What's a scrapbooker to do? Snap pictures of the person scrambling away, then create a "Sometimes You Just Can't Get the Perfect Picture" page. That's what Leah Fung of San Diego, California, did!

LEAH FUNG

Supplies *Corrugated paper:* DMD, Inc.; *Metal letters, metal plate, snaps and eyelets:* Making Memories; *Rubber stamps:* Hero Arts; *Fabric:* Custom Cut; *Alphabet beads:* Westrim Crafts; *Ring tag:* Avery; *Craft wire:* Toner Plastics; *Other:* Hemp and thread.

The Art of the Overlap

Afraid to break visual lines in your layout? Don't be! Page accents that overlap can add visual variety and a sense of cohesiveness. Here, Jamie Waters of South Pasadena, California, added interest by overlapping other page elements with patterned paper, cardstock strips, a photo, a metal-rimmed tag, letter accents, a tag, and a punched-out circle and brads.

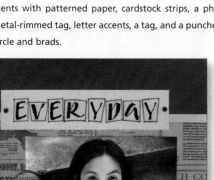

JAMIE WATERS

Supplies *Patterned paper:* 7 Gypsies; *Computer font:* Garamond, Microsoft Word; *Letter stickers:* Wordsworth; *Metal-rimmed tag:* Avery; *Mesh:* Magic Mesh, Avant Card; *Scrabble tiles:* Scraps Ahoy; *Brads:* Boxer Productions.

Fiber Storage

Save too many loose fibers, and even with their rich colors and tantalizing textures, this dream supply can turn into a storage nightmare. Do what Patricia Flores of Miami, Florida, does: store the loose fibers in compartmentalized, handy protectors! You can use a professional version like that shown below, or use a trading-card holder (nine compartments) or a recipe-card holder.

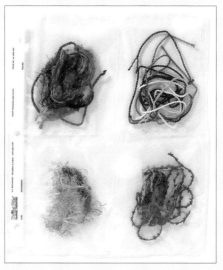

about a boy

Three scrapbookers capture his charm

LILAC CHANG OF SAN MATEO, CALIFORNIA, treasures these photos of her youngest son, Itay, discovering his yarmulke, the traditional cap worn by Jewish males. "Itay was having a great time getting his yarmulke just right on his head," shares Lilac. "I love that these photos capture his playfulness and curiosity as he discovers his path in life and Judaism."

Lilac created the layout below to document this special time in her son's life. She shared it with CK's editors, wondering how other scrapbookers would treat these special shots of her son. We asked Hall of Famers Tracy Miller and Tracie Smith to create layouts that showcase Itay's charming personality, as well as his discovery of an important religious symbol.

"Our Little Chazan"

by Lilac Chang
San Mateo, CA

SUPPLIES

Patterned papers: Ever After Scrapbook Co (stripe) and Karen Foster Design (newspaper)

Rubber stamps: Postmodern Design and DeNami Design

Computer fonts: Typist and Wendy, Microsoft Word

Metal letter and brads: Making Memories

Hat pin and star studs: Memory Lane

Paint: Lumiere, Jacquard Products

Stamping ink: Ranger Industries

Stencil: Ma Vinci's Reliquary

Punch: Family Treasures

Slide mount: Manto Fev

Metal plate: 7 Gypsies

Ribbon: Ink It

LILAC'S APPROACH

In Hebrew, "chazan" means someone who leads prayers, explains Lilac. "These photos of my son reminded me of a little chazan, so I chose that as the title for my layout."

A chazan typically sings prayers, so Lilac chose music paper for her background. To add interest to the focal-point photo, she sanded and inked it, then adhered ornate photo corners to the right-hand side. Lilac accented the layout with an aged circle charm that looks like the top of a yarmulke, and personalized it with Itay's initial.

ARTICLE BY KIM SANDOVAL

Itay, you manage to bring happiness and laughter to everything you do. At Hanukkah this year, you were fascinated with your yamaka and were trying to figure out just exactly why it was staying on your head. Once you got yours down, you offered to put one on everyone else.

you bring **happiness &laughter** to everything you do

Hanukkah 2002

"You Bring Happiness"
by Tracy Miller
Fallston, MD

SUPPLIES
Paper and letter stickers: SEI
Computer fonts: Bernhard Modern (title) and Bookman Old Style (journaling), downloaded from the Internet

TRACY'S APPROACH

Itay's facial expressions were so cute, Tracy wanted to keep the focus on the photos. She converted the shots to black and white so the colors wouldn't compete with Itay's adorable face. She enlarged the focal-point photo and placed it in the upper-left corner of the layout so it would be the first element to draw the eye.

Tracy chose rich neutral colors for the background, arranging them in a clean, color-blocked design. She framed the photos with thin white mats to help them stand out against the background. Playful circle accents echo the shape of Itay's yarmulke, and a bold title, taken from Lilac's journaling, leads the eye through the spread.

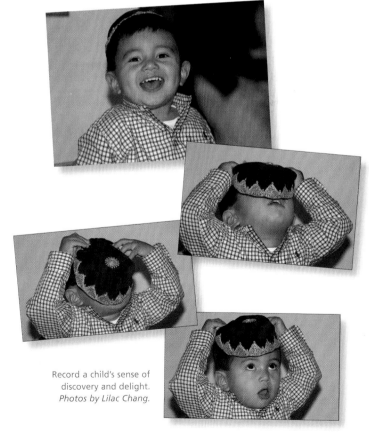

Record a child's sense of discovery and delight.
Photos by Lilac Chang.

"Hanukkah Joy"

by Tracie Smith
Smithtown, NY

SUPPLIES

Velvet: Hot Potatoes

Swirl rubber stamp: Stampin' Up!

Stamping ink: ColorBox, Clearsnap

Metal photo corners: Making Memories

Pens: Zig Millennium (black), EK Success;
Stampin' Up! (burgundy); Creative
Memories (silver)

Computer font: CK Extra, "Fresh Fonts"
CD, *Creating Keepsakes*

Antique brass squares: Magic Scraps

Acrylic paint: Folk Art

Other: Heart charm and jump ring

TRACIE'S APPROACH

When Tracie saw these photos of Itay playing with his yarmulke, the first thing that came to mind was "What a sweet tatteh shaneh!" Tracie's mother-in-law uses this Yiddish phrase (it means "pretty baby") with the sweetest affection for her grandchildren. Tracie knew it was a perfect fit for Itay and his joyful smile.

Tracie had velvet on hand that matched Itay's yarmulke. She embossed the velvet with a swirl image to create texture. She also used the velvet as a mat for the focal-point photo and as a background for the right-hand page. To add dimension, Tracie included torn mats and accents, as well as antique brass squares. ♥

From Chaos to Order

10 easy steps to photo organization

Whenever I teach a scrapbooking workshop, someone usually asks me how to organize photos. This is a perpetual concern among scrapbookers. I've seen shoeboxes stuffed with photos still in their envelopes from the processing lab; I've seen large boxes overflowing with loose photos.

These pictorial memories also get shoved into the kitchen drawer, the office desk, the bedroom nightstand and the hall closet. Some people develop elaborate organization systems but don't follow through because the systems are too complicated.

The would-be organizer in the workshop usually follows up with: "Will you do it for me?" I graciously decline, but offer to coach her through the process. I can empathize with feeling overwhelmed after looking at a pile or box or drawer of unorganized pictures. In the past, I spent many hours organizing my photos and negatives. I've since learned that organizing your photos isn't hard (time-consuming maybe, but not hard) if you follow 10 simple steps.

BY PATTI COOMBS

ILLUSTRATION BY PIERO CORVA

Step 1

Get over the mental block.

OK, I know organizing your photos can feel on par with a prison sentence, but if you follow a plan, the process can be fun. It can also be a learning experience.

Start by reminding yourself how important it is to preserve and protect your photos and memories. Enjoy the memories that come back to you as you work—and take notes! Notice how your life and surroundings have changed. Marvel at how much the trees in the neighborhood have grown. Laugh at the old hairstyles and outfits. Commit now to organize your photos *and* enjoy the process.

Work at the project a step at a time, and don't worry about getting it all done at once. Reward yourself as you complete segments of the project.

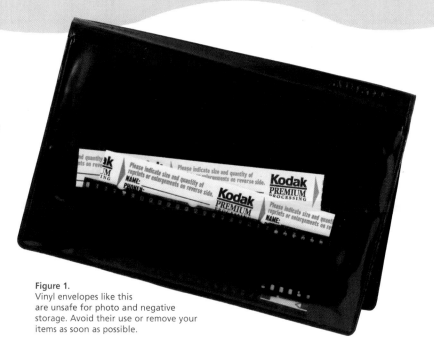

Figure 1.
Vinyl envelopes like this are unsafe for photo and negative storage. Avoid their use or remove your items as soon as possible.

Step 2

Gather everything together.

Let's get started. Gather all of your pictures and negatives into one location. Give yourself plenty of time to find everything. Look under the bed, in cubbyholes, kitchen cabinets, the glove compartment in your car and anywhere else you may have stashed pictures. If you have pictures already grouped together, leave them in their containers but bring them to your working area.

The next steps are easier if you can work somewhere where you can leave the project out until you finish. (Make sure it's out of reach of small children!)

Step 3

Categorize your pictures.

Separate your photos into the following categories:

- Heritage photos
- Snapshot photos
- Professional portraits
- Photos in magnetic albums
- Polaroid-type photos
- Negatives
- Photos to toss (it's OK to throw away a photograph!)

As you sort through your pictures, make sure you don't lose any information that will help you label and date the pictures. For example, if your photographs are still in processing envelopes, check for a date stamp. (This tells you that these pictures were taken before that date.) If you pull negatives from these envelopes, file them according to the date.

Carefully and systematically remove photos from magnetic albums, annotating any information on the pages as you go. Magnetic albums are acidic and will harm your photographs and other documents! So will vinyl envelopes (Figure 1).(For more information about the dangers of magnetic pages and how to safely remove pictures from them, see "Rescue Your Photos from Magnetic Mayhem" in CK's January/February 1999 issue.)

Place Polaroid-type photos in photo sleeves (or plastic sandwich bags) to shield other photos from the processing chemicals. Add them to the appropriate pile.

Give special care to heirloom photos that have started to deteriorate. Have negatives made of these photos, then store them properly to prevent further decay. (We'll cover negative sorting and storage later.)

Step 4

Divide photos into manageable groups.

Here are some category suggestions for subdividing your pictures:

- Side of the family (your side, his side, etc.)
- Individual family unit
- Individual person
- Residence
- Decade

Place
Stamp
Here

*Thanks in large part to World Wildlife Fund's
support, Africa's rhino population has increased by
nearly 13 percent since 1999.*

To:

photo on front © G.Ellis/GLOBIO.org

World Wildlife Fund
1250 Twenty-Fourth Street, NW
Washington, DC 20037
www.worldwildlife.org

WWF

♻ *Printed on recycled paper*

WFE182

- Year
- Generation (grandparents, parents, children, etc.)
- Period of life (baby, preschool, school, college, marriage, career, retirement, etc.)
- Themes or events (vacations, holidays, etc.)

Step 5
Continue to subdivide.

Unless you have tens of thousands of pictures, you can start to separate your photos into manageable groups for later filing in albums. You should also be able to see more clearly which pictures go together for future scrapbook layouts.

Step 6
Label your photos.

Never label photos with a ballpoint pen or a felt-tip marker! For today's resin-coated photos, I prefer the Photographic permanent marker by Illustrator because it dries quickly. Use a soft graphite pencil for labeling paper-backed photos. These pens and pencils are not expensive—don't cut corners by using something else. (See "The Lowdown on Labeling Photographs" in CK's May/June 1999 issue.)

Some detective work may be needed at this point. Do your best to label each picture, even if you only know a name or approximate year. I've seen many people get to this point and quit. All of their work was wasted.

For one-of-a-kind, irreplaceable pictures without back-up negatives, put the pictures in protective sleeves and label the sleeves.

Step 7
Set up a storage system.

Store your photos in acid-free products in a safe environment (Figure 2), away from heat, light and moisture. Make sure your system is one you will remember and maintain; make it fit your style. It's time to sort your photos again. I use three groups:

Figure 2. Store photos in a safe, secure holder designed for their safety. *Photo holder by Generations.*

- **Active photos.** These are my soon-to-be-scrapbooked photos. I store them in tilt bins with my other scrapbooking supplies. Each batch has a separate transparent sleeve, which makes them easy to find when I'm ready for them.
- **Inactive photos.** These photos are stored in an album with pocket pages so my family can still enjoy them before they are scrapbooked. Becky Higgins' "Power Scrapbooking" article in CK's April 2002 issue gives a similar suggestion for storing your photos. She puts her photos in page protectors with a sheet of cardstock.

You can also store your inactive photos in acid-free storage boxes. Place your photo batches in photo sleeves or partially sealed sandwich bags, then in the boxes. Use index dividers to keep your categories organized within each box. Or, store them in a filing cabinet. Acid-free filing supplies are also available. (See sidebar on page 110 for manufacturers.)
- **Give-away photos.** I use a small accordion file for pictures I plan to give away or use for other projects. I use many of them in birthday cards for my extended family members.

Photo and Negative Storage Manufacturers

Pocket Pages and Albums

- C-Line Products (*www.c-lineproducts.com*)
- Pioneer Photo Albums (*www.pioneerphotoalbums.com*)
- Print File, Inc. (*www.printfile.com*)
- Vue All (available through camera, scrapbook and online stores; distributed by *www.hpmarketingcorp.com*)
- Light Impressions (*www.lightimpressionsdirect.com*)

Storage Containers

- Generations (*www.generationsnow.com*)
- Highsmith (*www.highsmith.com*)
- Kokuyo (*info@kokuyo-usa.com*)
- Leeco Industries (*www.cropperhopper.com*)
- Pioneer Photo Albums (*www.pioneerphotoalbums.com*)
- Light Impressions (*www.lightimpressionsdirect.com*)
- Print File, Inc. (*www.printfile.com*)

Binders for Negative Storage

- Vue All (available through camera, scrapbook and online stores; distributed by *www.hpmarketingcorp.com*)
- Light Impressions (*www.lightimpressionsdirect.com*)

Negative Storage Pages and Envelopes

- Light Impressions (*www.lightimpressions-direct.com*)
- Print File, Inc. (*www.printfile.com*)
- Vue All (available through camera, scrapbook and online stores; distributed by *www.hpmarketingcorp.com*)
- C-Line Products (*www.c-lineproducts.com*)
- The Sentimental Playground (*www.photo-pockets.com*)

Photo Sleeves and Acid-Free Filing Supplies

- Light Impressions (*www.lightimpressionsdirect.com*)
- The Sentimental Playground (*www.photo-pockets.com*)

Other Online Sources

- *www.archivalplus.com*
- *www.iconusa.com*
- *www.pfile.com*
- *www.lineco.com*

The Ins and Outs of Negative Storage

The debate rages about the archival quality of negative sleeves: Are they archival or are they not? My photo finisher recommends acid-free sleeves from Crown Photo Systems (*www.crownphoto.com*), which manufactures 85 percent of the negative sleeves used in the photo processing industry.

Looking for another opinion? Check out *SOS—Saving Our Scrapbooks*. This CK publication contains information on identifying unsafe plastics. Between the two, I feel comfortable leaving my negatives in the sleeves from the processing lab. (As a side note, I doubt the brittle sleeves used in the past are acid free.)

Storage Ideas

Still trying to figure out how to store your negatives? Here are two easy options:

❶ Group the index print and negatives together in the pocket of an acid-free photo page. Make sure the binder is also acid free.

❷ Store the negatives in acid-free pages in a mini photo album (such as one by Pioneer Photo Albums).

From past experience, negatives can still get bent when stored in standing binders. To avoid damaged negatives, store the binders so the pages hang from the rings.

Quick tip: Mark the spot you remove a negative from with a Post-It note flag so you can easily find where to replace the negative.

Suffocate Your Negatives

A professional photographer told me to store my negatives as airtight as possible. She told me that file cabinets filled with negatives actually survived a fire at a portrait studio because the cabinets were so well packed.

On that recommendation, I decided to reorganize my negatives. I transferred them to pages manufactured by Print File, then labeled them with a photographic marker. I can fit four index prints on

Sept 1981

Figure 3. Use your photo negatives to help you date when pictures were taken. *Examples by Patti Coombs.*

Step 8
Organize, label and store your negatives.
Negatives are fragile and must be handled with care. To help preserve your negatives, store them in protective sleeves. Index prints make negative retrieval much easier. (Negatives shouldn't be cut apart, even to sort by person or event.)

Filing my negatives by date has really helped me label some of my photos. For example, while working with an undated photo of my daughter, I looked through my negatives and found that the photo was taken between a family birthday and Halloween (Figure 3). This dated the picture within a few weeks. (See sidebar on negative storage.)

Step 9
Keep it up.
Divide, label and store your photos and negatives as soon as you get them from the processor. Stay up-to-date with your film developing. Don't wait until you have 15 rolls that need to be developed.

Step 10
You did it!
Sit back and enjoy the memories and the peace of mind. I hope these steps help you feel like you have a personal coach helping you organize your photos and negatives. I'll be cheering for you! ♥

each pocket page. The corresponding negatives follow the index prints in separate pockets. I put them in a folder using brads, then date the folder. Next, I slide the bar from an old hanging file folder through the fold of the folder. The folders can be packed tightly in a file box or cabinet. (Light Impressions sells a negative storage system similar to the one I use.)

The middle of the second drawer from the bottom is the safest place for negatives to survive a fire. Packing the drawer tightly eliminates extra air. For added protection, place regular files in front of and behind your negative files.

If you don't access your negatives very often, consider storing your negatives in a separate location. I make a lot of reprints, so I prefer to store my negatives at home.

Acid-Free Envelopes?
Are your negatives safe in paper envelopes from the processor, even if they don't have sleeves? I tested a variety of photo envelopes with a pH testing pen. Some envelopes tested acid free, but others did not. Acid-free envelopes are readily available. However, if you are going to purchase something to protect your negatives, the sleeves make retrieval much easier.

Older Negatives
For negatives that pre-date the 1950s, check *SOS—Saving Our Scrapbooks* for important information. They are made of hazardous materials and are flammable as the chemicals break down.

Postscript: I recently met a woman who had just reprinted all of her mother's old negatives. Many were from the 1940s. She said the photo processor couldn't believe the good condition of the negatives. I asked how her mother had stored the negatives, and the woman said they were crammed in a box. This tells me that the lack of air circulation helps prolong the life of a negative.

Cookin' up
Quick Pages
Go easy, with great results

by Tracy White
Illustration by Stacy Peterson

✳ **After a long day filled with stressful deadlines, you're probably ready to unwind with your favorite hobby—scrapbooking.** Instead, upon arriving home, you find a heap of laundry and the standard question "What's for dinner?" How on earth will you get some scrapbooking done?

If Superwoman could use a break tonight, never fear—we've cooked up scrapbook pages that are so quick to create you can scrapbook while you're making dinner! (We've even included quick-and-easy recipes that'll give you more scrapping time.) With these pages and recipes, you'll be able to satisfy your scrapbooking urge *and* your family's hunger!

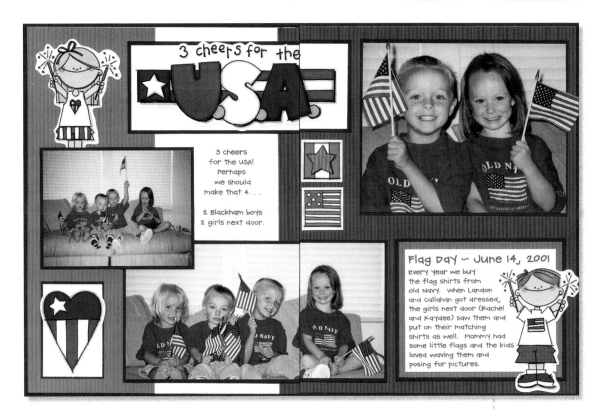

3 cheers for the **USA**

3 cheers
for the USA!
Perhaps
we should
make that 4. . .

2 Blackham boys
2 girls next door.

Flag Day ~ June 14, 2001
Every Year we buy
the flag shirts from
old Navy. When Landon
and Callahan got dressed,
the girls next door (Rachel
and Kaydee) saw them and
put on their matching
shirts as well. Mommy had
some little flags and the kids
loved waving them and
posing for pictures.

Keep your accents from "floating" by grounding them on journaling and accent blocks. *Pages by Jennifer Blackham.* **Supplies** *Patterned paper, title and accents:* All About Me, Pebbles in my Pocket; *Computer font:* Doodle Basic, Cock-A-Doodle Design, Inc.

HANDS ON
ATLANTA

Hands On Atlanta is an annual volunteer event where thousands of volunteers from all over the metro area perform work at hundreds of needy locations.

This year, GE's 200 or so volunteers worked at SciTrek - painting, landscaping, and cleaning. Vic was a painting team leader. Aidan and I visited for awhile, but he was much too interested in playing to let me help out (we did clean some spilled paint off the carpet, though!)

After the work was done, we went to the huge "Thank You" picnic in Centennial Olympic Park. Boxed lunches, live entertainment, and ice cream bars galore (Aidan's favorite part). The only downside was that it was SO hot and miserable - I didn't last very long. Vic let Aidan cool off in the fountains, then headed home, exhausted.

OCTOBER
2002

Tearing paper along the edge of a metal ruler creates subtle texture. *Page by Lisa Russo.* **Supplies** *Patterned paper:* The Paper Loft; *Circle tag and brads:* Making Memories; *Computer fonts:* Copperplate Gothic Light, Microsoft Word; Gill Sans Light, downloaded from the Internet.

Secret Ingredient

Make your pages feel as good as "comfort food" by dividing your background into thirds.

Secret Ingredient

Let complementary colors work to your advantage. The red (green's complement) brings the eye to the most important aspects of the layout: the photo, title, date and journaling.

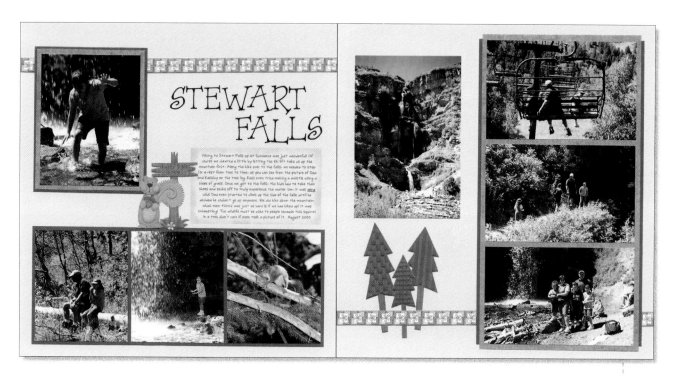

Unify your layout by carrying a border to both sides. *Pages by Kerri Bradford.* **Supplies** *Border and accents:* Embossible Designs, We R Memory Keepers; *Letter stickers:* Provo Craft; *Computer font:* CK Jot, "The Art of Creative Lettering" CD, *Creating Keepsakes.*

Secret Ingredient

Let pre-printed accents help you "cook" up a quick layout.

Secret Ingredient

If your layout looks a little boxy, use computer fonts with a crooked baseline. Or, hand stamp your titles with alphabet stamps—the look will breathe life into a geometric layout.

Give patterned paper a handmade look by pen-stitching around its design. *Page by Shelley Sullivan.* **Supplies** *Patterned paper:* SEI; *Rubber stamps:* PSX Design; *Pen:* Zig Writer, EK Success.

Get more use out of enhancements by trimming and using portions of them. *Pages by Kristy Banks.* **Supplies** *Title, accents and border:* My Mind's Eye; *Mesh:* Magic Mesh, Avant Card; *Computer font:* CK Handprint, "The Best of Creative Lettering" CD Combo; *Letter stickers ("soccer"):* Provo Craft; *Page template:* Close To My Heart.

Secret Ingredient

Page templates make putting together scrapbook pages a snap. Note that Kristy used the same template to make the second page of her layout; she simply turned it on its side!

Secret Ingredient

Throw out the recipe and use free-form shapes to dress up your layout.

Look at the world around you for accent ideas. Jackie got the idea for the grid accent from a quilt her mother made. *Page by Jackie Bonette.* **Supplies** *Computer font:* Garamouche, Impress Rubber Stamps; *Brads:* Boxer Scrapbook Productions; *Mesh:* Magic Mesh, Avant Card.

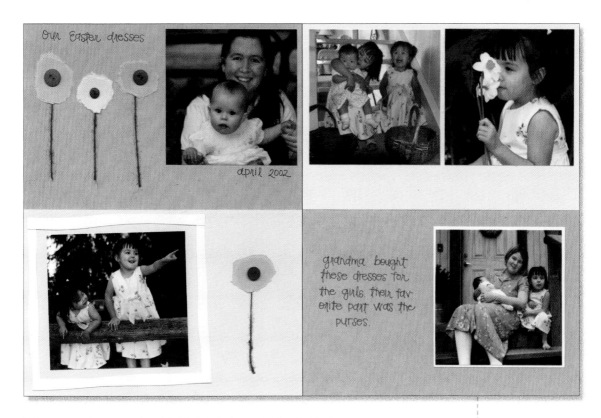

Put your scraps to use—create a delightful photo frame with four hand-cut strips of paper. *Pages by Sarah Kang, photos by James Tunnell.* **Supplies** *Buttons:* Hillcreek Design; *Pen:* Zig Writer, EK Success; *Thread:* DMC.

Secret Ingredient

The recipe is simple: tear four circles, add four buttons, adhere four pieces of string and you've got a bouquet of flowers.

Want a custom look but short on time? Attach elements with mixed-media items like buttons and eyelets. *Page by Kristy Banks.* **Supplies** *Title:* My Mind's Eye; *Eyelets:* Doodlebug Design; *Buttons:* Provo Craft; *Computer font:* CK Handprint "The Best of Creative Lettering" CD Combo, *Creating Keepsakes*.

Secret Ingredient

Spice up your layout by placing the title and border down the center. The variety will surprise and delight people who look through your album.

T w o   T h u m b s   U p

august 14

Save time—you don't need to mat every photo. *Pages by Tara Whitney.*
Supplies *Circle cutter:* Creative Memories; *Circle punches:* Marvy Uchida;
Computer font: Just Plain Little, from *www.twopeasinabucket.com.*

Secret Ingredient

An easy-to-make circle border can bring rhythm
and line to a layout.

Secret Ingredient

Add a hint of whimsy by tearing only one edge of
a photo mat.

Letter stickers make dramatic titles in little time. *Page by Kerri Bradford.*
Supplies *Letter stickers:* Provo Craft; *Computer fonts:* CK Fun (journaling), "The
Art of Creative Lettering" CD, *Creating Keepsakes*; Garamouche (quotes), Impress
Rubber Stamps; *Brads:* Making Memories.

Select a monochromatic color scheme to keep a layout unified. *Pages by Gaylene Steinbach.* **Supplies** *Computer font:* CK Primary, "The Art of Creative Lettering" CD, *Creating Keepsakes*.

Eyelet "bullet points" help emphasize journaling. *Page by Tara Whitney.* **Supplies** *Pen:* Zig Writer, EK Success; *Eyelets:* Doodlebug Design; *Word tile:* FunLogic.

Secret Ingredient

Shorten "cooking" time by matting multiple photos on one strip of paper.

Secret Ingredient

Create the illusion of photo mats by placing photos close to one another. This works especially well when working with complementary colors like the orange background paper and the blue photos in this layout. ♥

kids, gardening and a girl's room

Five great looks from one sketch

WISH SCRAPBOOK DESIGN could be more flexible? This column's for you! You'll find a brand-new sketch, plus examples of how five scrapbookers—Angie Cramer, Anne Heyen, Linda Porter Jones, Kimberly Stone and I—used the same concept to create five different layouts.

The Sketch

This sketch is designed to showcase up to 13 photographs. Talk about making the most of

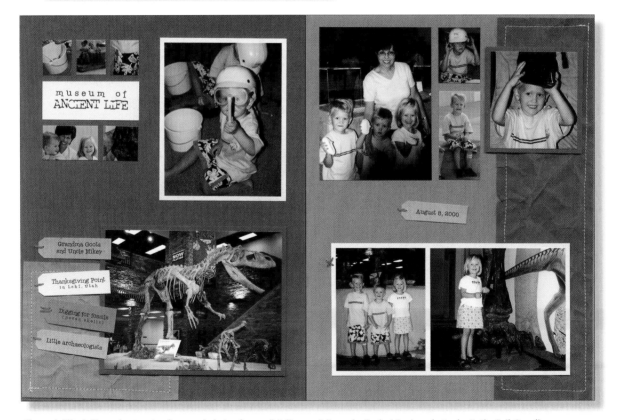

Figure 1. Trim leftover fragments of cropped photos for small "glimpses." *Pages by Becky Higgins, photos by Kathy Feil.* **Supplies** *Computer fonts:* CK Stenography and CK Gutenberg, "Fresh Fonts" CD, *Creating Keepsakes. Idea to note:* Becky crumpled sections of cardstock for a "rougher" touch and sewed them to the page.

ARTICLE BY BECKY HIGGINS

Figure 2. Celebrate your child's hobby by taking close-up pictures of him in action. *Pages by Angie Cramer.* **Supplies** *Patterned paper:* Provo Craft; *Stickers:* Kathy Davis Collection, Colorbök; *Snaps:* Making Memories; Embroidery floss: DMC; *Computer font:* CK Journaling, "The Best of Creative Lettering" CD Combo, Creating Keepsakes.

your space! The title is surrounded by small photos, which can be substituted with other designs if you don't have enough photos. The bottom left corner of the layout has room for journaling, along with a little extra space at the far right. You can still fit an additional five photos in this format.

The Approaches

After drawing this layout design, I posted the sketch on our web site and invited CK readers to submit their layouts (see sidebar for more information). I asked the scrapbookers to keep their page designs similar to the sketch. Other than that, they were free to use any photos, colors, tools or supplies they desired. Here's how we each chose to implement the sketch.

"Ancient Life Museum"

by Becky Higgins

I used this month's sketch to scrapbook a friend's trip to a museum with her family (Figure 1). Instead of including lengthy journaling as shown in the sketch, I used key words instead to highlight the memories of the day.

Because the layout includes so many photos, I kept the background solid and simple. I used three colors (rustic red, golden tan and brown) throughout. All of the journaling is done on subtle shades of neutral colors.

Figure 3. Use hand-trimmed squares to create a look that's as hip as your page subject! *Pages by Anne Heyen.* **Supplies** *Patterned paper and vellum:* Paper Adventures; *Letter stickers:* SEI, Inc.; *Computer font:* Vintage, downloaded from *www.twopeasinabucket.com.*

"Happy Birthday, Gammy"

by Anne Heyen
New Fairfield, CT

Anne achieved a fresh look (Figure 3) by incorporating an almost geometric theme into the design. She mounted her main photograph on patterned paper with crooked blocks. She repeated those accents throughout the layout by cutting some of her matting slightly crooked to coordinate with the crooked blocks.

"Plant a Garden"

by Angie Cramer
Redcliff, AB, Canada

Angie adapted the design to her 8½" x 11" pages (Figure 2). Instead of using small photos, she chose gardening stickers to complement her theme. She mounted the stickers on white cardstock, then cut them into tag shapes and adhered snaps to the top of each one. She used snaps on her journaling blocks as well, to provide continuity throughout the layout.

Figure 4. Add a homemade touch to spring pictures by highlighting them with fabric-like papers, buttons and torn edges. *Pages by Linda Porter Jones.* **Supplies** *Patterned paper:* Karen Foster Design (blue plaid) and Sweetwater (flowers); *Vellum:* Bazzill Basics; *Computer fonts:* Lemon Chicken and Gigi, downloaded from the Internet; *Buttons and eyelets:* Making Memories.

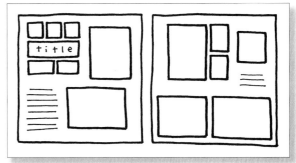

"Let Spring Begin"

by Linda Porter Jones
Long Beach, CA

The lovely photos take center stage on Linda's layout in Figure 4! With plaid and floral papers and a touch of vellum and buttons, Linda achieved a look that's almost as pretty as her girls.

Because Linda didn't have pictures that worked well for the small blocks around the title, she used extra blocks to "extend" the title. Patterned paper and buttons dress up the other blocks. Notice how Linda personalized the design by including journaling on the photo mat.

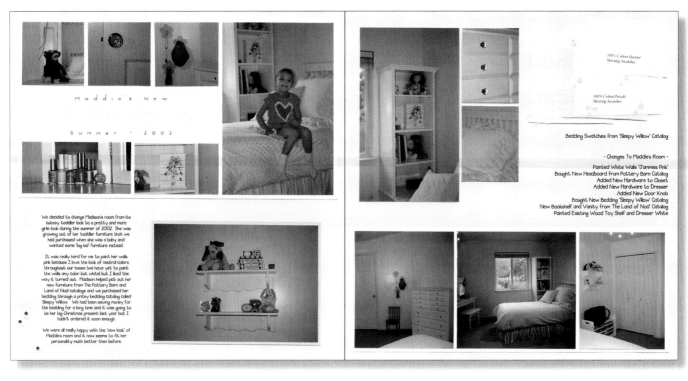

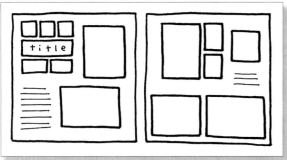

Figure 5. When documenting a room makeover or other creative project, include swatches of fabric, paint chips and other decorating elements. *Pages by Kimberly Stone.*
Supplies *Computer fonts:* CK Newsprint (title), "Fresh Fonts" CD, Creating Keepsakes; Think Small (subtitle) and Plain Jane (journaling), downloaded from *www.twopeasinabucket.com*; *Flower punch:* Marvy Uchida; *Gems:* Swarovski and Impress Rubber Stamps; *Other:* Fabric swatches.

"Girlie Room"

by Kimberly Stone
Westland, MI

Kimberly kept the "all girl" layout in Figure 5 simple and clean. The design lends itself perfectly to her photos—elements from her daughter's newly decorated room. Note how she cut small blocks from larger pictures. She replaced the photo on the top right with fabric swatches used to redecorate the room. Kimberly also printed her journaling directly on the background cardstock and added tiny flowers for an extra-girlie touch. ♥

family, friends and vacations

Six great looks from one sketch

Figure 1. A continuous border across your layout helps draw your viewer through both pages. *Pages by Becky Higgins.* **Supplies** *Patterned paper:* Lasting Impressions for Paper; *Border and fish stickers:* Ever After.

WISH SCRAPBOOK DESIGN could be more flexible? This column's for you! You'll find a sketch, plus examples of how six scrapbookers—Juilien Jiang, Nia Reddy, Lauren Hartman, Sande Krieger, Jill Knight and I—used the same concept to create six different layouts.

The Sketch

This sketch features up to nine photographs and three journaling blocks. A vertical photo tops the upper left corner of the left page, with two small photos (or embellishments) overlapping its lower right edge. A horizontal

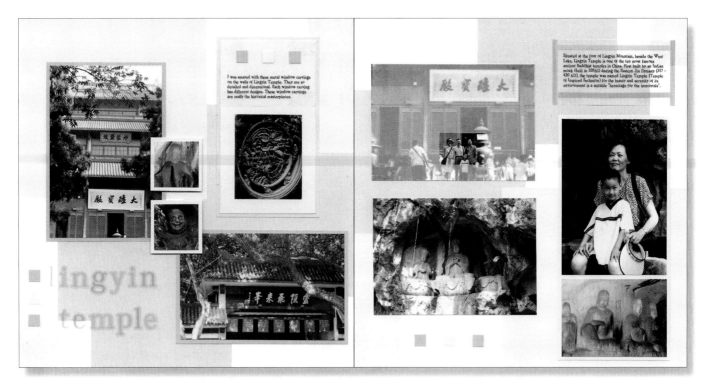

Figure 2. Clean lines and muted colors help keep the attention on your photos. *Pages by Juilien Jiang.* **Supplies** *Patterned paper:* SEI, Inc.; *Vellum:* Bazzill Basics; *Stickers and letter stickers:* SEI, Inc.; *Square punch:* Paper Shapers, EK Success; *Computer font:* CK Constitution, "Fresh Fonts" CD, *Creating Keepsakes.*

photo in the bottom right corner of the page adds balance to the left page.

Journaling spaces fill the two empty spaces on the left page, along with another small photo in the top space. On the right page, two horizontal photos are stacked on the left side of the page. The sketch includes two smaller matted photos on the right side, with a journaling block above.

The Approaches

I posted this sketch on our web site and invited CK readers to submit their layouts (see sidebar for more information). I asked the scrapbookers to keep their page designs similar to the sketch. Other than that, they were free to use any photos, colors, tools or supplies they desired. Here's how we each chose to implement the sketch.

"Deep-Sea Fishing"
by Becky Higgins

Pictures from my husband's fishing trip worked well with this particular design (Figure 1). I highlighted my focal-point picture with a thicker mat and included my title on the journaling block at the top. Instead of using additional journaling in the bottom left corner, I included journaling with the bottom picture on the right-hand side. I then placed my subtitle at the top right of the layout. The theme-appropriate border stickers enhance my background combination of solid and patterned cardstock.

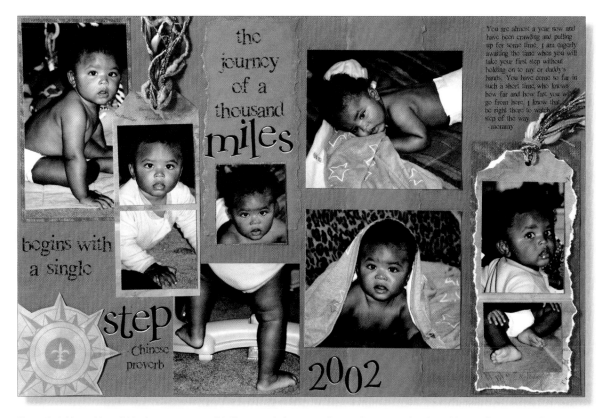

Figure 3. Add an old-world feel to your pages with fiber, mottled paper and torn edges. *Pages by Nia Reddy.* **Supplies** *Patterned papers:* Sonnets by Sharon Soneff, Creative Imaginations; Bravissimo!, Emagination Crafts; *Letter stickers:* Sonnets by Sharon Soneff, Creative Imaginations; *Fiber:* Fibers by the Yard; *Pigment ink:* ColorBox, Clearsnap; *Computer font:* Crack Babies, downloaded from the Internet; *Pop dots:* All Night Media. *Ideas to note:* Nia used map paper to create her tags. For the compass accent, she cut the pattern from the same map paper.

"Lingyin Temple"

by Juilien Jiang
San Jose, CA

Juilien had a lot of photos from her trip to the Lingyin Temple in China, and this sketch helped her fit a variety of photo sizes on one layout (Figure 2). She found the photo and journaling mat on the left page perfect for journaling about a specific photo.

Juilien printed the journaling at right on vellum to continue the soft lines from her patterned paper. The sticker border helps define the journaling block. To tone down a photo with a busy background, Juilien layered it with vellum and cut a square out of the center to frame her subjects.

"A Thousand Miles"

by Nia Reddy
Brooklyn, NY

Nia dressed her layout up with handmade tag accents, fiber and decorative papers from the Sonnets line by Creative Imaginations (Figure 3). She added dimension by placing pop dots under various accents, such as the compass embellishment in the lower left corner and also the tag at far right. Note how the torn and gold-inked turquoise paper complements the patterned paper and draws your eye through the entire layout.

Figure 4. Use a panoramic photo as a page accent or border. *Pages by Lauren Hartman.* **Supplies** *Background paper:* K & Company; *Sandstone paper and vellum:* Paper Pizazz; *Fern panoramic:* Lauren's photo; *Square embellishments and tag:* Mini Fresh Cuts, EK Success; *Round tag:* Impress Rubber Stamps; *Pen:* Le Plume 2, Marvy Uchida; *Craft wire:* Artistic Scrapper; *Beads:* ShipwreckBeads.com; *Fibers:* On the Surface and DMC; *Metallic rub-ons:* Craf-T Products; *Chalk:* Stampin' Up!; *Embossing ink:* Top Boss, Clearsnap; *Embossing powder:* JudiKins; *Letter stickers:* Provo Craft; *Computer font:* CK Print, "The Best of Creative Lettering" CD Combo, *Creating Keepsakes.*

"Patience"

by Lauren Hartman
Seattle, WA

Lauren wanted a very natural look for these pictures of her son at the park, so she chose mossy green paper to link the photos (Figure 4). She accented her left focal photo by double-matting it and threading craft wire and charms through the top. The torn fern border is actually a photo Lauren took using a panoramic setting on her camera. She added more green to the layout with cropped sections of Mini Fresh Cuts by Rebecca Sower.

Figure 5. Black-and-white tones create unity among photos with many different colors. *Pages by Sande Krieger.* **Supplies** *Patterned paper:* American Crafts (sunshine), Art Impressions (yellow wash) and Provo Craft (green); *Colored vellum:* Provo Craft; *Letter stickers:* me & my BIG ideas; *Rubber stamp:* Hero Arts; *Stamping ink:* Stampin' Up!; *Computer font:* Angelina, downloaded from the Internet; *Star eyelets:* The Card Ladies; *Filigree nailheads:* Jest Charming; *Wire hands:* Westrim Crafts; *Linen:* Beverly's; *Letter cubes:* Source unknown; *Embroidery floss:* DMC; *Pop dots:* All Night Media; *Other:* Craft wire. *Idea to note:* Sande scanned color photos, then printed them as black-and-white photos.

"McKean's Girl Friends"

by Sande Krieger
Salt Lake City, UT

Nine-year-old McKean Krieger has a lot of friends who just happen to be girls, and this sketch gave Sande the inspiration she needed to show her son's friendship with them (Figure 5). To keep the smaller photos at left from getting lost

in the larger matted photo, Sande matted them with green linen and mounted them with pop dots.

Sande mounted star eyelets, laced embroidery floss through them, then threaded them with moveable beads. The wire hands at bottom right add a finishing touch to this colorful layout.

Figure 6. Add simple touches such as handprints and bows to make a lasting impression. *Pages by Jill Knight. Photos by Echoes of Light Photography and Jill Knight.* **Supplies** *Patterned vellum:* EK Success (grass gold) and Liz King (grass blue); *Vellum:* Paper Adventures; *Computer fonts:* Monotype Corsiva, Microsoft Word; *Embossing ink:* VersaMark, Tsukineko; *Embossing powder:* JudiKins; *Brass brads:* Magic Scraps; *Ribbon:* Shades of Elegance. *Ideas to note:* Jill stamped embossing ink on her children's hands, then pressed them onto vellum. She filled in the non-inked spaces, sprinkled embossing powder over the surface, then heat-embossed it. She trimmed the vellum to size and mounted it under her yellow patterned vellum for a soft accent. Jill used scraps from her cropped photos as borders under the vellum at bottom right.

"A Mother's Blessing"

by Jill Knight
Centerville, OH

Jill kept her layout (Figure 6) very simple and true to the sketch. The yellow ribbon accents around her journaling and the small bows help soften the straight edges of each matted photo. The ribbon also complements the bow in Jenna's hair.

Note how the embossed hand accents balance the two opposing corners of the layout. For Jill, they're beautiful reminders of how small her children were at this time. ♥

Highlight the little things—good and bad—that comprised your traveling experiences. *Page by Allison Strine.* **Supplies** *Patterned paper:* Karen Foster Design (background and waves); Renae Lindgren (green), Creative Imaginations; *Computer fonts:* Splurge (title) and CAC Norm Heavy (journaling), downloaded from the Internet; *Stamping ink:* Ranger Industries; *Embossing powder:* Suze Weinberg; *Colored pencils:* Prismacolor, Sanford.

My sister Jennifer just finished a twenty-hour car ride with two preteens. When I asked how stressful the journey was, she replied, "It was great. The kids just watched movies the whole way." What a difference 30 years makes! When I was a kid, long car rides were all about entertaining ourselves. We certainly didn't have a television in the car, or even an audio cassette player. Airbags were long in the future, and seat belts were optional. Instead we listened to Dad singing off-key renditions of "Show Me the Way to Go Home." We played endless games of "Find the License Plate" and "I Spy."

While these snapshot memories are just small clues to what traveling was like for me in the mid 60s, I'm happy to keep track of these "little things" that are part of vacations today. As you think about how to capture your vacation memories, consider the following questions:

◆ How did you get to your destination? Did you drive or fly? How did you entertain yourselves on the car ride? Did you play any games in the car, listen to certain music or watch T.V.?

◆ Who packs the suitcases in your family? How about loading the car?

◆ What do you bring home from a trip?

◆ What are some of the "firsts" that happened on your trip? Did someone dare to try a new food or go parasailing?

◆ Vacations are always learning experiences. What lessons did you learn? What will you do differently next time?

◆ What was your favorite meal, and how much did it cost?

—by Allison Strine

a new brother, july 4 and more

Five great looks from one simple sketch

WISH SCRAPBOOK DESIGN could be more flexible? This column is for you! You'll find a sketch, plus examples of how five scrapbookers— Allison Landrum, Ali Edwards, Susan Crawford, Aime Davis and I—used the same concept to create five different layouts.

The Sketch

This sketch is pretty standard when it comes to the number of pictures used on the layout—six. You'll find ample room for a title and subtitle on the left and journaling spaces on both pages. The

Figure 1. Keep the design clean and simple for a quick approach. *Pages by Becky Higgins.* **Supplies** *Tags:* The Paper Loft; *Vellum:* Paper Adventures; *Nailheads:* Westrim Crafts; *Pen:* Zig Writer, EK Success.

ARTICLE BY BECKY HIGGINS

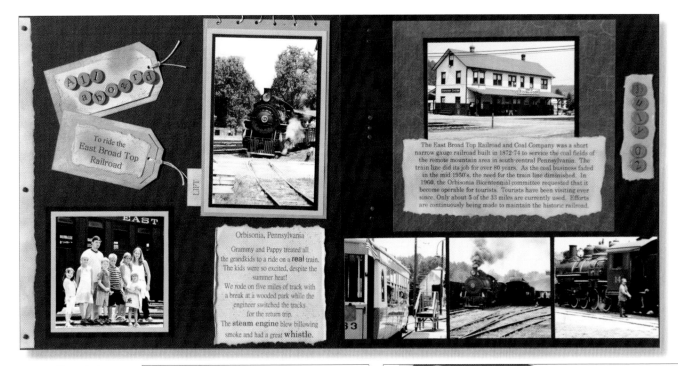

Figure 2. Age your pictures by tearing edges and adding rustic colors to your layout. *Pages by Susan Crawford.*
Supplies
Patterned paper: Colorbök; *Eyelet letters and numbers:* Making Memories; *Computer fonts:* Batang, Arial and Times New Roman, Microsoft; *Rubber stamps, stamping ink and craft wire:* Stampin' Up!; *Other:* Hemp and brads. *Idea to note:* Susan included other pictures beneath the vertical train photo and included a lift tag.

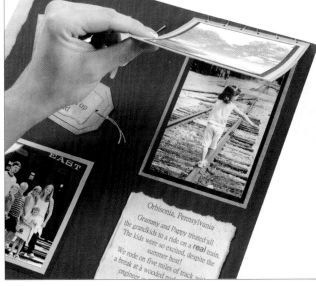

photo placement is balanced and lets you use a variety of photo sizes. The sketch is designed to lend itself to any theme.

The Approaches

I posted this sketch on our web site (at *www.creatingkeepsakes.com/magazine/your work*) and invited CK readers to submit their layouts (see sidebar for more information). I asked the scrapbookers to keep their page designs similar to the sketch. Other than that, they were free to use any photos, colors, tools or supplies they desired. Here's how we each chose to implement the sketch.

"Samuel"

by Becky Higgins

For my layout, I stuck with a simple, uncluttered style. This layout only took between 15–20 minutes to create. With minimal "fluff" and the use of clean lines and appropriate colors, the focus remains on the pictures.

Figure 3. Remember to scrapbook more than just events. Create a layout about your child's hobbies, gifts and passions. *Pages by Ali Edwards.* **Supplies** *Patterned paper:* Magenta; *Computer fonts:* Arial Black, Microsoft Word; American Typewriter Condensed ITC, downloaded from the Internet. *Idea to note:* Ali scanned letters from a Scrabble game.

"All Aboard"

by Susan Crawford
Virginia Beach, VA

I love the rich colors that accompany Susan's black-and-white photos of her family's train experience. She added a rustic touch with tearing and inking techniques. Susan opted to keep her three lower right photos straight instead of toggled.

"Read for Pure Joy"

by Ali Edwards
Eugene, OR

Ali wanted to portray her son's love for books, and this sketch worked well as a springboard for her layout. Although her title is not contained in blocks, Ali still placed it in the upper left corner of the layout. Her trio of elements at bottom right also works well as an alternative to the three photographs suggested by the sketch.

Figure 4. Celebrate your family's holiday celebrations with an all-American color scheme. *Pages by Allison Landrum.* **Supplies** *Red paper:* Colorbök; *Vellum and paper wire:* DMD Inc.; *Circle punch:* Provo Craft; *Flag accents:* Wallies, McCall's; *Stamping ink:* VersaColor, Tsukineko; *Computer font:* Garamouche, Impress Rubber Stamps; *Lettering template:* Provo Craft; *Mini brads:* American Pin & Fastener; *Eyelets:* Making Memories (red) and unknown (blue); *Chalk:* Craf-T Products; *Foam adhesive squares:* Making Memories (small) and Therm O Web (large); *Stars and tags:* Allison's own designs.

Ideas to note: To give her page a rustic, aged look, Allison chalked and inked the tags and torn edges. She sanded the red paper and used brown ink on the edges of the title and photo mats. Allison machine-stitched the mat on the left, then cut up the flag accents to use as star accents and strips.

"Fourth of July"

by Allison Landrum
Austin, TX

Allison created a 12" x 12" layout based on the proportionally smaller sketch, as did the other scrapbookers featured this month. She created her title with template letters placed in tags and made a folded strip out of her subtitle.

Figure 5. Creative techniques can help enhance black-and-white photos of an all-American boy. *Pages by Aime Davis.* **Supplies** *Patterned paper:* All My Memories; *Corrugated paper:* DMD Inc.; *Computer font:* CK Journaling, "The Best of Creative Lettering" CD Combo, *Creating Keepsakes; Tags:* Fresh Cuts, EK Success; *Stamping ink:* Fresco, Stampa Rosa; *Other:* Brads, eyelets and pop dots.

Idea to note: Aime aged her pictures by stamping her inkpad directly on the pictures. She also used the same technique on the background cardstock.

"All American Boy"

by Aime Davis
Riverton, UT

The rustic approach here makes Aime's layout a standout, along with her "All-American" color choices. Note how she added an antique touch by roughing up copies of her black-and-white photos with ink blotches and torn edges. Aime chose to turn her trio of photos into tag elements for a more interesting look. ❤

Sporting events can inspire powerful emotions. Share how the action touches you on a layout. *Page by Allison Strine.* **Supplies** *Computer font:* China Cat, downloaded from the Internet; *Clip art:* Microsoft Design Gallery Live; *Alphabet stickers:* me & my BIG ideas; *Stamping ink:* ColorBox, Clearsnap, Inc. *Idea to note:* Allison manipulated the clip art using Microsoft Picture It! 2002, then aged the images and the alphabet stickers with sandpaper and ink.

Embarrassing confession #376: I cry during baseball games. Yep, every single time my husband takes me to a ball game, as we stand and sway with thousands of other fans, ankle-deep in peanut shells, bellowing out the song that fans have sung for over a hundred years, that incredibly *American* song, "Take Me Out to the Ball Game," I get all choked up and the occasional tear dribbles down my cheek. Sports can touch us in powerful and even magical ways, and these events and emotions are well worth scrapbooking.

Consider creating sports layouts that answer the following questions:

◆ As a child, what was your favorite sport and why?

◆ When you go to a ball game, what emotions do you experience during the different parts of the game?

◆ As you drag your daughter to her fifth soccer practice in five days, think about why you're doing it. What does it mean to you, and to her, to be involved in sports?

◆ What kinds of things do you do to culti-vate your (or your kids') love for sports?

◆ What is your favorite sporting moment of all time? Was it watching the U.S. hockey team overcome all odds to win an Olympic medal? Or seeing your son get up after being tackled hard on the football field? How did this moment affect you?

◆ What are your hopes, dreams and predictions for your young athletes?

◆ What are some of your memories of family members' sports experiences?

—by Allison Strine

the farm, football and fall

Five easy ideas for this month's sketch

WISH SCRAPBOOK DESIGN could be more flexible? This column's for you! You'll find a sketch, plus examples of how five scrapbookers—Patty McAnally, Silvia Arizaga Kolsky, Jane Rife, Shannon Rippeth and I—used the same basic concept to create five different layouts.

The Sketch

Between seven and eight photos will fit on the layout, but this is flexible. Note how the

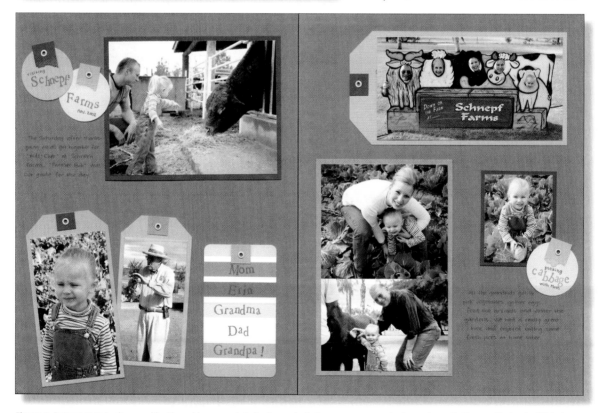

Figure 1. Repeat certain shapes—like the cabbages and circles here—to help carry across part of your layout's theme. *Photos by Michele Kennedy, pages by Becky Higgins.* **Supplies** *Tags:* SEI; *Eyelets:* Emagination Crafts; *Letter stamps:* PSX Design; *Stamping ink:* Tsukineko; *Pen:* Pigma Micron, Sakura.

ARTICLE BY BECKY HIGGINS

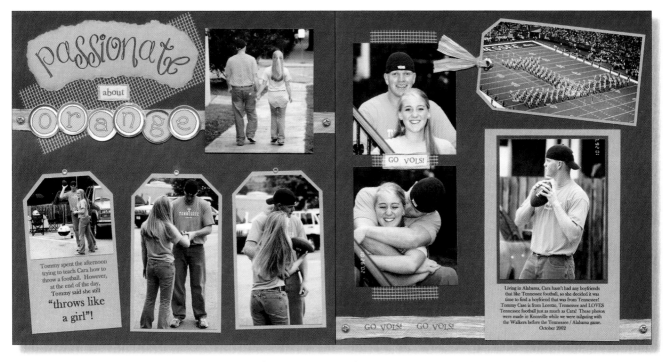

Figure 2. Fall is time for football. Scrap your favorite fans and their passion for the sport. *Pages by Patty McAnally.* **Supplies** *Paper yarn:* Twistel, Making Memories; *Mesh:* Magic Mesh, Avant Card; *Phillips-head eyelets and silver eyelets:* Making Memories; *Computer fonts:* 2Peas Pancakes ("Orange") and 2Peas Beautiful ("Passionate"), downloaded from *www.twopeasinabucket.com*; Garamouche ("about") and Old Baskerville (journaling), downloaded from the Internet; *Chalk:* Craf-T Products; *Tags:* Patty's own design; *Other:* Metal-rimmed tags.

placement of the journaling in the last of the three tags (see left page) is only a suggestion. You can place photos in all three positions or use only two of the tags for journaling. Also, note that the two touching horizontal photos on the right-hand page can be separated slightly.

The Approaches

I posted this sketch on our web site (at *www.creatingkeepsakes.com/magazine/your_work*) and invited CK readers to submit their layouts. I asked the scrapbookers to keep their page designs similar to the sketch. Other than that, they were free to use any photos, colors, tools or supplies desired. Here's how we each chose to implement the sketch.

"Schnepf Farms"
by Becky Higgins

As if the design didn't have enough tags, I added three more! I couldn't resist balancing the look of all those rectangles with a few circles, and the tags I found seemed like the perfect fit. Basing my color palette on the product I used, this page was a cinch to put together.

Figure 3. Sprinkle your layout with pearl beads for an elegant touch. *Pages by Silvia Arizaga Kolsky, photos by Bill Stockwell.* **Supplies** *Patterned paper:* Anna Griffin; *Metallic paper:* Accu-Cut Systems; *Textured paper:* Bravissimo, Emagination Crafts; *Vellum:* Paper Adventures; *Computer fonts:* Goddard Demo (title and journaling) and Garton ("Bride"), downloaded from the Internet; *Dress sticker:* Jolee's by You, Sticko; *Grosgrain ribbon:* Wright's; *Tags:* Silvia's own design; *Other:* Beads.

"Becoming a Bride"

by Silvia Arizaga Kolsky
Reno, NV

Silvia wanted a formal look, so she used a monochromatic color scheme and pearl beads. To give her black-and-white pictures a "warmer" feel, she added a hint of red with the Variations tool in Adobe Photoshop. Since the pictures speak for themselves and are part of a larger album, Silvia included minimal journaling.

"Passionate About Orange"

by Patty McAnally
Decatur, AL

Fall means football season in Patty's house. She added zing (and a more masculine feel) to her title block by layering chalked vellum and metal-rimmed tags over mesh. The screw eyelets also add to the manly theme. The orange paper yarn accents help call attention to the orange highlights in each photo.

Figure 4. Add a hint of fall by chalking your layout with earthy tones. *Pages by Shannon Rippeth.* **Supplies** *Computer fonts:* CK Elegant ("September"), "Fresh Fonts" CD, *Creating Keepsakes*; BernhardModBT ("Song") and TypoUprightBT (journaling), downloaded from the Internet; *Colored pencils:* Prismacolor, Sanford; *Fibers:* Adornaments, EK Success; *Burlap ribbon:* Jo-Ann Crafts; *Chalk:* Craf-T Products; *Other:* Craft wire, beads, jute and brads. *Idea to note:* Shannon strung beads onto twisted wire, then used it to frame the window in the burlap ribbon.

"September's Song"

by Shannon Rippeth
Quaker City, OH

Shannon's children were delighted to see their first Ohio fall. Her daughter thought the trees were on fire. By using natural colors for her background, Shannon kept the focus on her pictures. Note how she chalked her journaling and poem and used earthy fibers to add an autumn tone.

September's Song

The September song is played on the chords

Of winds rustling through the trees,

Creating a melody low and sweet

Of whisperings in the breeze.

There is rhythmic harmony in the leaves

That, turning yellow and brown.

Are keeping tuneful and lyrical time

As they come tumbling down.

—by Virginia Katherine Oliver

Figure 5. Scrapbook a page about your night out with friends. *Pages by Jane Rife.* **Supplies** *Gold paper:* Metropolis Paper Company; *Patterned paper:* Brother/Sister Design Studio; *Handmade paper and eyelets:* Creative Imaginations; *Mulberry paper:* Yasutomo; *Mosaic tiles:* Sarah Heidt Photo Craft; *Photo corners:* Jolee's Boutique, Sticko; *Fibers:* On The Surface; *Metal mesh:* ScrapYard 329; *Leaf charms:* Boutique Trims; *Gold hot glue:* Embossing Arts Co.; *Computer fonts:* Carpenter ICG (title) and Angelina, downloaded from the Internet; CK Script (journaling), "The Best of Creative Lettering" CD Combo, *Creating Keepsakes.*

"Life Is Delicious"

by Jane Rife
Hendersonville, TN

A recent outing took Jane and her monthly dinner-club friends to an Italian restaurant. To complement its ambiance on her layout, Jane chose earthy background and patterned papers. Note the details—tiles, charms and fiber—that help carry her theme throughout the layout. ♥

Need an "antiqued" accent for a heritage page? Try rubbing an ink pad over a length of ribbon. *Page by Lynne Montgomery.* **Supplies** *Patterned papers:* Anna Griffin (floral), Autumn Leaves (hearts); *Computer fonts:* CK Bella, "The Best of Creative Lettering" CD Vol. 4, *Creating Keepsakes*; Technical, Microsoft Word; *Stamping ink:* Ancient Page; *Tags:* American Tag Co.; *Other:* Ribbon and charms.

Have you ever wanted to use a particular ribbon on a heritage layout, only to find it looks too clean, crisp and stark next to your photos? I have. I tried to "antique" my ribbon by tea-staining it, but the technique doesn't work well on ribbons with any kind of finish. Then I discovered that I can create an "old world" feel on ribbons of any kind with just a permanent ink pad.

It's easy to do. First, lay your ribbon on a piece of wax paper and rub the ink pad over it. (My favorite color to use for this technique is Sandalwood by Ancient Page.) If your ink pad is new, touch the ribbon ever so slightly or you'll transfer too much ink. Keep applying the ink until the color is fairly even and you reach the desired shade. Within minutes, the ribbon will be dry and ready to be attached to your page.

—by Lynne Montgomery

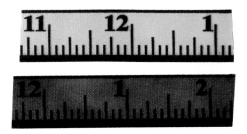

autumn days

Get 13 photos on one layout

WISH SCRAPBOOK DESIGN could be more flexible? This column's for you! You'll find a sketch, plus examples of how five scrapbookers—Heather Uppencamp, Rebecca Stanford, Tracy Whitney, Nancy McKinney and I—used the same concept to create five different layouts.

The Sketch

This sketch accommodates 13 photos, with 10 various-sized photos on the lower half of the layout. The photo arrangement can be changed as needed, yet still preserve the integrity of the design. The three main photos along the top carry a lot of visual weight, making them the strongest photos. Journaling space is provided in a strip on the left-hand page.

The Approaches

I posted this sketch on our web site (*www.creating-keepsakes.com/magazine/your_work*) and invited CK readers to submit their layouts. I asked the scrapbookers to keep their page designs similar to the sketch. Other than that, they were free to use any photos, colors, tools or supplies they desired. Here's how we each chose to implement the sketch.

"Christmas Pictures"
by Becky Higgins

Supplies *Patterned cardstock:* The Crafter's Workshop; *Tags:* O'Scrap!, Imaginations, Inc.; *Alphabet stamps:* PSX Design; *Stamping ink:* Tsukineko; *Brads:* Karen Foster Design; *Brown pen:* Zig Writer, EK Success.

"Autumn"
by Heather Uppencamp
Provo, UT

Supplies *Patterned paper:* Sharon Ann Collection, Déjà Views, The C-Thru Ruler Co.; Karen Foster Design; *Vellum:* Provo Craft; *Mesh:* Maruyama, Magenta; *Leaf punch:* Marvy Uchida; *Rubber stamps:* Craft Stamps; *Stamping ink:* ColorBox, Clearsnap; *Computer font:* Smargana, downloaded from the Internet; *Embossing powder:* Stampendous!; *Fibers:* Fibers By The Yard. *Ideas to note:* Heather punched leaves from patterned paper, stamped them with leaf stamps, then heat-embossed them with gold embossing powder. When she ran out of a specific color of mesh, she heat-embossed another color with gold.

"Kimbell Museum"
by Rebecca Stanford
San Antonio, TX

Supplies *Transparency:* 3M; *Eyelet letters:* Making Memories; *Pastels:* Design NuPastel; *Computer font:* Kabel BK BT, WordPerfect; *Pen:* Zig Writer, EK Success. *Ideas to note:* To create the "concrete" wall background, Rebecca sanded white cardstock, chalked it, then drew joints and holes with a black pen. She printed her journaling on a transparency.

"October"
by Tracy Whitney
Marion, NY

Supplies *Patterned paper:* Bo-Bunny Press; *Vellum:* DMD, Inc.; *Eyelets:* Making Memories; *Colored pencils:* Lyra; *Die cut:* Carolee's Creations; *Computer fonts:* Verdana (journaling), Microsoft Word; 2Peas Stained Glass (title), downloaded from *www.twopeasinabucket.com*.

"Nevada Desert"
by Marie-Ève Trudeau
Sainte-Julie, QC, Canada

Supplies *Embossing powder:* Ranger Industries; *Pigment ink:* Clearsnap; *Rubber stamps:* Magenta; *Acrylic paints:* Pebeo; *Other:* Polymer clay.

Ideas to note: Marie-Ève created the sand look by mixing two embossing powders, then sprinkling the mixture over glue. She made the handprint marks with pigment ink. ❤

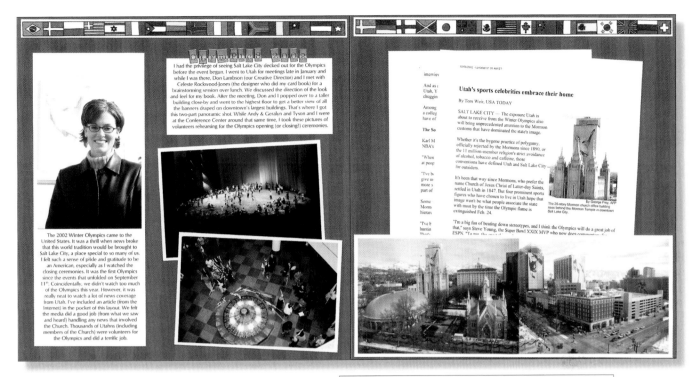

Figure 2. Create a panoramic effect by taking side-by-side pictures and matching them up on your layout. *Pages by Becky Higgins.* **Supplies** *Patterned paper:* Lasting Impressions for Paper; *Stickers:* Stampendous! (letters) and The New Kids on the Block (border); *Computer font:* Optimum, downloaded from the Internet.

The Sketch

This simple layout includes five photos and room for memorabilia. Two of the photos are placed side by side on the right-hand page on a large strip of cardstock, which also acts as a pocket. Many sizes of memorabilia can fit into this large pocket. The other three pictures are placed on the left-hand page as shown. The title and all the journaling also appear on this side of the layout.

The Approaches

I asked Cindy and Jenny to keep their page designs similar to the sketch. Other than that, they were free to use any photos, colors, tools or supplies they desired. Here's how we each chose to implement the sketch:

"Let's Go"
by Cindy Schow

Cindy did a great job adapting the 12" x 12" sketch to fit this 8½" x 11" layout (Figure 1). To mimic the look of tracks left in the snow from a snowmobile, Cindy crimped the paper to add texture to her photo mat and pocket border. She also used "dotlets" to resemble rivets. Note how Cindy used just one photo on the pocket instead of two.

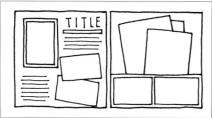

Figure 3. Headed for the slopes? Be sure to gather ski tags and pamphlets for your scrapbook. *Pages by Jenny Jackson.* **Supplies** *Computer fonts:* PC Ratatat (journaling), "A Gathering of Friends Vol. 1" HugWare CD, Provo Craft; Flowerchild ("Skiing"), downloaded from the Internet; *Snowflake buttons:* Dress-It-Up; *Glue dots:* Glue Dots International.

"Olympics"

by Becky Higgins

I opted to keep the title small and discreet (Figure 2), which left more room for journaling. I combined my journaling below the vertical photo on the same white cardstock where the photo is mounted.

I didn't include space between my two pictures on the memorabilia pocket because I took the pictures with the intent of creating a panoramic view of Salt Lake City dressed up for the Winter Olympics. As a finishing touch, I added world flag border stickers along the top of the layout.

"Skiing"

by Jenny Jackson

Coincidentally, Jenny and Cindy both used snow-related pictures and chose blue as their main color! Jenny also adapted the concept to the smaller format (Figure 3). She separated her title from the journaling with a torn strip of cardstock, adorned with snowflake buttons. Jenny hung her ski tag from a snowflake button next to the memorabilia in her pocket, which holds a pamphlet and map of the ski trails. ♥

What does family coming together for the holidays mean to you? Preserve your thoughts on a scrapbook page. *Page by Allison Strine.* **Supplies** *Patterned paper:* Karen Foster Design (photo frame), Magenta (background); Bo-Bunny Press (title letters); *Circle punch:* EK Success; *Stickers:* Magenta; *Rubber stamps:* Above the Mark, Planet Rubber (tags); *Stamping ink:* Ranger Industries; *Embossing powder:* Suze Weinberg; *Computer fonts:* CAC Leslie (title) and Pamela (captions, tags), downloaded from the Internet; CK Print, "The Best of Creative Lettering" CD Vol. 1, *Creating Keepsakes; Fibers:* Rubba Dub Dub; *Clip art:* Microsoft Design Gallery Live.

There's nothing like the cozy, almost magical feeling that comes when the entire family joins together to celebrate a special holiday. However, if your family is anything like mine, you're scattered across the country.

When we only see some of our loved ones a few times a year, time spent together for special occasions is extra precious. Future generations will want to know the efforts we go through to keep our families intact. Why not create a scrapbook page describing the logistics behind getting the family together for a holiday? Use these ideas as a starting point:

◆ How far did loved ones travel in order to join the family at a holiday?

◆ What sacrifices were made in preparing for the trip, and what does that mean to you?

◆ Describe the worst part of traveling. Was the plane delayed? Did anyone get a flat tire?

◆ How have some loved ones changed since you saw them last?

◆ When did you plan this trip? Was it a last-minute decision or one you've had planned since the last holiday?

◆ Why did everyone make the effort to join together at this time of year?

◆ What holiday did everyone choose to spend together this year, and why?

◆ Who is the mastermind behind the family's plans to get together?

—by Allison Strine

first birthday, twins and a dentist

Three great looks from one sketch

WISH SCRAPBOOK DESIGN could be more flexible? This column's for you! You'll find a brand-new sketch, plus examples of how three scrapbookers—Amy Williams, Anita Matejka and I—used the same concept to create three different layouts.

The Sketch

Look at the sketch, and you'll see that this no-nonsense layout is designed to include six

Figure 1. Hang your photos with fibers and buttons for a more homemade feel on your layout. *Pages by Becky Higgins, photos by Michele Kennedy.* **Supplies** *Fiber:* FiberScraps; *Buttons:* Magic Scraps; *Adhesive for attaching buttons:* Glue Dots International; *Letter stickers:* SEI, Inc.; *Fine-point pen:* Pigma Micron, Sakura; *Computer font:* CK Jot, "The Art of Creative Lettering" CD, *Creating Keepsakes.*

ARTICLE BY BECKY HIGGINS

Figure 2. A small touch of ribbon adds a sweet feeling to precious pictures. *Pages by Amy Williams.* **Supplies** *Computer fonts:* CK Bella (journaling), "The Best of Creative Lettering" CD, *Creating Keepsakes* and Doodle Do (title), Cock-A-Doodle Design, Inc.; *Pen:* Slick Writer, American Crafts; *Hearts:* Amy's own design; *Other:* Ribbon.

photos. The creative touch? Dangle photo elements like pictures hanging on a wall.

The simple design features one large block on the left page, which houses the main photo. Two smaller photos and the title span the bottom length of the main photo. Two vertical photos are staggered on the right page, and the journaling block (along with one more small photo) runs along the bottom of that page.

The Approaches

I asked Amy and Anita to keep their page designs similar to the sketch. Other than that, they were free to use any photos, colors, tools or supplies they desired. Here's how we each chose to implement the sketch. Note the birthday, baby and dentist themes.

"Erin's First Birthday"
by Becky Higgins

I chose a solid-colored cardstock since the pictures were fairly busy (Figure 1). To help the pictures stand out from the plum background, I matted the photos and title with paper in a light shade of violet. I used fibers and buttons that blend with the same color scheme.

I created my title with letter stickers, then added different fibers and buttons to my layout to add interest. My journaling strip is torn on the top and bottom edges to "soften" the overall look and decrease the harshness of so many straight lines.

Figure 3. A little metal here and a little metal there is easy to implement with wire and nailheads. *Pages by Anita Matejka.* **Supplies** *Patterned papers:* Karen Foster Design (dark blue) and Treehouse Designs (striped); *Vellum:* Paper Adventures; *Silver metallic paper:* Close To My Heart; *Metal letters and nailheads:* Making Memories; *Computer font:* Teletype, Microsoft Word; *Craft wire:* Westrim Crafts; *Other:* Clips from a photo-processing lab.

"Not One, but Two"
by Amy Williams

The photos of Amy's twin daughters called for a feminine touch, so she chose white ribbon to create her "hanging element" (Figure 2). Instead of using another element to secure the ribbon, Amy threaded it through the back of the layout and tied little bows to the front. She included a sweet poem for her journaling and labeled the individual pictures of the girls.

"Open Wide"
by Anita Matejka

Anita had wonderful photos of her daughter's first visit to the dentist (Figure 3). Her "hanging element" was craft wire, secured with nailheads and clips. She typed her journaling on vellum and set it apart with dark-blue, crooked strips of cardstock on the top and bottom edges.

Note how Anita's layout is 12" x 12" even though the sketch is designed for 8½" x 11" pages. The ideas you see here and throughout the magazine can easily be adapted to the size of your choice! ♥

B abies are some of my favorite subjects to photograph. They're so small and cuddly, and they don't talk back yet! From precious black-and-whites of their cute baby parts to everyday snapshots, pictures of your little one will quickly fill your albums. Here are a few tips to help you take photos you'll love:

◆ **Focus on your subject.** And, no, baby isn't always the subject. Narrow it down—is it the gleeful smile, the "pick me up" look, or hands outstretched for a favorite toy?

◆ **Go vertical.** Out of habit, we tend to leave the camera in the natural-feeling horizontal position. But for most portraits, vertical is a better fit. Look through your camera both ways and decide which one fills the viewfinder the most with your subject.

◆ **Remember lighting.** One of the best places to take photographs is inside by a north-facing window (or any window on an overcast day). If you're outside on a bright, sunny day, find shade from a tree or wait until the sun sets a bit before starting a portrait session.

Remember, the moments will go by quicker than you ever expect, so be sure to capture each and every one you can!

—by Anita Matejka

PHOTOS BY ANITA MATEJKA

"She may be the face I can't forget, the trace of pleasure or regret,
May be my treasure or the price I have to pay...
She may be the song the summer sings, may be the chill the autumn brings,
May be a hundred different things within the measure of a day.

She may be the beauty or the beast, may be the famine or the feast,
May turn each day into a heaven or a hell...
She may be the mirror of my dreams, the smile reflected in a stream
She may not be what she may seem inside her shell.

She may be the reason I survive, the why and wherefore I'm alive,
The one I'll care for through the rough in many years.
Me, I'll take her laughter and her tears and make them all my souvenirs
For where she goes I've got to be...the meaning of my life is she."   ~Elvis Costello

Figure 1. Shift your template to emboss an entire rectangle, then brush with walnut-colored rub-ons to create an elegantly textured photo mat. *Page by Denise Pauley.* **Supplies** *Patterned papers:* Design Originals (brown floral) and Rainboworld (leaves); *Computer font:* CK Constitution, "Fresh Fonts" CD, *Creating Keepsakes; Embossing stencil:* TSC Designs; *Metallic rub-ons:* Craf-T Products; *Brass frame:* Ink It; *Other:* Antique brass heart.

dry emboss it!

Make an elegant impression

The first time I dry embossed, I was amazed. Inspired by a beautiful card at a stamp store, I skeptically purchased a brass template and a stylus. I brought them home for what I figured would be an afternoon of futility and frustration.

I held the template and a sheet of cardstock up to a window, then ran my stylus around the image. The result? A perfectly embossed flower accent. My reaction? "Wow, this actually works!" A few years and several embossing templates later, I'm still hooked on dry embossing and its elegant and eclectic effects.

Getting Started

If you're hesitant to try dry embossing because you think it's too expensive, time-consuming or difficult, think again. All you really need to start are:

- A stylus (most are double-sided with sizes for regular or detail work)
- A template (brass, plastic, or even one you create yourself)
- A light source (try a light box or even a window on a sunny day)

For my light source, I use a Crayola model purchased at a toy store. I love how it runs on batteries and I can use it anywhere.

How to Dry Emboss

Dry embossing can be completed in three easy steps:

❶ Place template (also called a stencil) on a light source. Tack the template down if desired.

❷ Place cardstock over template, front side down if you have a preference at all.

❸ Trace edge of shape with stylus.

ARTICLE BY DENISE PAULEY

Dry embossing
is a perfect way to add dimension and drama without much bulk.

Tips to Help You

To make the process even smoother:

♦ When choosing a stylus, use the largest size the design will accommodate. Although a smaller tip is necessary for detailed images, a larger size lets you emboss quickly without the danger of puncturing your page.

♦ Before you begin, run your finger or a piece of wax paper over the area you plan to emboss. This will help the stylus glide more smoothly.

♦ Go over the design lightly several times. Avoid pressing too hard, too fast, which could also result in micro tears.

Cool Effects To Try

Now that we've got the basics covered, let's look at some cool effects you can achieve with dry embossing. The images can go from simple to sophisticated to shabby, depending on the treatment you give them.

Use dry embossing to design anything from little accents to large photo mats (Figure 1), borders, backgrounds and more. Find inspiration in one of the following examples, or experiment to create even more cool looks!

Dark Paper

Dark paper poses a particular challenge when dry embossing. Since the light won't penetrate the paper, it's impossible to see the image that needs to be traced. To combat this, simply place your cardstock over the template, firmly rub your fingernail or a burnisher over the general area until an outline appears, then use the stylus to fill in the details of the design. (If you flip the cardstock over and discover an incomplete portion of the design, simply line the template back up from the front and carefully turn it back over to go over any missed spots.)

An easier option? Find cardstock that has a white center. Whatever its shade, light will still seep through. Another advantage to this type of cardstock? You can create a shabby, distressed look after embossing by roughing up the images with sandpaper, allowing a bit of the white to show through (Figure 2).

Figure 2. Emboss, then gently sand, white-centered cardstock for a funky finish. *Example by Denise Pauley.* **Supplies** *Flower template:* ScrapPagerz 4 Basic Shapes With Envelopes Template, GoneScrappin.com, *Eyelet letters:* Making Memories, *Stamping ink:* Fluid Chalk, Clearsnap; *Tag:* American Tag.

Figure 3. Trace your topper onto vellum for a two-toned, dimensional effect. *Page by Tammy Lombardi.* **Supplies** *Vellum:* Paper Adventures; *Computer fonts:* Scriptina and Whimsy, downloaded from the Internet; *Photo-tinting oils:* Marshall's; *Ribbon:* C.M. Offray & Son; *Chalk:* Craf-T Products; *Eyelets:* Making Memories; *Other:* Studs.

Lettering

Get additional mileage from your lettering templates by using them to design dry-embossed titles as well. You can even make custom templates.

Joanne Moseley of Aurora, Ontario, Canada, likes to write her letters on heavy cardstock in the size and configuration needed, cut them out with an X-acto knife, then use the template to emboss the letters directly onto her background page. To enhance the dimension, she adds a touch of metallic rub-ons for a hint of shimmer.

Vellum

Embossing on vellum yields a lovely result. The stylus not only creates a raised image, but also lightens the color of the vellum to produce a nice, two-tone effect.

To emboss "Sophia" in Figure 3, Tammy Lombardi of Valrico, Florida, sized and reversed her title in Microsoft Word. Next, Tammy placed the printout on top of something with give (like a mouse pad), and positioned the vellum face-down over that. She then traced the lettering with a stylus to complete the elegant title. You can also try this technique with clip art, stamped images or even freehand designs.

Impressions

Change the look by letting the backside of embossed images face up. You'll still have great texture, and a bit of chalk around the edges will add even more interest to the piece. Or, instead of a template, try tracing around punch pieces to get images that are inset into the cardstock.

Here's another idea to try: Punch a square from a sheet of thick cardstock, then use the hole as an embossing template. Punch a smaller square, then tack the punch piece onto your light box. Position your cardstock so the square is in the center of the larger one you just embossed. Trace the shape, then flip the cardstock over. You'll end up with a mini "frame" for smaller accents or title letters (Figure 4).

Figure 4. Combine the positive and negative sides of embossed shapes to create frames for accents and title letters. *Example by Denise Pauley.* **Supplies** *Mesh paper:* Maruyama, Magenta; *Flower stencil:* TSC Designs; *Letters:* Squigglebets, Creative Imaginations; *Square punches:* Family Treasures; *Alphabet stamps:* PSX Design; *Ink:* Dauber Duo, Tsukineko; *Paint:* Plaid Enterprises; *Brad and tag:* Making Memories; *Chalk:* Craf-T Products.

Coloring

Adding color to dry-embossed designs is a wonderful way to enhance their definition. After embossing, flip the cardstock over, reposition the template on the front of your image, then apply color to specific areas, masking off those you'd like to keep plain.

Depending on the mood of your layout, experiment with acrylic paint, pigment powder or ink applied directly to your design (Figure 5). You can also try chalk, rub-ons, watercolors, pens, pencils and more. Lasting Impressions for Paper also offers software that coordinates with their templates and allows you to add color even before embossing.

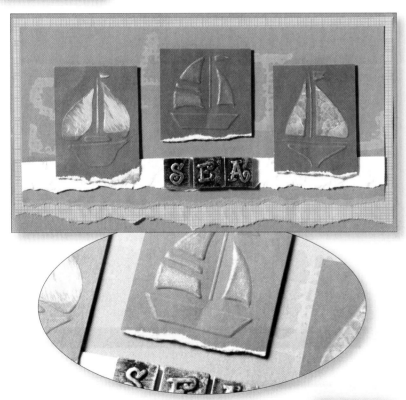

Figure 5. Experiment with a variety of coloring techniques to produce an effect that suits your layout. *Example by Denise Pauley.* **Supplies** *Patterned paper:* Chatterbox; *Sailboat stencils:* Lasting Impressions for Paper; *Alphabet stamps:* Reliquary, Ma Vinci; *Letter tiles:* Savvy Tiles, Creative Imaginations; *Stamping inks:* Dauber Duo, Tsukineko; Perfect Adhesive, Ranger Industries; *Paint:* Plaid Enterprises; *Pigment powder:* Perfect Pearls, Ranger Industries.

Metal

Embossing metal mesh can result in a funky, industrial look that'll make your 3-D images shine. To get good definition, you'll need to go over the image several times. (You can even trace the backside of the image with a marker and back the shape with a lighter shade of cardstock to help it stand out more.)

Make the most of your templates by varying which parts you choose to emboss. You can even mix and match! Create a design comprised of embossed mesh and embossed cardstock pieces like that in Figure 6.

Figure 6. Metal mesh gives extra sheen and shabby style to dry-embossed accents. *Example by Denise Pauley.* **Supplies** *Patterned paper:* Chatterbox; *Metal mesh:* American Art Clay Co.; *Door and topiary stencil:* Lasting Impressions for Paper; *Title tag:* Scrapbook ID, Chatterbox; *Fasteners:* Scrapbook Nails, Chatterbox; *Pen:* Slick Writer, American Crafts; *Metallic rub-ons:* Craf-T Products.

Dimension

Give dry-embossed images even more punch by adding another layer. Whether you add micro beads, glitter, tinsel and more, you can apply just enough extras to highlight a single area, or you can apply complete coverage for a total facelift.

For a quick and easy faux tile effect like that in Figure 7, dry emboss a set of squares onto cardstock. Dab embossing ink over the top and apply a few layers of thick embossing enamel.

Dry embossing is a perfect way to add dimension and drama without much bulk. With a few tools and a couple of dry runs, you'll discover it's quick and easy to get the image you want, every time. With a variety of techniques to update embossed looks, your accents are guaranteed to make the perfect impression! ♥ →

Figure 7. Adding extras can double the dimension and produce some funky faux looks. *Example by Denise Pauley.* **Supplies** *Patterned paper:* The Paper Loft; *Leaf stencil:* Lasting Impressions for Paper; *Square punch:* PaperShapers, EK Success; *Embossing powder:* Ultra Thick Embossing Enamel, Suze Weinberg, Ranger Industries; *Tag:* American Tag; *Fiber:* Rubba Dub Dub, Art Sanctum; *Charm:* Embellish It, Boutique Trims; *Chalk:* Craf-T Products; *Brad:* Avery Dennison.

It's quick and easy to get the image you want, every time.

With a few tools

and a couple of dry runs, you'll discover dry embossing is quick and easy and guaranteed to make the perfect impression.

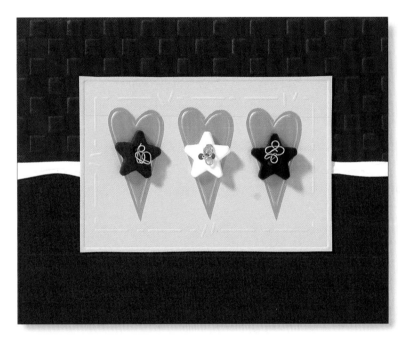

Share Your Patriotic Spirit with an Embossed Card

Feeling patriotic this time of year? Continue the celebration by using your stencils to make an embossed card! Following are two fun ideas from the book *Elegantly Embossed Vol. 2* by Jennifer Harkema, Elegantly Embossed (703/361-9299).

"RED, WHITE AND BLUE"
Supplies *Silver paper:* Lasting Impressions for Paper; *Other cardstock:* Chantilly Lace; *Star buttons and floral wire:* From craft store; *Templates:* L961 heart and ticking border, B261 ribbon border and L969 check background.

"USA"
Supplies *Pre-embossed background paper and silver cardstock:* Lasting Impressions for Paper; *Cardstock for letters:* Chantilly Lace; *Dangling star border:* From craft store; *Templates:* M1 alphabet and square frames, Lasting Impressions for Paper.

Transfer It!

Move a favorite image to fabric, canvas, paper and more

THE ART of transferring images has fascinated me for years. It all started when my husband's aunt quilted us a beautiful wall hanging, complete with childhood pictures and our wedding-day portraits sewn into the quilt.

My aunt's next gift? A collaged picture quilt of my twins when they were about six months old. Those chubby cheeks make me smile every time I see the quilt. The photographs maintained excellent quality even after being transferred to fabric.

Fast forward several years, and you'll find image transfer one of today's hottest artistic techniques. With the right supplies you can put images on a variety of surfaces and textures, and since scrapbooking is all about photographs, image transfer is right up your alley and mine! Here's how to get started.

by Karen Burniston

3 Questions

BEFORE DIVING INTO an image transfer project, ask yourself three questions:

What? What do you want to transfer? Typical items are photographs, clip art, drawings, digital images, magazine images, text and ads.

Where? Where do you want to put the image? Typical "receiving surfaces" are paper, glass, clay, book covers, wood, fabric or canvas.

How? Which method will you use for transferring the image? We'll cover several techniques (easy to advanced) in this article.

Mirror-imaging. You'll want to become familiar with mirror-imaging before doing image transfer (some techniques require it, while others don't). With mirror-imaging, the item to be transferred is "flipped" electronically in one of three ways: software that handles this automatically (many packages do), a special printer setting (if your printer driver supports it), or using the "flip horizontal" or "mirror image" setting on a copy machine.

After the item is transferred, it will appear in its original orientation. You can skip this step if the direction an image faces doesn't matter to you or if you're making a transparent transfer that can be used in either orientation.

Do a Tape Transfer

PACKING TAPE TRANSFERS may be the easiest and most cost-effective way to transfer images. All that's needed is a color or black-and-white photocopy of an image, regular clear packing tape, a burnishing tool and water. *Tip:* When making photocopies, be sure to use a copier with toner. Many "copiers" marketed for home use are actually inkjet printers, which don't work for this method. A laser printer is another option, since it uses toner.

Transparent image. With the packing tape method, you'll end up with a transparent image. Because you can use either side, mirror-imaging is not required.

Width of tape. Another consideration is the width of the packing tape (generally about 2"). To do larger images, you can place several pieces of tape side by side, but the seams will be visible. To create seamless transfers, reduce the original images to 2" wide, or you can use clear contact paper instead, which comes in larger sheets.

Ready to give the packing tape method a try? The step-by-step instructions here will help you become familiar with the technique.

Figure 1. Use rubber stamps and packing tape transfers to create an artsy collage look. *Page by Karen Burniston.* **Supplies** *Cork paper:* Creative Impressions; *Metal mesh:* ScrapYard 329; *Tagwear and extreme eyelets:* Creative Imaginations; *Eyelet charms:* Making Memories; *Brads:* Magic Scraps; *Key charm:* Once Upon a Charm; *Manila shipping tag and metal-rimmed tags:* American Tag; *Ink pads:* Adirondack, Ranger Industries; *Embossing powder:* Stampendous!; *Rubber stamps:* Rubber Baby Buggy Bumpers (background writing on first three tags), Hero Arts (background writing on fourth tag, small swirl, square), PSX Design (small letter stamps), Magenta (flower), Cherry Pie (large swirl), Twenty-Two (swirly star) and Wordsworth (letter stamps for title).

Step-by-Step Packing Tape Method

To transfer images with packing tape:

(1) Make a color photocopy of transfer items. *Tip:* For photos, line up six 4" x 6" photos on a copy machine, choose "photo," select 8 ½" x 11" as the paper size, then reduce the image to 50%. Each image will be 2" wide, perfect for packing tape. Most glossy magazine ads don't need to be photocopied first, but you may want to make backup copies on a copy machine.

(2) Cut out the image you wish to transfer. Cover the image with packing tape and burnish in both directions with a bone folder or other tool.

(3) Soak the image in a bowl of warm water for at least five minutes.

(4) Start rubbing the white (non-tape) side under running water to remove all the paper. You can rub with firm pressure, but do not scrape or gouge the image as you may damage it.

(5) Once all the paper is removed, blot the area dry with a towel. You'll be left with a transparent image on the packing tape. Attach it to your project as you would a transparency, with clear glue, fasteners or a gel medium.

Now that you've got the basics down, "go to town" with the transfer idea. For the layout in Figure 1, I added packing tape transfers of my kids' "age four" photo shoot over rubber-stamped tags. Note how the stamped backgrounds are visible through the transfers for a fun collage look.

Figure 2. Use Mod Podge for a gel transfer to a tag. *Tag by Karen Burniston.* **Supplies** *Gel medium:* Mod Podge; *"Love" accent:* Alphawear, Creative Imaginations; *Star charm:* Making Memories; *Rubber stamps:* Above the Mark (compass), Cherry Pie (large swirl), Magdalaina (script), PSX Design (letter stamps for "K" and "E"), *Ink pads:* Adirondack, Ranger Industries; *Other:* Fibers.

"Gel It" with Gel Transfers

LOOK IN MOST arts and crafts stores, and you'll find several gel mediums that are great for image transfer. Some common brands are Soft Gel Gloss, Mod Podge and Golden GAC 800. They can be used to create memorable results like those in Figure 2. For this method, you'll need mirror-imaged toner photocopies. After making the photocopies:

1. Trim the photocopy you wish to transfer. Apply one coat of gel medium to the photocopy and 3–6 coats to the receiving surface (such as clay, wood, glass and paper).

2. Place the photocopy face-down into the gel surface while still wet, then burnish to remove air bubbles. Allow the gel to dry for several hours or overnight.

3. Once the gel is dry, use a wet sponge to gently remove the paper.

If desired, seal the transfer with another coat of gel medium.

Another idea for gel transfers? Pour or foam brush the gel directly onto the photocopy, then allow it to dry for several hours or overnight. Once dry, soak the piece in warm water for several minutes and rub off the paper. You'll be

Figure 3. Lay a gel decal transfer over a photograph with patterned paper sandwiched in the middle. *Pages by Allison Strine.* **Supplies** *Gel medium:* Omni-Gel, Houston Art; *Metal-rimmed tag, scrapbook accent and white letter stickers:* Sonnets, Creative Imaginations; *Letter stamps:* Wordsworth (title) and Junque (subtitles); *Cork:* Magic Scraps; *Brads:* Making Memories; *Grass photo:* Shotz, Creative Imaginations; *Patterned paper between gel and photos:* 7 Gypsies.

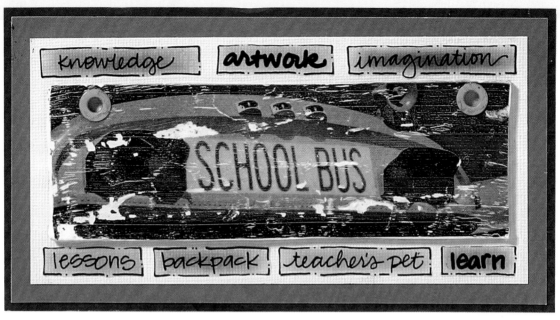

Figure 4. Transfer your image to polymer clay with a transparency and a gel medium. *Title block by Allison Strine.* **Supplies** *Gel medium:* Omni-Gel, Houston Art; *Polymer clay:* Sculpey; *Photograph and stickers:* Creative Imaginations; *Other:* Eyelets.

left with a semi-transparent "decal" image suitable for mounting to any surface. Use an additional gel medium as an adhesive.

Omni-Gel by Houston Art (*www.houstonart.com*) is a wonderful gel product for either method. It dries relatively quickly (15–20 minutes per coat), and will transfer inkjet-printed images, saving the step of photocopying. Also, as you apply the coats, if you brush gels in a swirly motion you can mimic the look of an oil painting on canvas (Figure 3).

Transparencies

You can also use gel mediums to transfer inkjet images that have been printed onto transparency film. Purchase transparency film designed for inkjet printers and print out the images you wish to transfer. *Note:* Be sure to mirror-image any text so it will appear correctly after transferring. Then, follow these steps:

1. Apply gel medium to the receiving surface, then place the transparency ink-side down into the gel.

2. Burnish well and check the transfer process by carefully peeling up a corner of the transparency.

When the transfer is complete, peel away the transparency. You may be able to make a fainter second transfer using the same transparency. Experiment! You can use this technique to transfer a transparency image to clay and paper (Figures 4 and 5).

Figure 5. Create a "library card" journaling pocket with a transparency and a gel medium. *Pocket by Allison Strine.* **Supplies** *Gel medium:* Golden's Soft Gel (Semi-Gloss); *Stickers:* K & Company; *Rubber stamp:* Cat's Life Press; *Stamping ink:* StazOn, Tsukineko; *Library card pocket:* Anima Designs; *Computer font:* CK Elusive, "Fresh Fonts" CD, *Creating Keepsakes; Other:* Button and microscope slide.

Figure 6. Use a blender pen to transfer an image to a tag. *Tag by Karen Burniston.* **Supplies** *Manila shipping tag and jewelry tag:* Avery; *Brads and press-ons:* Creative Imaginations; *Faux wax seal:* Sonnets, Creative Imaginations; *Mesh:* Magic Mesh, Avant Card; *Blender pen:* Chartpak; *Other:* Fibers and black beads.

Transfer It with a Blender Pen

FOR THIS METHOD, you'll need a blender pen containing Xylene. Common brands are Chartpak and Sanford. *Warning:* These blender pens have strong fumes. Use them outdoors or in a well-ventilated area.

After creating toner photocopies that have been mirror-imaged:

1. Trim the image you wish to transfer, then place it face-down onto the receiving surface.

2. Apply the blender pen to the back of the photocopy, pressing firmly and saturating the back of the paper. Further burnish the image with a bone folder or other tool.

3. Peel up the paper to view the transferred image. Continue applying the blender pen and burnishing until you're satisfied with the intensity of the transfer. Create a lovely image like that in Figure 6.

Use an Inkjet Iron-On Transfer

Nowadays, you can find a variety of mediums designed for inkjet printers. One of the easiest to use is iron-on transfer sheets. They can be purchased in any office supply store, and they come with complete instructions.

In general, you'll want to group several images together to reduce waste on the sheet. Text will need to be mirror-imaged to transfer correctly. Check your printer settings for "flip horizontal" or a similar command in your software program. As an alternative, The Vintage Workshop (see web site at *www.thevintageworkshop.com*) offers a type of iron-on sheet that works like a sticker. This means you don't need to reverse your images and text.

Whichever type you choose, after printing the images, cut out the one you wish to transfer. Follow the instructions for transferring to fabric, and note that the white areas are actually transparent, so colored fabrics and surfaces will alter the look of the image. (You may like the effect, so experiment with different colors and textures.) After ironing the transfer to the surface, carefully peel away the backing sheet.

Print on Fabric and Canvas

THE VINTAGE WORKSHOP offers printable media in canvas and fabrics. Paper backing sheets allow the fabric to be fed right into an inkjet printer and printed directly, saving the step of transferring the images (Figure 7).

You can also make your own printable fabric by ironing the waxy side of freezer paper to thin, fringe-free fabric. Carefully run it through an inkjet printer and allow the ink to dry thoroughly. Set with an iron using parchment paper or a thin cloth between the iron and the printing. Peel away the freezer paper, and you're left with printed cloth.

Figure 7. Print images directly onto canvas sheets designed for inkjet printers. *Tag by Allison Strine.* **Supplies** *Canvas paper:* The Vintage Workshop; *Mesh:* Magic Scraps; *Tiles for "Eva":* Savvy Tiles, Creative Imaginations; *Collage items:* ARTChix Studio; *Fibers:* Adornments, EK Success; *Stamping ink:* ColorBox, Clearsnap; *Other:* Image.

Answers to Commonly Asked Questions

IMAGE TRANSFERS are definitely cool, but they can be a little intimidating as well. Increase your confidence and know-how with the information that follows.

Q How long will image transfers last? Are the transfers safe for my scrapbook?

A It depends on the method. Packing tape and contact paper are questionable, so don't let the transferred images touch or overlap important photos. (Better yet—work with duplicate photos.) Gel mediums are very safe, especially if you encapsulate the transfer under a sealer coat. Direct printing methods depend on your specific printer and the medium you're printing to. Refer to your printer manual and the medium's packaging for information about longevity. With any non-fabric project, a

coat of sealer spray or gel will ensure longer life.

Q Where can I learn more about image transfers?

A You can find some books on the market, but your best bet with anything new is the Internet. Type "image transfers" or "photo transfers" in a search engine and explore the sites that come up. Some Yahoo! groups are dedicated to the art of image transfer. Go to *www.yahoogroups.com* and search for "image transfer."

Q Are there other techniques I can try?

A Of course! For example, a company called Lazertran makes transfer sheets that produce wonderful transfers on special surfaces. You can also find transfer techniques that use Polaroid emulsion, water

transfers, fusible webbing transfers and liquid polymers.

Q What if I can't get all the paper off or my image is distorted or blurred?

A Sounds like a winning transfer to me! Remember, image transfer involves an artistic, somewhat imperfect look that's supposed to appear more subtle than an actual photograph or imagery.

Experiment with "distressing" your transfers even further with stamps, inks, painting, tearing and layering. For an artistic look, layer two transparent transfers (gel decal or packing tape) over each other.

As for the leftover white paper, do your best to remove it all with water, even rewetting it if you notice residual after drying. If you can't remove it all, layer the transfer over white or light paper to make the residual less noticeable.

Elevate your scrapbook page to a new art form by using photo canvas. With a little know-how and care, you can include canvas board as well. *Page by Carol Wingert.*
Supplies *Photo canvas:* Avery; *Canvas board:* Fredrix; *Stamping ink:* Fresco, Stampa Rosa; *Copper:* Art Emboss, Amaco; *Rubber stamps:* JudiKins (leaf) and Wordsworth (keyhole); *Computer fonts:* CK Gutenberg and CK Newsprint, "Fresh Fonts" CD, *Creating Keepsakes;* *Key:* Stampington & Co.; *Cotton cording and fibers:* Memory Lane; *Stippling ink:* Nick Bantock, Ranger Industries; *"Barcelona" paper:* Ink It!; *Metallic rub-ons:* Craf-T Products.

How about a Twist and a Stretch?

ARTISAN'S CHOICE offers two fun products that are a slightly different take on image transfer. The first is a kit for creating your own rubber stamps at home using any imagery, including a photograph. Refills are available.

The second is a photo transfer kit that works somewhat like gel transfers, but is heat set instead of air dried. The resulting transfers are even stretchy! Check out these kits at *www.artisanschoice.com*, or check your local fabric and craft stores.

Hopefully you're now inspired to try some image transfers of your own. Although we've shown you several fun looks using image transfers on scrapbook pages and accents, don't feel like you have to stop there. Use transferred images on cards, altered books, frames, pillows, quilts, clay and more. With so many products and techniques available, you can put a photo anywhere your imagination takes you!

Creating with Canvas

4 Tips to Try Today

by Carol Wingert

WOULD YOU LIKE to make a photograph look like an artist's oil painting? You can—without lifting a brush! With today's computer technology and a product like Avery's Canvas Photo Fabric, you can reproduce your photos on canvas and be confident they're archivally safe. Plus, they're relatively inexpensive when compared with original art.

Following are some of my favorite tips:

• When working with canvas, choose photos that are actual portraits, close-ups of faces, or contain one or two people. You'll get a formal look yet retain the impact of the canvas.

• Age your canvas by sponging or stippling ochre, sepia, or black dye-based inks on the surface. Avoid pigment inks (they take longer to dry). Allot extra drying time since canvas takes longer to dry than paper.

• Canvas is flexible—roll it to create a scrolled effect for your page layout.

• Scan or copy fabrics or favorite papers (including gift wrap) onto photo canvas to create memorable backdrops for your photos.

Give canvas photo fabric a try, and next time you're asked, "Wow, who did these pictures?" you can proudly take credit for them! ❤

chalk talk

I have a little toolbox (and when I say "little," I mean "huge") that holds all of my essential supplies—adhesives, tools and embellishments that I use nearly every time I scrap. The problem is, whenever I become obsessed with a new product, I have to make room in the overcrowded organizer by taking something else out.

Despite the constant influx of trends and techniques, I turn to some items again and again, and chalk is one of them. Functional and fun, chalks are the perfect medium to add highlights and dimension to punch art, die cuts, clip art and torn accents. With a few swipes, you can alter the appearance of stickers, enhance hand-cut lettering, or simulate the look of airbrushed elements with stencils or stamps. And, with a little experimentation, it's easy to uncover additional applications for chalking.

The Basics

Whether you're just discovering chalk or simply need a little refresher, here are a few basics. Chalk can be applied with just about anything—eye shadow applicators, cotton swabs, mini pom-poms, cotton balls, tissue or brushes. Pazzles (*www.pazzles.com*) makes a custom chalk applicator that's especially popular. While some scrapbookers use their fingertips to apply chalk, avoid this whenever you can. Skin can transfer natural oils.

Build up color with a slow swirling motion, adding layer upon layer to achieve deeper tones. Create blends by applying the lighter shade first, then working the darker color into it to develop a third shade as the two combine. Or, blend colors before you apply chalk to paper by dipping into one shade, then rubbing the applicator immediately onto a second or third shade. If you make a mistake while chalking, simply correct it with a chalk eraser, sold in craft and art supply stores. (A regular white eraser will work in a pinch.)

To set the chalk, you can coat it with a spray fixative (check for archival safety first). I generally find it

Learn the basics, then try these twists

sufficient to simply burnish the design. To do this, flip the completed image over and rub it firmly on a piece of scrap paper. The excess chalk will either be pressed into your design or transferred to the other sheet. Chalk will also be sealed when applied with a blender pen or water.

New Twists To Try

It's time to put this classic back in the spotlight. With chalk palette in hand, let's add new twists to traditional techniques to create interesting backgrounds, titles and accents.

◆ **Marbling.** Chalk and water are all you need to design an eye-catching, colorful background. Simply fill a shallow pan (such as an acrylic box frame) with about a half-inch of water.

Scrape 2–3 colors of chalk onto the surface, swirling together just once (if you stir too much, the colors will blend completely and won't create the marbled look). Drop a sheet of cardstock onto the water, then lift out immediately and let the paper dry. (If the cardstock begins to warp, place it under a heavy book to flatten.) After a bit of practice, you'll

BY DENISE PAULEY

Figure 1. Create eye-catching marble backgrounds with water and wisps of chalk. *Page by Denise Pauley.* **Supplies** *Rubber stamps:* Art Impressions; *Stamping ink:* Ancient Page, Clearsnap; *Chalk:* Craf-T Products; *Pen:* Zig Writer, EK Success; *Charm:* Embellish It, Boutique Trims; *Fiber:* Rubba Dub Dub, Art Sanctum; *Pop dots:* All Night Media; *Other:* Brass frame.

Figure 2. Stamped images add dimension to a chalked, faux suede background. *Page by Denise Pauley.* **Supplies** *Vellum:* Paper Adventures; *Rubber stamp:* Serendipity Stamps; *Stamping ink:* VersaMark, Tsukineko; *Letters:* Bradwear, Creative Imaginations; *Pen:* Zig Millennium, EK Success; *Chalk:* Craf-T Products; *Brads and page pebble:* Making Memories; *Pop dots:* All Night Media.

create cardstock with vibrant swirls of color (Figure 1).

◆ **Suede Stamping.** Turn plain cardstock pretty by applying chalk in small swirls to achieve a plush, velvety look. To add more dimension, try this popular technique: coat a rubber stamp with VersaMark ink and press the stamp in random spots on the page (the ink will "remove" the chalk, leaving a slick watermark). Enhance the look by brushing

chalk over portions of the stamped images (Figure 2).

Other options: Erin Lincoln of Frederick, Maryland, discovered this technique also works well when chalking over glue that has dried until it's tacky, while Nicki Smith of Omaha, Nebraska, brushes chalk over light-colored pigment ink to enhance its color and dimension.

◆ **Variety with Vellum.** By applying chalk to vellum, you can

achieve effects that go from funky to elegant. Add interest to a plain vellum title by crumpling it and brushing chalk on the creases. Freehand a design by "painting" on vellum with chalk and a blender pen. Simulate the look of hand-drawn designs by stamping with clear ink and gently smearing chalk over the image. Or try all of the above to create an eclectic collage (Figure 3).

◆ **Stained Glass.** Chalks and dark cardstock combine for beautiful effects, giving the appearance of stained glass or soft velvet. In her layout "Take Time to Smell the Flowers," Joanne Moseley of Aurora, Ontario, Canada, fills stamped images and a hand-drawn design with chalk for a lovely, rich look (Figure 4). Another technique Joanne finds effective is applying a thick layer of chalk to dark cardstock, then "lifting" the color off with a VersaMark pen to handwrite title lettering.

♦ **Altered Embossing.** Step up heat-embossed images with a single layer of chalk! Simply emboss a stamped design with white powder, brush with a contrasting color of chalk, and rub to remove excess chalk and add shine (Figure 5).

Try this technique with Liquid Appliqué as well, adding color after the image has been puffed with a heat gun. Nancy Rogers of Baton Rouge, Louisiana, did this to customize the accent colors in Figure 6. See also portions of the collage in Figure 3.

Figure 3. Vellum gets revamped with a variety of chalking techniques. *Page by Denise Pauley.* **Supplies** *Vellum:* Paper Adventures; *Corrugated paper:* DMD Inc.; *Computer fonts:* CK Wanted and CK Constitution, "Fresh Fonts" CD, *Creating Keepsakes; Rubber stamps:* Hero Arts; *Stamping ink:* Perfect Medium, Ranger Industries; *Chalk:* Close To My Heart; *Liquid appliqué and blender pen:* Marvy Uchida; *Brads:* American Tag.

Figure 4. Achieve beautiful effects when chalking on dark cardstock. *Pages by Joanne Moseley.* **Supplies** *Lettering template:* Wordsworth; *Rubber stamps and embossing ink:* Close To My Heart; *Embossing powder:* Stamp 'n Stuff; *Chalk:* Craf-T Products; *Pen:* Staedtler.

Figure 5. Add subtle color to heat-embossed images for an ultra elegant touch. *Example by Denise Pauley.* **Supplies** *Rubber stamp:* Stampin' Up!; *Stamping ink:* Dauber Duo, Tsukineko; *Embossing powder:* Ranger Industries; *Chalk:* Stampin' Up!; *Fiber:* Adornaments, EK Success; *Beads:* Blue Moon Beads; *Tag:* American Tag; *Other:* Poetry bead.

◆ **Fingerpainting.** Here's a quick and easy way to create a funky background finish with your fingers if desired. Apply several coats of chalk (either single colors or blends) to heavy cardstock. Spritz with water until the colors begin to run, then use your fingertips to draw swirls, squiggles or straight lines into the wet chalk. Allow the design to dry completely (Figure 7).

◆ **Watercoloring.** Applying chalk with a blender pen is a simple way to achieve the look of watercolors and set your chalk. For bold color, use the pen to pick up chalk directly from the palette to design freehand images or to add highlights to textured paper.

For a more subtle effect, apply chalk to cardstock, then blend in from the edges to fill in stamped designs or template lettering (Figure 8). Another method? Try using an embossing pen instead of a blender pen, then heat-emboss with clear powder to add extra pizzazz.

◆ **Textured Tie-Dye.** Add texture in two seconds with this simple chalking technique. Start with a piece of thick cardstock (the heavier, the better). Add swatches of two colors in various places, then run the cardstock under water until soaked.

Carefully crumple the cardstock into a ball, then flatten it and let it dry. The colors will run together and into the creases, creating a rippled, tie-dye look. Punch or cut accents from the sheet, or use it as a contrasting background for

Figure 6. Chalking over Liquid Appliqué results in eye-catching color and dimension. *Pages by Nancy Rogers.* **Supplies** *Chalk:* Inkadinkadoo; *Liquid appliqué:* Marvy Uchida; *Daisy punch:* Punch It; *Computer fonts:* Scriptina (title) and Quigley Wiggly (journaling), downloaded from the Internet; *Paper yarn:* TwistArt, Emagination Crafts. *Idea to note:* Nancy only had two colors of liquid appliqué, so she colored the white with chalk to match the colors on her daughter's shirt.

a stamped image chalked to a wispy airbrushed effect (Figure 9).

◆ **Fossilized Leaves.** Create a funky accent for fall pages by "trapping" chalked leaves under a layer of mica. Stamp images with VersaMark ink, then gently add several shades of chalk for more dimension. Adhere a layer or two of mica over the top to add the finishing touch to your rustic design (Figure 10).

As you can see, chalking is one technique that never goes out of style. Turn to this old favorite the next time you're in the mood to create new looks for your layouts. Whether your style is shabby, cute, elegant or eclectic, chalk is a tried-and-true way to add a lot of look to your layouts. ❤

Figure 7. Use a simple "fingerpainting" technique to design funky background patterns. *Example by Denise Pauley.* **Supplies** *Chalk:* Close To My Heart; *Pewter frame:* Making Memories; *Mesh:* Coastal Netting, Magic Scraps; *Starfish:* Magic Scraps.

Figure 8. Brush chalk with a blender pen to create a "watercolored" title. *Example by Denise Pauley.* **Supplies** *Handmade paper:* Creative Imaginations; *Lettering template:* Kiki, ScrapPagerz.com; *Vellum sticker:* Shotz Thoughts, Creative Imaginations; *Chalk:* Craf-T Products; *Blender pen:* Marvy Uchida; *Tag:* Making Memories; *Other:* Wire and beads.

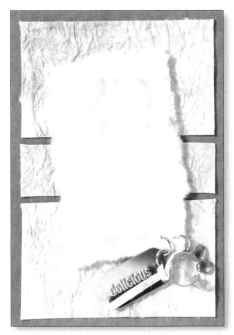

Figure 9. Crumpling wet, chalked cardstock allows colors to bleed together for a touch of tie-dye. *Example by Denise Pauley.* **Supplies** *Textured cardstock:* Club Scrap; *Rubber stamp:* A Stamp in the Hand; *Stamping ink:* VersaMark, Tsukineko; *Chalk:* Stampin' Up!; *Dog tag:* Chronicle Books; *Beads:* Blue Moon Beads; *Jump rings:* Darice; *Pop dots:* All Night Media.

Figure 10. Achieve the look of fossilized leaves with chalked images under a layer of mica. *Example by Denise Pauley.* **Supplies** *Patterned paper:* Mustard Moon; *Rubber stamps:* Maple and Rose Leaves (Rubber Stampede) and Snow Bush (Hero Arts); *Stamping ink:* VersaMark, Tsukineko; *Chalk:* Craf-T Products; *Mica:* USArtQuest; *Adhesive:* Perfect Paper Adhesive, USArtQuest; *Studs:* Dritz.

peach

sandalwood

lemon ginger

comfre y

lavender

coconut

amber

aloe

cocoa butter

j. kostecki

collage craze

Top talents show how to carry off **collage** in style

Utah's climate is rather dry, and I go through lotion like crazy. Whenever I shop with my friend Nan, we always stop at Bath & Body Works to check out the latest lotions. I'll find a scent I like and apply a little "here." I'll find another lovely scent and apply a little "there." Soon, I'm covered with different lotions from fingertips to elbows. I can't distinguish the scent of one lotion from the next—it's mixed together in fruity harmony.

Collage is something like my lotion excursions—a little bit of this, a little dab of that—carefully layered elements that create a pleasing whole. Is there a method to this madness? You bet! Get ready to slather yourself with great ideas from the following collage pages, accents and tips.

by **LORI** Fairbanks
Illustration by **JENNY** Kostecki

Tag by *Faye Morrow Bell.* **Supplies** *Paper clip:* Boxer Scrapbook Productions; *Paris label:* Hot Off The Press; *Airmail label and postage stamps:* Limited Edition Rubber Stamps; *Mini tag charm and ticket stubs:* Collage Joy; *Brads:* American Pin & Fastener; *Other:* Beaded chain, postage stamps and paint chip. *Ideas to note:* Faye created her tag from a paint chip. She used a cropped postage stamp to reinforce the tag hole.

Page by *Faye Morrow Bell.* **Supplies** *Patterned paper:* 7 Gypsies (definitions) and unknown (gingham); *Rubber stamp:* Stampers Anonymous; *Stamping ink:* Stampin' Up!; *Gears:* Hillman; *Postage stamps:* Limited Edition Rubber Stamps; *Computer fonts:* Arial, Microsoft Word; Plastique and Mom's Typewriter, downloaded from the Internet; 2Peas David Walker, downloaded from *www.twopeasinabucket.com; Photo corners:* Making Memories; *Brads:* American Pin & Fastener; *Alphabet cutouts:* Hot Off The Press; *Other:* Metal picture hangers.

Design your collage around a color scheme, such as a monochromatic or analogous design.

• Choose a key color for a monochromatic collage design. Select accents and embellishments in shades, tints and tones of that color. The more color values you use, the more interesting and eye-catching the results!

• An analogous scheme refers to neighboring colors on a color wheel, such as green and blue-green. First, select two (or more) analogous colors. Build your collage with shades, tints and tones from your selected colors. Because the colors are related, the result is pleasing to the eye.

—*Faye Morrow Bell*
Charlotte, NC

Faye's
color scheme tips

Tag by *Faye Morrow Bell.* **Supplies** *Tag:* Making Memories; *Rubber stamp and stamping ink:* Stampin' Up!; *Craft wire:* Hot Off The Press; *Fibers:* Fiber Accents by AIC (green) and On The Surface (coral); *Fern punch:* The Punch Bunch; *Postage stamp and clock charm:* Limited Edition Rubber Stamps; *Embroidery floss:* DMC.

Jenni's
tips for effective collage

Collage is all about play! No need for straight lines and perfect handwriting. Give yourself permission to experiment with unfamiliar colors and textures.

• Repetition is an important design principle. Repeat colors and textures to help unify your layout.

• Keep your eyes open for possible embellishments. Recycle old letters, labels, stamps and even broken jewelry pieces. Here's your opportunity to be really creative and preserve a piece of history, too!

—*Jenni Bowlin*
Mt. Juliet, TN

Photo mat by Jenni Bowlin, photo by Alan Clark. **Supplies** *Patterned paper:* Anna Griffin; *Alphabet stamps:* PSX Design ("a" and "m") and Turtle Press ("F"); *Scrabble letter:* Limited Edition Rubber Stamps; *Typewriter key:* ARTchix Studio ("L"); *Computer font:* Courier New ("Y"), Microsoft Word; *Metal alphabet stamps:* Pittsburgh Press; *Other:* Trim, button, jewelry settings and sheet music.

Tag by Jenni Bowlin. **Supplies** *Patterned paper:* 7 Gypsies; *Label:* Vintage Dennison, Manto Fev; *Alphabet stamps:* Hero Arts; *Walnut ink:* Postmodern Design; *Other:* Handmade paper, vintage jewelry settings and book locket.

Page by Jenni Bowlin. **Supplies** *Foam stamp:* Plaid Enterprises; *Rubber stamp for diamond border:* Postmodern Design; *Slide, label and bingo piece:* Manto Fev; *Metal tape:* USArtQuest; *Eyelets:* Making Memories; *Paper flowers:* The Robin's Nest Press; *Other:* Fabric swatches. *Idea to note:* The quote is from the lyrics to "Seven Years" by Norah Jones.

Page by Rebecca Sower.
Supplies *Paints:* Lumiere, Jacquard Products; *Crackling medium:* USArtQuest; *Stucco gel:* Liquitex; *Hand-dyed ribbons:* Flights of Fancy; *Word eyelet:* Making Memories; *Alphabet stickers:* Nostalgiques, Sticks by EK Success; *Rubber stamp:* Rubber Baby Buggy Bumpers; *Embroidery floss:* DMC; *Other:* Artificial flowers, beads, tissue and hairpin, words cut from vintage books.

Rebecca's
tip for meaningful collage

Accent by Rebecca Sower.
Supplies *Rubber stamp:* Limited Editions Rubber Stamps; *Letter stickers:* Nostalgiques, Sticko; *Copper tape:* USArtQuest; *Paint:* Lumiere, Jacquard Products; *Chain:* Making Memories; *Embroidery floss:* DMC; *Other:* Library pocket, key, watch face, brad and postage stamps.

Collage is more than just cutting and pasting bits of paper and embellishments. It's about telling a story through symbolism. When I assemble collage art, I use pieces that have a specific purpose for being there.
—*Rebecca Sower*
Cedar Hill, TN

Julie's
tips for collage beginners

If you're new to collage scrapbooking, start small. Try an accent, tag or title. As you get more comfortable with the process, create a card, photo mat or page border. Soon, you'll complete entire collage layouts!

• You don't need to fill your entire page with collage. It's OK to design "mini-collages."
• Inventory your paper and embellishments. See how many combinations you can create! I begin by layering different types of embellishments and "create" as I go until I like the result.
• Rubber stamps and shadowing inks add great design and texture without the bulk.

—*Julie Scattaregia*
Carmel, IN

Tag by Julie Scattaregia. **Supplies** *Stamping ink:* Archival Ink, Ranger Industries; *Rubber stamps:* Stampabilities (compass) and Limited Edition Rubber Stamps (dated visit pass); *Alphabet stamps:* Stamp Craft and Hero Arts (squares); *Chalk:* Craf-T Products; *Circle punch:* McGill; *Ribbon:* C. M. Offray & Son; *Craft wire:* Artistic Wire Ltd.; *Page pebble:* Making Memories; *Other:* Safety pin and washers.

Page by Julie Scattaregia. **Supplies** *Patterned paper:* 7 Gypsies; ScrapHappy (postcards), Design Originals; K & Company (brown); *Vellum:* The Paper Company (white) and Paper Pizazz (brown); *Computer fonts:* CK Carbon Copy, "Fresh Fonts" CD; CK Script and CK Journaling "The Best of Creative Lettering" CD Combo, *Creating Keepsakes; Eyelets, brads, eyelet phrase and metal photo corners:* Making Memories; *Stamping inks:* Archival Ink, Ranger Industries (sepia) and Close To My Heart (black); *Embossing powders:* Stampendous! and Suze Weinberg; *Rubber stamps:* Stampin' Up! (postmark, stamp and pen), Stampendous! (marble texture) and Hero Arts (Italian poetry); *Fibers:* Adornments, EK Success; On The Surface; *Round tag:* PaperCuts; *Tags:* Deluxe Designs; *Buttons:* Theresa's Hand-Dyed Buttons; *Ribbon:* C. M. Offray & Son; *Photo corners:* Canson; *Hinges:* Demis Products; *Other:* Letter tiles, ruler, tulle and frame.

Page by Julie Turner. **Supplies** *Patterned papers:* Anna Griffin and 7 Gypsies; *Tissue:* Hallmark; *Canvas:* Jo-Ann Crafts; *Decoupage medium:* Perfect Paper Adhesive, USArtQuest; *Acrylic paint and rubber stamp:* Plaid Enterprises; *Stamping ink:* Ranger Industries; *Metal photo corners and tinker pin:* 7 Gypsies; *Envelope:* Anima Designs; *Tassel:* Paper Parachute; *Other:* Button and embroidery floss.

Idea to note: Julie journaled on notebook paper, folded it, then tucked the paper behind a photo in the envelope.

Pocket accent by Julie Turner. **Supplies** *Patterned papers:* Anna Griffin and 7 Gypsies; *Library pocket:* Silver Crow Creations; *Decoupage medium:* Perfect Paper Adhesive, USArtQuest; *Acrylic paint:* Plaid Enterprises; *Eyelets:* Making Memories; *Frame:* Michaels; *Other:* Fiber.

Idea to note: Julie rubbed the frame and eyelets with white paint to dull the shiny finish.

Julie's antiquing tips

Apply acrylic paint or an antiquing medium to your layout or accent for an antiqued look. Here's how I created a whitewashed look on my layout and pocket accent:

1. Apply a decoupage medium to your cardstock, then adhere your background papers. Roll a brayer over the papers to remove bubbles. Let the papers dry.

2. Paint a coat of matte-finish decoupage medium over the entire surface. Let it dry.

3. Thin the white paint with water. Lightly brush the solution over the surface (the decoupaged undercoat helps the paint spread).

4. Wipe away any excess paint. The paint creates a whitewashed patina that softens the background papers.

—*Julie Turner*
Gilbert, AZ

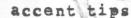

Allison's
accent tips

Save like a packrat! It helps to categorize your "stuff" in tubs. This "stuff" can include scrap papers, postage stamps, tickets and stubs, pieces of photographs, greeting cards, sheet music, unsuccessful accent attempts and more. My secret to successful collage is to gather more than I think I'll need.

• To keep your eye moving around the artwork, don't overuse color. It's best to keep the intensity (brightness or dullness) and value (lightness or darkness) the same for each color in your collage.

• Start with a nature-themed layout. Fibers, leaves, shells and dried flowers work well. Don't be too judgmental about your efforts—you can't go wrong with a nature collage!

—*Allison Strine*
Atlanta, GA

Tag by Allison Strine. Supplies *Patterned paper, poemstones and stickers:* Sonnets, Creative Imaginations; *Other:* Fibers.

Page by Allison Strine. Supplies *Patterned papers:* SEI (background) and K & Company (book cover); *Stickers:* Sonnets, Creative Imaginations (title) and SEI (journaling); *Stamping ink:* ColorBox, Clearsnap; *Pen:* Milky Lunar, Pentel; *Computer font:* Modern 20, downloaded from the Internet; *Metal heart:* Anima Designs; *Other:* Buttons, needle, thread and magazine cutouts.

Idea to note: "The Good Wife's Guide," a clipping from a 1955 issue of *Housekeeping Monthly*, inspired this fun page by Allison. You can download the article at *http://web.pdx.edul~singlem/goodwife.html.*

Pages by Nicole Gartland. **Supplies** *Patterned paper:* Paper Pizazz; *Computer fonts:* CK Elegant and CK Extra, "Fresh Fonts" CD, *Creating Keepsakes; Embroidery floss:* DMC; *Punches:* Marvy Uchida and McGill; *Pens:* American Crafts; *Other:* Collage clips.

Card by Nicole Gartland. **Supplies** *Rub-ons:* Alphawear and Bradwear, Creative Imaginations; *Collage picture:* ARTchix Studio; *Rubber stamp:* Rubba Dub Dub, Art Sanctum; *Stamping ink:* ColorBox, Clearsnap; Ranger Industries; *Embossing powders:* Ranger Industries and Suze Weinberg; *Lettering template:* Puzzle Mates; *Punch:* McGill; *Leaf detail:* Mynah Bits.

Nicole's
tips for successful collage

Successful collage is all about placement—a balance between photos and objects is crucial.

• It's important to allow elements to overlap, even just slightly, without hiding too much.
• Straight angles often keep collage from becoming too visually chaotic.
• Collage is recycling, scrapper style! Grab scraps of paper from your desk or the last letters from a sheet of stickers. Use a leftover cutout on a card or tag.

—Nicole Gartland
Portland, OR

Tear-ific!

BY TRACIE SMITH
ILLUSTRATION BY PASCAL GARNIER

I drive a bus to nursery school, and every day I pick up a little boy named John. He has the brightest smile and biggest brown eyes I've ever seen. He boards the bus each morning with a little bear named Bing Bing. If you saw this bear, you'd think he'd been pulled from a dumpster! He's tattered and torn, but to John, Bing Bing is everything. He's unique because he's worn, has a missing right eye, and his nose now looks like a mustache.

I feel the same comfortable familiarity each time I rip a piece of patterned paper. It looks a little different than the time before, and tearing adds an aged feeling of warmth to a page or card. Tearing is also an easy way to add texture and depth.

Love the look of tearing but timid about giving it a try? Relax! Once you do it a time or two, tearing becomes second nature. There's not really a "right" or "wrong" way. See what works well for you. I'll share how I tear, plus provide tips and techniques that'll be fun for those of you who are old hands at tearing paper.

The Basics

Okay, select a piece of paper and I'll walk you through the tearing process. (Or, turn to page 189 for step-by-step visuals). Here's how I proceed:

1. I roughly measure the area where I want the ripped edge to be. For example, if I'm adding a 2" ripped border to the bottom of my layout, I pencil in a tiny mark at the 2" point and start from there.

2. I grasp the paper in my left hand, keeping my thumb forward. (*Note:* I'm right-handed. If you're left-handed, doing the opposite may yield the best results.)

3. With my right hand, I slowly rip the paper as I pull it back toward my body. It's easier to keep the tear straight if I use my left thumb as a guide, slowly moving my finger down the paper as I pull. *Tips to note: If you need an ultra-straight tear, CK assistant editor Lori Fairbanks recommends scoring your paper first, then ripping along the scored edge. If you want added control, take a cotton swab, dampen it with* water, then "trace" where you want the tear to be. You'll find the moistened paper easy to work with.

Tearing paper for a journaling or title block? Measure the area first, then tear while rotating the piece counterclockwise with your other hand. Add the completed block to your page for a relaxed yet artistic look.

Cardstock vs. Patterned Paper

Most cardstocks are dyed through, while most patterned papers are limited to color on the top layer. Ripping cardstock will give you a subtle, textured look, while tearing patterned paper will yield a textured, white edge. If you're curious what the results will be before you tear, simply turn your paper over and see what the back looks like. If the back of your paper is white, you know that the color on the other side is only on the top layer.

Mats and Frames

A torn frame or photo mat can really help a photo stand out (Figure 1). When ripping a photo mat, adhere the photo first, then rip around it. When creating a torn frame, first mark the measurements for the inside opening. Next, using sharp scissors or a craft knife, cut an "x" in the center. Gently peel the paper back, tearing along the marked lines. After you've torn the center, decide how large you want the completed frame to be. Measure it and tear.

Figure 1. Create an eye-catching frame with foam core and torn, patterned-paper strips. *Page by Tracie Smith.* **Supplies** *Patterned paper:* Carolee's Creations; *Tag and metal heart accent:* Making Memories; *Pen:* Zig Millennium, EK Success; *Brush marker and hemp:* Stampin' Up!; *Craft wire:* Artistic Wire Ltd.; *Transparency film:* 3M; *Foil tape:* Olive Wimple; *Adhesives:* Glue Dots International (frame), Mod Podge (decoupage) and Stampin' Up! (title block); *Other:* Denim.

Figure 2. Use torn, patterned-paper squares to build a dramatic background. *Page by Alannah Jurgensmeyer.* **Supplies** *Patterned papers:* Karen Foster Design and Magenta; *Watercolor paper:* Canson; *Computer fonts:* Glitter Girl and Pancake, both downloaded from www.twopeasinabucket.com; *"Joy" sticker:* Wordsworth; *Fibers:* On the Surface, EK Success and Scrappin' Dreams; *Circle conchos:* Scrapworks; *Star brads:* Creative Imaginations; *Circle tag:* Making Memories; *Square eyelets:* The Stamp Doctor; *Powder:* Pearl-Ex, Jacquard Products.

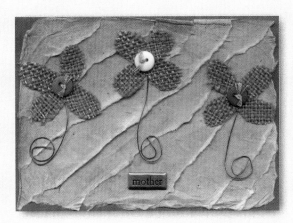

Figure 3. For a different approach, try torn diagonal strips on your next project. *Card by Tracie Smith.* **Supplies** *Handmade paper:* Kate's Paperie; *Metal "mother" eyelet:* Making Memories; *Buttons:* Theresa's Hand-Dyed Buttons; *Craft wire:* Artistic Wire Ltd.; *Other:* Burlap.

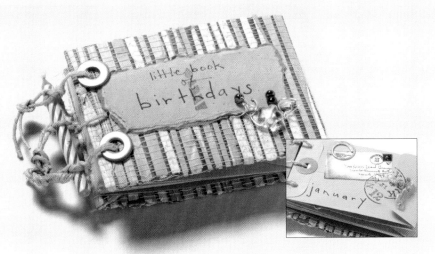

◀ Try this technique by Julie Turner: Mix Perfect Paper Adhesive with Pearl-Ex powder to create a "wash." Next, brush the wash over a watercolor paper background. Once it's dry, add other page elements.

Decoupage

With its lighter weight, patterned paper is perfect for decoupage. To create the frame in Figure 1, I cut the frame's dimensions in foam core with a craft knife. I then ripped strips of patterned paper, keeping a nice, textured edge on both sides of the strips. I "painted" Mod Podge on the back of my first strip with a sponge brush.

While the glue was still wet, I wrapped the frame with the strip. I continued with the patterned paper strips until the entire frame was wrapped. Upon completing the task, I coated the entire finished frame with a thin coating of Mod Podge.

Tip: Don't limit yourself to strips—you can use this technique for borders, backgrounds or page accents. The layout in Figure 2 is an eye-catching example of how squares can be used to create a whimsical background.

Layered Strips

Layering torn strips of cardstock can give you a one-of-a-kind backdrop for an entire layout. Or, use the technique for a title or journaling block. You can use horizontal, vertical and even diagonal strips (see Figure 3) and change the colors to fit the mood of your page. For a subtle yet classy color change, adhere three small sheets of cardstock together and rip them at the same time (see Figure 4).

Figure 4. Adhere three or more pieces of cardstock together before ripping for a subtle yet sophisticated effect. *Sample by Tracie Smith.* **Supplies** *Handmade grass cloth paper:* Kate's Paperie; *Beads:* Magic Scraps; *Pen:* Zig Millennium, EK Success; *Rubber stamp and stamping ink:* Stampin' Up!; *Craft wire:* Artistic Wire Ltd.; *Other:* Hemp and candle.

Mosaics

Enjoy playing with paper? Create intricate mosaic designs from torn paper. Note how in Figure 5, artfully torn and arranged pieces of cardstock blend to create a page reminiscent of an impressionistic painting.

To achieve this look, Shannon Taylor drew a rough sketch on her background paper. She then tore other pieces of paper into small pieces and glued them to the sketch, starting at the top and overlapping slightly. After completing her mosaic, Shannon outlined the sand castle with embroidery floss to make it stand out from the beach.

Note how Shannon outlined the sun in Figure 6 as well. These tags are the perfect size to color copy and use for projects such as cards, calendars and gift bags.

Editor's note: This technique provides a great way to use those extra scraps of paper.

Relief Tearing

Want to try something new? Consider relief tearing. Look at Erin Lincoln's layout in Figure 7, and you'd never guess that the only piece of white cardstock is inside the bookplate. By using removable tape, Erin strategically ripped the top layer of patterned paper off, exposing the white underneath. She used the relief technique for her photo mat, journaling strips and heart accent.

Figure 5. Add just the right texture with torn paper mosaics. *Page by Shannon Taylor.* **Supplies** *Computer font:* Kidprint, downloaded from the Internet; *Embroidery floss:* DMC; *Pen:* Zig Writer, EK Success; *Starfish:* Magic Scraps; *Glue dots:* Glue Dots International; *Seashells:* Mementoes from trip. *Idea to note:* Enlist the help of a child to tear paper into small to medium pieces.

Figure 6. Mosaic tags make adorable additions to scrapbook pages. *Samples by Shannon Taylor.* **Supplies** *Embroidery floss:* DMC; *Other:* Fibers.

Torn Edges

While torn edges add texture, they can be showpieces as well. Consider adding chalk, watercolors, glitter, beads, foil flakes or embossing powder to your white edges. And don't forget that your photos are made with paper, too. You can bring focus to a duplicate photo by tearing one or even all of the edges. This can be a bit intimidating the first time, so be sure to use a photo from an extra set of prints.

The next time you want to give a scrapbook page a comfortable, "lived in" look, tear your paper for artistic effect. People will love it as much as John loves Bing Bing! ❤

Figure 7. Heartfelt journaling, photographs and page accents are highlighted beautifully with this "relief" tearing technique. *Page by Erin Lincoln.* **Supplies** *Patterned paper:* Mustard Moon; *Computer font:* 2Peas Jack Frost, downloaded from *www.twopeasinabucket.com;* *Buttons:* Making Memories; *Mesh:* Magic Mesh, Avant Card; *Other:* Bookplate and brads.

Steps for Paper Tearing

Practice to get a feel for how different kinds of paper will tear. Once you get the hang of it, paper tearing is a technique you'll enjoy and use again and again!

▼ TEAR IT SIMPLY

If you're right-handed, hold the paper in your left, non-dominant hand (vice versa if you're left-handed). Hold the paper with your thumb and index finger. Gently tear with your free hand. Tear steadily and slowly in the direction of the grain for a straighter tear, or more rapidly for a modern, jagged look. *Note:* If the torn paper has a wide, jagged edge, you may be tearing against the grain. Rotate the paper a quarter turn (90°) and you'll be back on track.

▼ TEAR STRONG PAPER

Wet the paper with a small paintbrush or cotton swab where you plan to tear. This will weaken the paper. Next, tear or gently pull the paper apart. When the paper is completely dry, you won't see the water mark. Water is helpful when working with shapes, cardstock, fibrous mulberry and handmade papers.

▼ TEAR INTRICATE SHAPES

Sketch your design in pencil first. Brush with water to weaken along the lines. For greater ease, use a scoring blade or stylus and firmly press the stylus or blade against the paper or cardstock to graze it. Then tear the paper as directed in "Tear It Simply" at left.

Create one-of-a-kind accents with a watermark stamping technique. *Pages by Lynne Montgomery.* **Supplies** *Patterned vellum:* PrintWorks; *Embossed paper:* Lasting Impressions for Paper; *Patterned paper:* Paper Patch; *Computer fonts:* CK Bella (journaling), "The Best of Creative Lettering" CD Vol. 4 and CK Journaling (title), "The Best of Creative Lettering" CD Vol. 2, *Creating Keepsakes*; *Rubber stamp:* Close To My Heart; *Stamping ink:* VersaMark, Tsukineko; *Tag:* American Tag Co; *Other:* Ribbon.

Sometimes it's hard to find just the right patterned paper for a layout. Why not try creating your own? I love using this watermark technique to create patterned paper because it's easy and subtle. All you need is a rubber stamp and a VersaMark ink pad by Tsukineko. First, ink your stamp and stamp the image on your paper. The image created will be slightly darker than the shade of paper you've stamped on. This is called a watermark.

Besides making your own coordinating papers, you can also make your own page accents. Be creative and have fun with the different backgrounds and accents you can create with this technique—I know you'll love it as much as I do.

—by Lynne Montgomery

30 Lovely Looks with Embossing Powder

by Rebecca Sower

EMBOSS IT

f you're someone who thinks embossing powder is solely for rubber-stamping projects, you're in for a big surprise. I admit I love rubber stamps and find myself using them more and more in my scrapbooks. But I've also discovered a truckload of uses for embossing powder without ever picking up a rubber stamp.

When I first saw embossing powder work its magic, I knew it was something I wanted to learn to use. My mind instantly begin whirling with all the great projects I could create using this powdery medium. When I discovered all the many *types* of embossing powder available, I was delighted. I found metallic, glittery, pearlescent, translucent, clear and even some that changed colors when they were melted—what fun!

I can't share all the techniques and uses for embossing powder here for two reasons. First, it would take at least this entire magazine to cover all the great uses. Second, I don't know them all. *But* I'm on my way to discovering them, and I think once you see how much fun embossing powder can be, you'll want to join me.

The Basics

These are the items you need to create a heat-embossed image:

• **The surface you'd like to emboss.** This can be just about anything—from a brass fastener to cardstock to nylon screen.

• **A sticky substance.** Embossing powder needs a tacky surface to cling to until it's melted in place and hardened. I've used embossing liquid in these forms: embossing stamp pad, embossing markers and bottled embossing liquid. I've also used very tacky tape and double-sided adhesive paper (like the one manufactured by Grafix).

• **Heating source.** You'll get the best results with a heat tool made for embossing, but some people have had luck with an iron, a light bulb or even their toaster oven (be careful!).

• **Embossing powder.**

Figure 1. Change the look of brass fasteners with embossing powder. *Page by Rebecca Sower, photograph by Petra Carden.* **Supplies** *Embossing powders:* PSX Design; *Punches:* EK Success; *Square eyelets:* Details, Making Memories; *Pen:* Zig Writer, EK Success; *Other:* Vellum.

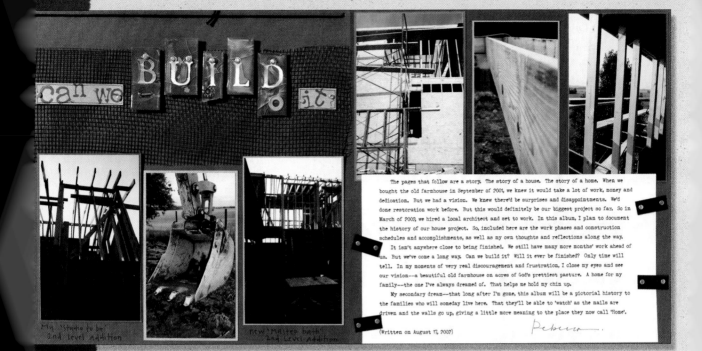

The pages that follow are a story. The story of a house. The story of a home. When we bought the old farmhouse in September of 2001, we knew it would take a lot of work, money and dedication. But we had a vision. We knew there'd be surprises and disappointments. We'd done restoration work before. But this would definitely be our biggest project so far. So in March of 2002, we hired a local architect and set to work. In this album, I plan to document the history of our house project. So, included here are the work phases and construction schedules and accomplishments, as well as my own thoughts and reflections along the way.

It isn't anywhere close to being finished. We still have many more months' work ahead of us. But we've come a long way. Can we build it? Will it ever be finished? Only time will tell. In my moments of very real discouragement and frustration, I close my eyes and see our vision—a beautiful old farmhouse on acres of God's prettiest pasture. A home for my family—the one I've always dreamed of. That helps me hold my chin up.

My secondary dream—that long after I'm gone, this album will be a pictorial history to the families who will someday live here. That they'll be able to 'watch' as the nails are driven and the walls go up, giving a little more meaning to the place they now call 'Home'.

(Written on August 17, 2002)

Rebecca

Figure 2. Layered and cracked clear embossing powder can take center stage for your page title. *Pages by Rebecca Sower.* **Supplies** *Embossing powder:* Ultra Thick Embossing Enamel, Suze Weinberg; *Metal letters:* Details, Making Memories; *Alphabet rubber stamps:* Turtle Press; *Screen:* Scrapyard 329; *Copper fasteners:* Impress Rubber Stamps; *Pen:* Zig Writer, EK Success; *Computer font:* Triumph Tippa, downloaded from the Internet; *Other:* String and miscellaneous small hardware.

HERE'S HOW

Follow these steps for using embossing powder:

• Apply the embossing powder to the surface you'd like to emboss. You can apply it with a rubber stamp, a paint brush or your finger.

• Quickly pour embossing powder over the tacky area, making sure you catch the excess with scrap paper (one jar of embossing powder will last an eternity if you catch and reuse your excess). Tap off the excess powder. You can use a soft paint brush to brush away the powder that's stuck outside the desired area if you wish, but most of the time I leave it—the splattery look is fun.

• Now you're ready to melt the powder with your heat tool. Ta-da!

Helpful Tips

Save time and trouble with these methods when using embossing powder:

• If you're working with a metal item, such as craft wire or a metal-rimmed tag, don't burn your fingers! Use craft pliers to hold your item in place while using the heat tool.

• To help the embossing liquid adhere better to shiny or metallic items such as brass fasteners and eyelets, gently rub the surface with steel wool first (see Figure 1).

• If you're embossing on paper that's lighter weight than cardstock, adhere a piece of cardstock to the back of the paper to prevent warping when heating.

• Embossing powder is very forgiving. If you make a mistake, you can usually just re-melt the powder and try again.

• Sue Settles, designer for Embossing Arts Co., suggests creating an embossing powder identification chart to view the versatility of each powder in your collection.

• Create embossing powder "recipes" by mixing coordinating colors together before sprinkling them on your project.

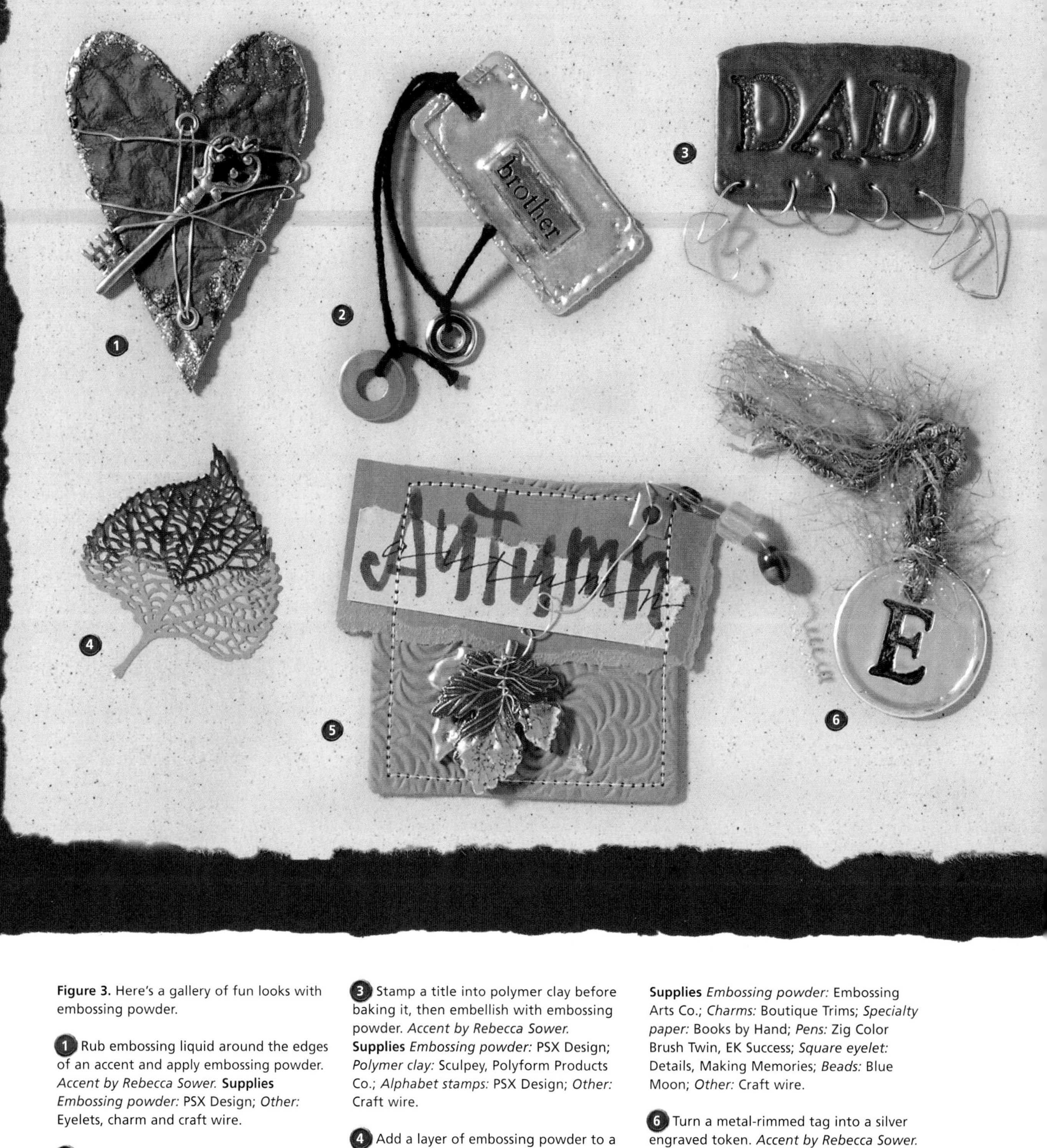

Figure 3. Here's a gallery of fun looks with embossing powder.

1 Rub embossing liquid around the edges of an accent and apply embossing powder. *Accent by Rebecca Sower.* **Supplies** *Embossing powder:* PSX Design; *Other:* Eyelets, charm and craft wire.

2 Sink a metal finding into a pool of melted embossing powder. *Accent by Rebecca Sower.* **Supplies** *Embossing powder:* Cloisonné (high-gloss granules); *Word eyelet and tag:* Making Memories; *Other:* Copper washer, snap and black cord.

3 Stamp a title into polymer clay before baking it, then embellish with embossing powder. *Accent by Rebecca Sower.* **Supplies** *Embossing powder:* PSX Design; *Polymer clay:* Sculpey, Polyform Products Co.; *Alphabet stamps:* PSX Design; *Other:* Craft wire.

4 Add a layer of embossing powder to a laser die cut. *Accent by Rebecca Sower.* **Supplies** *Embossing powder:* Stampendous!; *Laser die cut:* Provo Craft.

5 Make charms look like they've been dipped in gold. *Accent by Rebecca Sower.*

Supplies *Embossing powder:* Embossing Arts Co.; *Charms:* Boutique Trims; *Specialty paper:* Books by Hand; *Pens:* Zig Color Brush Twin, EK Success; *Square eyelet:* Details, Making Memories; *Beads:* Blue Moon; *Other:* Craft wire.

6 Turn a metal-rimmed tag into a silver engraved token. *Accent by Rebecca Sower.* **Supplies** *Embossing powder:* Embossing Arts Co.; *Fibers:* Adornaments, EK Success; *Alphabet stamp:* PSX Design; *Other:* Metal-rimmed tag.

7 Emboss a shrink-plastic heart accent. *Accent by Jamie Martin of Stampendous.* **Supplies** *All supplies:* Stampendous!.

8 Create a crackle finish over a cut-out accent. *Accent by Rebecca Sower.* **Supplies** *Embossing powder:* Ultra Thick Embossing Enamel, Suze Weinberg; *Cut-out accent:* FreshCuts, EK Success; *Fiber:* Adornaments, EK Success.

9 Decorate a die cut with glitter embossing powder. *Accent by Rebecca Sower.* **Supplies** *Embossing powder:* Embossing Arts Co.; *Die cut:* Cut-It-Up; *Beads:* Blue Moon Beads; *Eyelets:* Impress Rubber Stamps; *Other:* Craft wire.

10 Use your fingertip to create a fun embossed accent. *Accent by Rebecca Sower.* **Supplies** *Embossing powder:* Stampendous!.

11 Give metallic letters a whole new look with embossing powder. *Accent by Rebecca Sower.* **Supplies** *Embossing powders:* Stampendous!; *Metal letters:* Details, Making Memories; *Specialty paper:* Emagination Crafts; *Copper eyelets:* Im-press Rubber Stamps; *Other:* Picture wire.

12 Use embossed screen as an accent pocket. *Accent by Rebecca Sower.* **Supplies** *Embossing powder:* Stampendous!; *Cut-out accent:* FreshCuts, EK Success; *Screen:* Super Screen, Embossing Arts Co.; *Fiber:* Adornaments, EK Success; *Mini fasteners:* Doodlebug Design.

13 Encapsulate a charm under clear embossing powder. *Accent by Rebecca Sower.* **Supplies** *Embossing powder:* Ultra Thick Embossing Enamel, Suze Weinberg; *Charm:* Impress Rubber Stamps; *Circle punch:* EK Success; *Other:* Ribbon.

14 Flatten a piece of shaped wire with a hammer, then emboss! *Accent by Rebecca Sower.* **Supplies** *Embossing powder:* PSX Design; *Craft wire:* Artistic Wire Ltd.

15 Add highlights to corrugated cardstock accents. *Accent by Rebecca Sower.* **Supplies** *Embossing powder:* PSX Design; *Punches:* Family Treasures; *Other:* Vellum, craft wire and brass fastener.

16 Give an ordinary sticker a translucent look. *Accent by Rebecca Sower.* **Supplies** *Embossing powder:* Embossing Arts Co.;

Sticker: Colorbök; *Alphabet beads:* Impress Rubber Stamps; *Tiny beads:* Details, Making Memories; *Other:* Eyelets and craft wire.

17 "Float" microbeads or glitter under several layers of clear embossing powder. *Accent by Rebecca Sower.* **Supplies** *Embossing powder:* Ultra Thick Embossing Enamel, Suze Weinberg; *Punch:* EK Success; *Microbeads:* Beedz, Art Accents; *Other:* Craft wire and heart bead.

Figure 4. Stamp your page title into melted embossing powder. *Page by Rebecca Sower.* **Supplies** *Embossing powder:* Stampendous!; *Adhesive tape:* Terrifically Tacky Tape, Art Accents; *Alphabet rubber stamps:* Turtle Press; *Fibers:* Adornments, EK Success; *Photo corners:* Canson; *Pen:* Zig Writer, EK Success; *Other:* Wire and manila tag.

Go Online

Want even more embossing inspiration? Click your way to any of these helpful web sites:

www.embossingarts.com
www.allnightmedia.com
www.stampendous.com
www.docmartins.com
www.psxdesign.com
www.impressrubberstamps.com
www.rangerink.com
www.magentarubberstamps.com

Use Your Imagination

Here are some of my favorite uses for embossing powder. Try a few, then see what you can come up with:

• Your craft punches can be turned into awesome embossed accents. Simply punch a shape into a double-sided, peel-off adhesive sheet and emboss. If you want to punch a hole in your accent (to make it a tag, for instance), punch the hole before you emboss.

• One of my favorite embossing techniques is coating an accent with several layers of clear embossing powder (one layer at a time: melt-pour-melt-pour), waiting for it to cool completely, then bending the accent to crack the embossed layers (see Figure 2).

• You can embed flat items (charms, for example) into your embossing powder. Just place the charm onto a layer of clear embossing powder while it's still tacky, then continue with enough layers of clear powder until the charm is completely submersed beneath the melted powder.

• I like to press alphabet stamps into hot, melted embossing powder to create page titles (see Figure 4). If you press your stamp into an ink pad first, your title will be easier to read.

• Pam Hornschu of Stampendous! showed me how to layer several different colors of embossing powder (see Figure 5).

Figure 5. Create tile accents that look as if they came straight from Italy. *Accent by Pam Hornschu of Stampendous.* **Supplies** *All supplies:* Stampendous!.

Figure 6. Layer embossing powders for a colorful effect. *Page by Rebecca Sower.* **Supplies** *Embossing powders:* Stampendous!; *Rubber stamp:* Stampin' Up!; *Pen:* Zig Color Brush Twin, EK Success; *Square punch:* Marvy Uchida; *Watercolor paper:* Strathmore; *Other:* Wire, seed beads and button.

I tried my hand at Pam's technique and let that be the only accent on my layout. It's quite effective (see Figure 6).

• A cardstock frame coated with embossing liquid can be gorgeous. While the top layer of embossing powder is still soft from being melted, press a favorite rubber stamp into the frame a few times to create an ornate appearance (see Figure 7).

Now that you know how versatile embossing powder can be, give it a try. The powdery medium will enchant you, too! ♥

Figure 7. Create an ornate frame with cardstock and embossing powder. *Sample by Rebecca Sower, portrait by Dustine Wallace.* **Supplies** *Embossing powder:* Mark Enterprises; *Rubber stamps:* Limited Edition; *Other:* Ribbon and eyelets.

it's all clear

now imaginative, "see-through" ideas for your scrapbook pages

by Allison Strine

maybe it's because I've worn glasses my whole life, but I absolutely adore windows. Give me rose-colored spectacles any day of the week! Whenever I peek through the eyepiece of a camera or a pair of binoculars, I feel a sense of intrigue. I can't wait to view the wonders before me.

To capture that same feeling on paper, I've come up with transparent techniques for scrapbook pages. The techniques involve three items you wouldn't normally associate with scrapbooking, but don't let that scare you off. Clear your mind and some space on your scrapbook table. Get out those magnifying glasses and let's explore, shall we?

Microscope Slides

Remember eighth-grade biology, when you squeamishly peeked at your first cell under the discerning eye of a microscope? Well, microscope slides are back, and this time they're fun! Whether constructed of glass or plastic, microscope slides make irresistible canvasses for the artist inside. Following are fun, cool ways to use this unlikely product to create satisfying scrapbook pages.

Soldered Edge

With its balanced shape and size, a microscope slide makes an ideal background for small sticker words and images. Mount the slide on a tag or title block, then create a cool soldered edge (Figure 1) to boost visual impact. I've provided the steps in Figure 2.

Note: If you're using plastic slides, heat an edge of the plastic with a heat gun. (You want to see if the plastic melts.) If a molten blob of plastic isn't the look you wanted, skip the embossing powder and press foil or gold leaf to the tape instead!

Figure 1. Use embossing powder to create a faux soldered edge. *Page by Allison Strine, photo by Richard Marks.*

Supplies *Patterned papers:* Magenta (tag) and Wordsworth (photo mat); *Rubber stamps:* Junque; *Stamping ink:* ColorBox, Clearsnap; *Embossing powder:* Inkadinkadoo; *Brad and eyelet:* Creative Imaginations; *Mesh:* ScrapYard 329; *Bird microscope slide:* FoofaLa; *Punch:* Marvy Uchida; *Other:* Sticker, fibers and collage elements.

Figure 2. Create a soldered-edge effect in three simple steps.

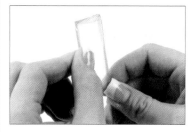

1. Wrap a ¼" wide strip of double-stick tape around the edge of the slide, folding in the corners.

2. Peel off the tape's release paper and dip the microscope slide into silver embossing powder. Tap the slide to get rid of excess powder.

3. The slide will be hot. Holding it with something other than your fingers, use a heat gun to melt the embossing powder. Add your stickers to the side that looks best.

Slide-Holder Booklets

Look out, scientists—here come scrappers! Microscope slides can be stored in special slide holders made of sturdy book board.

They're fun to play with and are perfect for storing memorabilia like postage stamps or pressed flowers.

Create a one-of-a-kind "memorabilia pocket" by covering a slide-holder booklet with your favorite papers. Next, personalize the booklet with stamps, handwriting, trinkets and baubles, then fill it with keepsakes you want to treasure (Figure 3).

Figure 3. Fashion a unique holder for fragile memorabilia. *Booklet by Allison Strine.*

Supplies *Slide holder, slides and alphabet letters:* FoofaLa; *Rubber stamp:* Cat's Life Press; *Stamping ink:* Ancient Page, Clearsnap; *Picture pebble:* Magic Scraps; *Patterned papers:* Legacy, Design Originals; *Other:* Postage stamps and magnetic poetry.

Transparent, Shallow and Proud of It

Love microscope slides? Examine these options:

- Make a collage using several small images and stickers.

- Sandwich pressed flowers between two slides.

- Stamp on glass or plastic with permanent ink. (Erase mistakes easily with rubbing alcohol.)

- Trim a photograph and tuck it behind a slide.

- Paint on slide holders with glass paint.

- Frame a finished slide with a metal bookplate.

- Punch a hole in plastic microscope slides and dangle them on a page. Feeling daring? Use a Japanese screw punch or a hand drill to make the hole in glass slides.

Glitter

Accentuate your slide holder with a brilliant glittery border (Figure 4). I've provided the steps in Figure 5.

Figure 4. Add glitter to adhesive for a glistening border. *Title block by Allison Strine.*

Supplies *Patterned paper:* K & Company; *Photo and stickers:* Creative Imaginations (words and photo) and Wordsworth ("Snow!"); *Glitter:* Magic Scraps; *Adhesive:* Glossy Accents, Ranger Industries.

Figure 5. Increase "sparkle" with a glitter-edged border you can create in three easy steps.

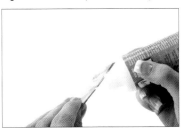

1. Trim photo to size and adhere to a microscope slide. Top the photo with a second slide, sandwiching the two with glue dots along the edge.

2. Holding the accent in the middle, squeeze a thin line of dimensional adhesive along the edges.

3. Pour a line of glitter onto a tray, then dip the slide into the glitter and let the adhesive dry.

Watchmaker Tins

Watchmaker tins are the tiny, glass-topped aluminum cases you'll find in scrapbook and art-supply stores. The tins are perfect for storing the bits and baubles we scrappers can't do without.

Of course, we scrappers also can't do without experimentation. Did you know the tin tops can be decorated and used as delicious page accents? Don't throw the tin bottoms away—just put a piece of plastic wrap over the tin and secure the plastic wrap with a rubber band. Read on for terrific effects with tin tops.

Fill 'er Up

Turn the lid glass-side down, leaving an adorable little opening just begging to be filled (Figure 6). Next, fill the opening with glass and alphabet beads, watch pieces, paper, glitter or anything small enough to fit inside. If you want to focus on a specific embellishment, just make sure it's larger than the others or a different color or texture.

Once you've arranged the items, pour in a "dries clear" adhesive (such as Diamond Glaze by JudiKins or Glossy Accents by Ranger Industries). Let the tin dry overnight for a permanent clear shine. For touch-me temptation, leave the opening as is (see letter "C" in Figure 7) or cover it with a piece of see-through mica or plastic (see letter "S" in Figure 7). *Hint:* Use glue dots to adhere tins to your page.

Tip It Over

For see-through storage, trace or punch a piece of sturdy cardstock the size of your tin. Apply double-stick adhesive to the cardstock base. Now you have a miniature 3-D artist's canvas to work on, and you can make a collage in that little circle.

Working from bottom to top, add your favorite tiny items. For a monochromatic look, use a single color of beads and buttons, accenting with white and silver. Carefully place the tin over the collage and glue with a thin line of adhesive.

Figure 6. Create a miniature collage with buttons and beads. *Tag by Allison Strine.*

Supplies *Patterned paper:* Legacy, Design Originals; *Rubber Stamp:* Stampington; *Stamping ink:* Ancient Page, Clearsnap; *Alphabet letters and fabric:* FoofaLa; *Other:* Needle, thread, buttons and beads.

Figure 7. Build a unique "altered alphabet" title with tin tops and odd letters. *Pages by Allison Strine, photos by Richard Marks.*

Supplies *Patterned papers and rubber stamps:* Wordsworth; *Stamping ink:* Staz-On, Tsukineko; *Sticker, poemstone, typewriter and computer key letters:* Creative Imaginations; *Pen:* Milky Gel Roller, Pentel; *Other:* Film negative, found alphabet letters, watch pieces and beads.

Tin-Tin Terrific

Use the actual tin as a decorating surface. A few possibilities?

- Decorate the glass top by stamping or painting on it.

- Paint the rim of the tin with acrylic paints.

- Color the tin with a permanent marker.

- Wrap a thin layer of tacky tape around the tin's edge and roll the tin in glitter (Figure 8).

Figure 8. Jazz up a tin with glitter, beads and more. *Title block by Allison Strine.*

Supplies *Patterned paper:* SEI; *Poemstones and brad rub-ons:* Creative Imaginations; *Mesh:* ScrapYard 329; *Beads:* Magic Scraps; *Photo corners:* Canson.

Transparencies

Transparencies are a fun way to expand your creative horizons. First, select the type that will best suit your needs. While inkjet transparencies can withstand heat, for example, they can be more costly. While more affordable, overhead transparencies can't be run through a printer. Find the transparency type that will work best for you. Next, try the following cool idea.

See Through This

Cover an entire page with a transparency, and you'll gain a layer to work with. Print or hand-write your journaling on the transparency for a clean, layered look, or attach miniature drawer pulls to the transparency like I did in Figure 10. The decorative pulls are functional—pull them and they reveal additional photos, journaling and accents.

To achieve the look of an embossed image over a photograph, follow the steps below (Figure 9). For a visual extravaganza, stamp and heat emboss directly on the transparency (see snowflake in Figure 10).

To create the fun look in Figure 11, I followed the steps illustrated in Figure 12. Give them a try!

Figure 9. Add dimension with an embossed image on a transparency layered over a photograph.

1. Position the photos on your layout, then decide where you want the stamped image. I chose to partially obscure a photo, which gave my layout a wintry look.

2. Use a permanent ink to stamp the image onto the transparency. Don't press or rock the stamp (the surface will be slippery). You can remove mistakes with rubbing alcohol.

3. Sprinkle embossing powder over the image and tap off the excess, using a dry brush to remove the powder you don't need.

4. Melt the embossing powder with a heat gun, moving it often so you don't melt the transparency.

Figure 10. Adorn a page with clear stickers on a preprinted transparency. *Pages by Allison Strine.*

Supplies *Transparencies:* Clearly Creative, Magic Scraps; *Glitter:* Magic Scraps; *Rubber stamps:* Hampton Art Stamps (textures), Hero Arts (small snowflakes) and Stampin' Up! (large snowflakes); *Stamping ink:* ColorBox, Clearsnap; *Embossing powder:* Stampendous!; *Stickers:* Wordsworth; *Word tiles:* Savvy Tiles, Creative Imaginations; *Pen:* Milky Gel Roller, Pentel; *Drawer-pull accents:* FoofaLa; *Photo corners:* Canson.

Figure 11. Use embossing powder to make an amazing see-through frame. *Accent by Allison Strine.*

Supplies *Patterned paper:* K & Company; *Transparency:* Clear Canvas, Magic Scraps; *Sticker:* Jolee's Boutique by EK Success; *Embossing powder:* Suze Weinberg.

Figure 12. A cool property of transparencies can be their strength under fire, as illustrated in the steps here.

1. Trim the transparency to size.

2. Apply embossing ink to the entire frame, then heat emboss with clear Ultra Thick Embossing Enamel (UTEE). Repeat for an extra thick look.

3. Apply another coat of embossing ink to the inside and outside edges.

4. Dip the frame's edges into gold UTEE and heat again.

To achieve the look of photographs on transparencies without printing them, try some of the lovely printed transparencies currently available. To achieve the look in Figure 13, I simply trimmed a transparency to size, then used it as a guide to make a color-blocked background. To accentuate my quote sticker, I backed it with tissue paper.

Take the plunge and adorn your scrapbook pages with super, see-through solutions. They're quite the "windows" of opportunity! ❤

Figure 13. Add texture and dimension with pre-printed transparencies. *Accent by Allison Strine.*

Supplies *Patterned papers:* 7 Gypsies, Creative Imaginations and Design Originals; *Transparency:* Clearly Creative, Magic Scraps; *Sticker:* Wordsworth; *Other:* Tissue paper and snaps.

time to shop

Ready to experiment with some transparent techniques? Following is a list of the suppliers discussed in this article. Don't forget to check local scrapbook and rubber stamp stores as well!

Microscope Slides
Glass and plastic microscope slides are available through medical and science supply stores. Or, check for slides at your local teacher supply store.

FoofaLa
402/330-3208
www.foofala.com

Science Stuff
800/795-7315
www.sciencestuff.com

Zefon International
727/327-5449
www.zefon.com

Watchmaker Tins
Watchmaker tins are also referred to as "bindi tins" and "glass-top tins." You can purchase these small round containers from the following suppliers:

BlissWeddingsMarket.com
866/445-4405
www.blissweddingsmarket.com

Lee Valley Tools, Ltd.
800/871-8158
www.leevalley.com

PaperZone.com
877/927-2737
www.paperzonestore.com

Profoundia
360/352-3474
www.profoundia.com

Stamp Studio
208/288-0300
www.stampstudioinc.com

Transparencies
You can find transparencies at office supply stores, scrapbook stores and more. Be sure to buy inkjet transparencies if you plan to print journaling or photographs.

CK safety check: Choose safe plastics such as polyester, polypropylene or polyethylene. If your transparency emits a definite chemical or plastic smell or is made from vinyl or acetate, this can destroy your photographs and scrapbook pages over time.

Artistic Expressions
219/763-1356
www.artisticexpressionsinc.com

Epson
800/873-7766
www.epson.com

Hewlett-Packard
888/999-4747
www.hp.com

Magic Scraps
972/238-1838
www.magicscraps.com

Adhesives
Clear, double-sided tape (acid free) works well for adhering clear embellishments to pages. Get a good hold with products like Magic Scraps' Scrappy Sheets and Scrappy Tape, Provo Craft's Art Accentz Terrifically Tacky Tape, or Suze Weinberg's Wonder Tape.

Magic Scraps
972/238-1838
www.magicscraps.com

Provo Craft
800/937-7686
www.provocraft.com

Suze Weinberg
732/761-2400
www.schmoozewithsuze.com

Bring the wonder of nature into your scrapbooks safely with the dried embellishments border. *Page by Lori Houk.* **Supplies** *Patterned paper:* Carolee's Creations; *Computer font:* Flowerchild, downloaded from the Internet; *Memorabilia pockets:* 3L Corporation; *Dried embellishments:* Fru Fru; *Other:* Fibers.

My kids, like most, are fascinated by nature. To commemorate our explorations at the park, I tucked the dried botanicals we gathered into memorabilia pockets to create a unique border. It's a creative—and safe—way to "bring the outdoors in" on a layout. Here's how it's done:

❶ Tear a strip of brown cardstock approximately the same width as the memorabilia pockets you're using in the border. Adhere the strip to the page.

❷ Place dried embellishments, such as flower petals, ferns, leaves, or even small seeds or twigs, inside memorabilia envelopes and seal the envelopes shut.

❸ Adhere the envelopes to the brown strip of paper, spacing them evenly.

—*by Lori Houk*

Cool Corners

GIVE YOUR PAGES A DISTINCTIVE EDGE

BY DENISE PAULEY • ILLUSTRATION BY RICHARD HULL

You know the feeling. The layout is done. Finished. The photos, title, journaling and accents are all in place, just as you envisioned them. You sit back, survey your work and think, "It still needs a little something, but what?" Try adding a cool corner or two!

Corners can adorn just about any page element—photos, journaling boxes or even the page itself. They can serve a purpose (such as holding photos without adhesive) or simply serve as additional ways to spruce up your layout. More than just triangles, "corners" can also be strips, strings, squares or a subtly curved embellishment that becomes a frame for your photograph (see my page at right).

Whichever type or size you choose, just consider your corner a mini canvas. It's a place to add one last dash of detail to enhance a layout's tone, theme or color scheme. I've included 24 more corner ideas below. Just because a space is small doesn't mean it can't be spectacular!

A gently curved accent can pull double duty as a photo corner. **Supplies** *Patterned cardstock:* Club Scrap; *Computer font:* ZapfHumnst BT, Microsoft Word; Spring, downloaded from the Internet; *Metallic rub-ons:* Craf-T Products; *Pop dots:* All Night Media; *Flowers:* Denise's own design.

Add a touch of elegance with a whimsical mini bouquet.

Supplies *Mulberry paper:* PrintWorks; *Paper flowers:* Impress Rubber Stamps; *Ribbon:* C.M. Offray & Son.

Steps:
1. Use needle to poke hole in photo corner.
2. Thread end of twine or wire up through hole, around flower stems, then back down through hole, binding flowers together and securing bouquet to page.

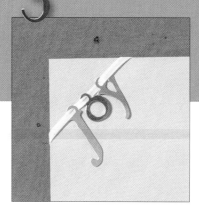

A few alphabet charms can add a bit of joy to your layout.

Supplies *Alphabet charms:* Making Memories; *Ribbon:* C.M. Offray & Son.

Secure a strip of vellum that can also serve as a caption.

Supplies *Silver paper:* Solum World; *Vellum:* Paper Adventures; *Computer font:* Cheapskate, downloaded from the Internet; *Rhinestone nailhead:* Westrim Crafts.

With a little embellishment, ticket stubs make trendy corners.

Supplies *Metallic rub-ons:* Craf-T Products; *Pop dots:* All Night Media.

Steps:
1. Brush ticket stubs with gold, bronze and platinum rub-ons.
2. Trim or tear edges to desired length.
3. Adhere with pop dots for dimension, or use eyelets or brads for an ultra-metallic look.

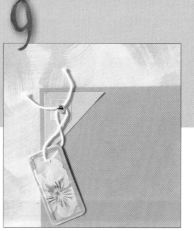

Use a corner to "anchor" another colorful, dangling accent.

Supplies *Patterned paper:* Magenta; *Pressed flower:* Nature's Pressed; *Tag:* Making Memories; *Brad:* American Pin & Fastener.

"Label" a memorable photo with a cool brass plate and alphabet stamps.

Supplies *Patterned cardstock:* Club Scrap; *Alphabet stamps:* PSX; *Inkpad:* Clearsnap; *Label holder:* Anima Designs; *Brads:* American Pin & Fastener.

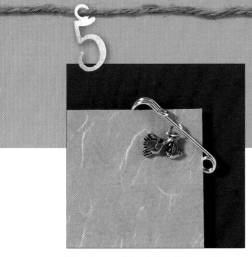

Use a large safety pin to add charm to your corners.

Supplies *Handmade paper:* Black Ink; *Safety pin:* KCraft; *Charm:* Blue Moon Beads.

Steps:
1. Attach charm to safety pin with jump ring.
2. Use strong, double-sided tape or glue dots to keep pin secured to corner.

Note: If you're concerned about metal touching your photo, adhere the safety pin to a strip of torn cardstock that can serve as a buffer. Or use the safety pin on a corner for your journaling or title box instead.

Mock Scrabble tiles can help you get a word in edgewise.

Supplies *Bronze paper:* Solum World; *Scrabble tiles:* Limited Edition; *Pop dots:* All Night Media; *Chalk:* Craf-T Products; *Other:* Handmade paper.

Steps:
1. Cut out the individual tiles that will form your word.
2. Chalk edges and attach with pop dots for added dimension.

Add a little love to your layout by creating a vellum envelope filled with heart stickers.

Supplies *Vellum:* Paper Adventures; *Stickers:* Treehouse Designs.

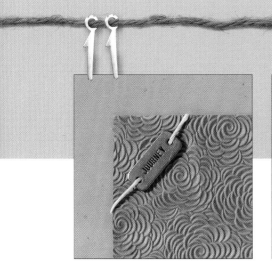

A shiny brass word tag can reflect the theme of your layout.

Supplies *Handmade paper:* Solum World; *Paper yarn:* Twistel, Making Memories; *Other:* Brass tag.

Strung beads provide a lot of look, whether funky, cute or extravagant.

Supplies *Beads:* Blue Moon Beads; *Craft wire:* Making Memories; *Other:* Handmade paper.

Use an elegant string of pearls to show off gorgeous wedding photos.

Supplies *Marble paper:* The Paper Company; *Pearls:* KCraft.

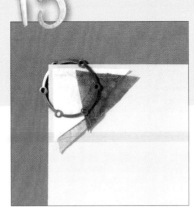

Design a tiny trellis to elicit the sweet feeling of spring.

Supplies *Punches:* 2Grrls (flower) and Fiskars (circle); *Butterfly:* Westrim Crafts.

Create a mini collage as an artsy touch.

Supplies *Handmade paper:* Black Ink; *Brass finding:* Anima Designs.

A small stamped image can make a big impression on a photo corner.

Supplies *Vellum:* Paper Adventures; *Embossing powder:* Cloisonné, Stampa Rosa; *Rubber stamp:* Hero Arts; *Embossing ink:* Ranger Industries.

Steps:
1. Apply embossing ink to cardstock.
2. Sprinkle with layer of embossing powder and heat with embossing gun.
3. While first layer is still hot, apply another coat of powder and heat until surface is smooth.
4. Press stamp into surface and hold firmly until cool, then remove carefully.

Pop up a punch made from embossed paper to add a little dimension.

Supplies *Handmade paper:* Solum World; *Punch:* McGill; *Pop dots:* All Night Media.

Tuck memorabilia into a suspended mini-pocket.

Supplies *Bronze and handmade paper:* The Paper Company; *Page protector:* Pioneer Photo Albums.

Steps:
1. Cut a corner from a page protector or memorabilia pocket.
2. Enclose memorabilia and seal pocket with adhesive of your choice.
3. Conceal sealed edge with a strip of cardstock or ribbon.

Need a corner to color coordinate with your photos? Use watercolors to paint your own!

Supplies *Watercolor sticks:* Rexel Derwent.

Weave dried flowers through mesh or netting to add a touch of nature.

Supplies *Mesh:* Magic Mesh, Avant Card; *Dried flowers:* Nature's Pressed.

Steps:
1. Attach mesh to cardstock corner and trim.
2. Weave sprigs of dried leaves or flowers through mesh and secure with extra glue if necessary.

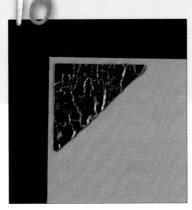

Achieve a risk-free industrial look by incorporating handmade, painted paper for a mock metallic finish.

Supplies *Metallic paper:* Unknown.

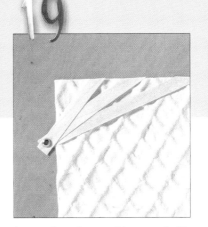

A spray of wood veneer strips secured with a brad is the right touch for home, boy or outdoor pages.

Supplies *Wood veneer:* Paper Adventures; *Brad:* American Pin & Fastener; *Other:* Handmade paper.

Photos get a winning look with stickers and die cuts that suit the sport.

Supplies *Grass die cut:* Li'l Davis Designs; *Sticker:* Kangaroo & Joey.

Layers and lots of sparkle can make your photo corners shine.

Supplies *Pearlized paint:* Radiant Pearls, Angelwings Enterprises; *Powdered pigment:* Pearl-Ex, Jacquard Products.

Steps:
1. Stipple a few shades of Radiant Pearls (or metallic paint) onto cardstock.
2. Sweep on a bit of Pearl-Ex powder for added shine and dimension.
3. Combine with strips of color-coordinated, torn cardstock for a multi-layered look.

Spread out a few punches to serve as a subtle corner accent.

Supplies *Patterned paper:* Provo Craft; *Punch:* The Punch Bunch; *Brad:* Impress Rubber Stamps.

photo corners

Add a classic look to your scrapbook pages

Whether they're dressy, modern or whimsical, photo corners add a touch of class to a layout. *Page by Catherine Scott, photos by Altus Photo Design.* **Supplies** *Patterned paper:* Hot Off The Press; *Vellum:* Paper Cuts; *Computer font:* Monotype Corsiva, Microsoft Word; *Photo corners:* Canson.

WHAT DO YOU PICTURE when you think of classic scrapbooks? I picture the albums handed down through the generations: black or cream backgrounds, thick paper with soft, uneven edges, and photos attached to pages with photo corners.

Although you may not even notice them at first glance, photo corners do wonders to physically and visually "anchor" pictures to a scrapbook page. Their clean, crisp look will never go out of style, no matter what era you're scrapbooking!

Whether you're after a modern, dressy look or an old-fashioned, worn look, there's a photo corner to suit your project—from paper to plastic, colored to metallic, even store-bought to handmade. And with all of the scrapbooking tools available, you can change the look of existing photo corners to match your pages exactly. Try painting white paper photo corners with watercolors, heat-embossing photo corners with a glossy embossing powder, or creating your own out of handmade paper.

And don't forget, photo corners aren't limited to "photos," either. You can use store-bought or handmade photo corners on accents, journaling blocks, and even on whole pages for that "put-together" look.

So, the next time you're looking at a page thinking, "It just needs … something," consider adding photo corners. Without stealing the show, they'll evoke a quiet sense of timelessness and completeness. What could be more appropriate for your memory albums? ❤

Use watercolors, stamping inks, embossing powder, chalks and other common scrapbooking tools to create custom photo corners for your pages. **"EASTER SUNDAY" Supplies** *Patterned paper:* Making Memories; *Computer font:* CK Leafy Capitals, "The Art of Creative Lettering" CD, *Creating Keepsakes; Colored pencils:* Memory Pencils, EK Success; *Watercolors:* Niji; *Photo corners:* Canson. **"LIGHTHOUSE" Supplies** *Lighthouse die cut:* Paperhouse Productions.

ARTICLE BY
CATHERINE SCOTT

variations on vellum

16 new looks that are sheer delight

Figure 1. Before you cut your serendipity squares, trim long, thin vellum strips to use as border accents. *Page by Karen Burniston.* **Supplies** *Patterned paper and letter stickers:* Sonnets, Creative Imaginations; *Self-adhesive cardstock:* Canson; *Vellum:* Shotz, Creative Imaginations; *Eyelet:* Creative Imaginations; *Shaved ice:* Magic Scraps; *Computer font:* CK Elegant, "Fresh Fonts" CD, *Creating Keepsakes; Other:* Fiber.

Translucent. Sheer. Filmy. Gossamer. Versatile. You know what I'm talking about. Vellum. You've used it for titles, journaling blocks, photo mats and accents. You've layered it, torn it, punched it, paper-pieced it and more. This ultra-cool paper definitely has staying power. What else can you do with this versatile product?

Check out the following techniques by 13 talented scrapbookers. Whether you're a new scrapbooker who has gazed longingly at the voluptuous stacks of vellum at your local scrapbook store or a pro with an enviable stash of this appealing staple, you're sure to find a new technique to try on your next page.

BY LORI FAIRBANKS

1 Over the Top

Direct the focus of your page to your photos by muting detailed photo mats and page accents with vellum overlays.

Serendipity Squares with Vellum

To make serendipity squares (Figure 1), rip different patterned papers into small pieces, then apply them to a sheet of self-adhesive cardstock. Continue until the sheet is mostly covered, then cut your desired shapes from the cardstock. To add more texture and shine to your accents, dip each square in shaved ice so the ice adheres to the adhesive cardstock.

Create a photo mat by evenly spacing smaller serendipity squares around the edges of your cardstock mat, leaving a thin margin. Adhere a piece of vellum over the entire mat.

Alternate serendipity squares on a tag in checkerboard fashion. Print your journaling on vellum, then trim it to fit over the tag. Attach a decorative eyelet and adorn it with fibers.

—Karen Burniston
Littleton, CO

Layered Vellum Border

❶ Tear ¾" from the left side of a 12" x 12" sheet of white vellum. Lay the sheet over your cardstock and photo, then tear a hole to reveal your photo. Curl the torn edges back with your fingers. Mount eyelets in the top and bottom left corners of the vellum to secure it to the layout.

❷ Tear various sized strips from the left edge of four shades of blue vellum. Layer them over the right side of the layout, then trim them to fit. Insert eyelets in the top and bottom of each strip to secure it.

❸ Remove the string from square vellum tags and place an eyelet in each tag hole. Cut out your vellum bubbles and attach them to the tags.

Thread fiber through the eyelets, then weave the fiber through the vellum layers. Randomly secure the fiber-threaded tags to the layout with glue dots. Secure the fiber to the back of the layout.

❹ Place more vellum bubbles behind the white vellum and journal over the top.

❺ Create your title with mounted eyelet letters.

—Shauna Berglund-Immel
Hot Off The Press

Figure 2. For polished journaling on 12" x 12" vellum, print your journaling on plain white paper, place it under your vellum, then trace the words with a dark gel pen. *Page by Shauna Berglund-Immel for Hot Off The Press.* **Supplies** *Vellum, vellum bubble cutouts and metallic paper:* Hot Off The Press; *Vellum tags and letters:* Making Memories; *Eyelets:* Impress Rubber Stamps; *Fiber:* Rubba Dub Dub, Art Sanctum; *Pen:* Gelly Roll, Sakura; *Computer font:* 2Peas Think Small, downloaded from *www.two-peasinabucket.com.*

Shadow Stamped Accent

To create this accent, stamp six squares on vellum using pastel-colored inks. Stamp words on cardstock strips, ink or chalk the edges, then adhere them to embossed cardstock. Stitch the stamped vellum to the embossed cardstock and attach a flower embellishment over the vellum.

Shortcut: Renee recreated her accent block using Mrs. Grossman's vellum panel stickers. She simply trimmed the stickers to size, then adhered them to her vellum.

Variation: For a subtle watermark effect on colored cardstock, try using VersaMark ink by Tsukineko.

—Renee Camacho, Nashville, TN

Figure 3. Create a muted geometric design with simple block stamps and pastel stamping ink. *Page and sample by Renee Camacho.* **Supplies** *Patterned paper:* Karen Foster Design; *Embossed paper:* Jennifer Handmade Paper Collection; *Vellum:* Paper Reflections, DMD Industries; *Handmade flower:* Savvy Stamps; *Alphabet stamps:* PSX Design (large) and Hero Arts (small); *Square shadow stamps:* Hero Arts; *Pop dots:* Making Memories; *Photo corners:* Canson; *Stamping ink:* ColorBox, Clearsnap.

2 Add Some Color

Add extra color to your vellum accent with embroidery floss, embossing powder or crystal lacquer.

Shadow Stitching

Looking for a new way to use those darling vellum tags? Choose a basic image and stitch an outline of that image with colored embroidery floss. Use a punched shape, small die cut, template or rubber stamp as your pattern. Fill in the back of the design by stitching your colored floss through the holes created by the outline stitches—the colors will show →

through as a shade lighter.

Shortcut: Running short on time? Color in the back of the outline with a broad-tipped pen.

—*Kim Morgan, Pleasant Grove, UT*

Figure 4. Stitch on vellum tags or accents with colored embroidery floss for a lovely effect. *Page by Kim Morgan.* **Supplies** *Vellum tags:* Making Memories; *Embroidery floss:* DMC; *Square punches:* Marvy Uchida and Family Treasures.

Embossed Highlights

After printing my journaling on yellow vellum, I took a sheet of paper and cut out rectangles to match the size of my words. I placed the "template" over the words, then used a cotton ball to chalk them. Next, with the "template" still in place, I stamped clear embossing ink over the words, sprinkled them with clear embossing powder, then heat-embossed them.

—*Shannon Jones, Mesa, AZ*

Figure 5. Add texture to your layout with crinkled cardstock and vellum. *Page by Shannon Jones.* **Supplies** *Vellum:* Paper Cuts; *Stamping ink:* Emboss It, Ranger Industries; *Embossing enamel:* Suze Weinberg; *Beads:* Hirschberg Schutz & Co.; *Craft wire:* Artistic Wire Ltd.; *Pen:* Zig Millennium, EK Success; *Chalk:* Craf-T Products; *Computer font:* Bradley Hand LTC, WordPerfect, Corel.

Lacquered Highlights

Use crystal lacquer on vellum to highlight key words in your journaling. Simply squeeze a few drops of lacquer on a piece of paper, lightly dip your paintbrush in it, then paint over the words you want to emphasize. (To prevent the vellum from puckering, apply a very light coat of lacquer.) You can also sprinkle glitter in the wet lacquer. Allow the lacquer to dry thoroughly before placing your layout in a sheet protector.

—*Tracie Smith, Smithtown, NY*

Figure 6. Add sparkle to your layout with crystal lacquer and glitter. *Page by Tracie Smith.* **Supplies** *Specialty cardstock and embroidery floss:* Making Memories; *Pens:* Zig Millennium, EK Success; *Vanishing ink pen:* Journaling Genie, Chatterbox, EK Success; *Colored pencils:* Prismacolor, Sanford; *Crystal lacquer, glitter, speckle stamp (title) and flower stamp (stitched flowers):* Stampin' Up!; *Other:* Fiber. *Idea to note:* Tracie used vanishing ink to stamp her flowers, then stitched the design before the ink disappeared.

3 Under Pressure

Vellum looks great dry embossed! The raised image whitens, creating a subtle, yet distinct look.

Stamped and Dry Embossed Card

Using a flower border stamp set that coordinates with my brass template, I used bleach to stamp a flower border along the edge of my card. I splattered a few extra drops of bleach on the card for a fun, random look. Next, I stamped pink flowers over the bleached flowers.

I tore a strip of white cardstock the length of the card and approximately 3" wide, folded it in half, then adhered it to the card's spine. Next, I tore a 1¼"-wide strip of vellum and dry embossed it with flowers and squares. I anchored it to the white cardstock with eyelets, then threaded ribbon through the eyelets. To finish it off, I attached a tag and tied the ribbon.

—*Sarah Seacrest, Stampin' Up!*

Editor's note: If you stamp on a scrapbook page with bleach, be sure to use duplicate photos on your layout. And, make sure you work in a well-ventilated area when using bleach. Use water to clean your stamps.

Figure 7. Add a decorative touch to a vellum envelope by dry embossing the flap. *Card by Sarah Seacrest for Stampin' Up!* **Supplies** *Rubber stamps:* Stampin' Up!; *Brass template:* Border Builders, Stampin' Up!; *Vellum, tags, stamping ink, eyelets, ribbon and envelope template:* Stampin' Up!

If this isn't a contented look, I don't know what is!

baby ball

Chandler's all-time favorite thing has to be balls. On this day he found a bat to carry around with his ball. He had such a hard time maneuvering to get them both in his hands at the same time. The bat was as big as he was and his little hand could barely hold the ball. Somehow he finally managed to get both of them and he walked around the back yard just as pleased as could be! July, 2001

Figure 8. Create an understated accent by dry embossing vellum adhered to cardstock. *Pages by Darcee Thompson.* **Supplies** *Vellum:* PaperCuts; *Computer font:* Doodle Print, "Page Printables" CD, Vol. 2, Cock-A-Doodle Design, Inc.; *Chalk:* Craf-T Products; *Embroidery floss:* JP Coats.

Dry Embossed Mosaic Accents

To create the subtle mosaic background above, I cut vellum into rectangles and ran them through my Xyron. Next, I trimmed the larger rectangles to size and mounted them, leaving spaces for smaller shapes, which I cut and pieced as I went. I left spaces open on the right for my mosaic lettering.

For the mosaic lettering, I traced the openings onto vellum where I had already printed the amply spaced letters.

After completing the background, I sketched the ball and bat on paper and traced the designs onto a blank stencil, then cut out the stencil. Next, I dry embossed the designs over the vellum and journaling. I chalked and stitched them to add dimension.

Shortcut: Create your vellum mosaic by using self-adhesive vellum by Emagination Crafts.

—*Darcee Thompson, Preston, ID*

Figure 9. Tie a ribbon around your journaling block for a simple, yet elegant touch. *Page by Sarah Seacrest for Stampin' Up!* **Supplies** *Rubber stamps:* Itty Bitty Backgrounds set, Stampin' Up!; *Brass template:* Fresh Flowers, Stampin' Up!; *Vellum, vellum cardstock, stamping ink, chalk and ribbon:* Stampin' Up!

Fashion original frames and accents for your pages with medium-gauge aluminum. *Page by Lynne Montgomery.* **Supplies** *Craft aluminum:* Art Emboss; *Rubber stamps:* PrintWorks; *Beaded chain:* Coffee Break Design, *Foam core:* Hunt; *Window screen:* Home Depot; *Corrugated embosser:* Marvy Uchida; *Stamping ink:* Ranger Industries; *Other:* Metal studs.

Get out those templates and embossing materials. This embossed-aluminum technique will put them to good use—and help you make some unique frames and accents for your pages.

First, you'll need to purchase some medium-gauge aluminum at your local craft store. The aluminum is soft and pliable, and comes in a few different colors. You can cut it with scissors, a paper trimmer or a craft punch, and you can easily poke a needle through it for sewing.

To create a design, simply cut a piece of aluminum to the desired shape and size. To emboss with a template, simply place the template on top of the aluminum and emboss. (Remember, when writing numbers or letters on the aluminum, write backward if you want the raised part of the design on the front of the accent.)

Be sure to use duplicate photographs with this technique if you're concerned about archival safety and want to overlap the aluminum onto a photograph (the aluminum could scratch the photo's emulsion).

—by Lynne Montgomery

Dry Embossed Accents

Dry embossed borders (Figure 9) lend a touch of elegance to any layout. For this layout, I embossed white cardstock for the top border, then chalked over the raised image. For the bottom border, I embossed cardstock weight vellum. I trimmed the wavy edge below the flowers to reveal the lavender cardstock behind it.

—Sarah Seacrest, Stampin' Up!

Dry Embossed Journaling

To create the embossed lettering, cut vellum into ⅜" strips. Open the label maker and feed the strips through the runner. (Experiment with the label maker to get the feel for how hard you need to pull the "trigger.") After embossing your strips, adhere them to the layout with glue dots.

Cut a hole out of the vellum envelope and set the photo in at an angle. Cut off the stems of the flowers and drop them in the envelope. I placed little flowers in the small silver concho frames and covered them with diamond glaze.

—Heidi Swapp, Mesa, AZ

Figure 10. Use a label maker to dry emboss journaling on vellum. *Page by Heidi Swapp.* **Supplies** *Patterned paper:* K & Company; *Vellum:* Autumn Leaves; *Flowers:* Savvy Stamps; *Conchos:* Scrapworks; *Diamond glaze:* Judikins; *Other:* Vellum envelope; *Label maker idea:* Debbie Crouse, *Designing with Notions* by Autumn Leaves.

4 Shining Through
Use colored vellum to create beautiful stained-glass accents.

Fast Stained Glass Accents

❶ For a 12" x 12" layout, cut two 6" squares from purple patterned paper. Adhere them in opposing corners on a sheet of blue patterned paper.

❷ Cut four 6" squares from different shades of vellum. Adhere one over each square of the background paper.

❸ Cut six strips of black paper measuring ⅛" x 12", then glue one over each seam where the vellums meet and along the outer edges of the background paper.

❹ Trim the pre-printed stained-glass vellum accent and adhere it to your layout. Cut two 2¼" x ¼" strips and two ¼" x 10¼" strips of →

Plant a little love,

Spring 2001

Mommy and Brandon

watch a miracle grow!

Figure 11. Soften patterned paper by covering it with pastel vellum. *Page by Shauna Berglund-Immel for Hot Off The Press.* **Supplies** *Patterned paper, vellum and stained-glass patterned vellum:* Hot Off The Press; *Pen:* Gelly Roll, Sakura; *Computer font:* CK Calligraphy, "The Best of Creative Lettering" CD Combo, *Creating Keepsakes.*

black paper, then attach them around the accent's edges.

❺ Adhere a ¼" strip of black paper around the edges of your photo. *Don't trim the overhanging strip!* Using the overhang as your starting point, attach ¼" strips of black paper around the photo in a grid pattern. Use Figure 11 as your guide. When you finish building the "window," frame it with ¼" strips and trim the excess pieces.

❻ Cut thin pieces of pastel vellum to fit behind each section of the window. Place adhesive behind the photo and adhere it to the background page.

—*Shauna Berglund-Immel*
Hot Off The Press

Stained Glass Shapes

Use vellum and paper wire to create stained-glass embellishments (Figure 12). Bend the paper wire into your desired shape. If you use a pattern, try using a wire jig to bend the wire. Glue a piece of vellum to the back of your shape, then trim the vellum around the paper wire. I've created ghosts, pumpkins, beach balls and even a fancy photo mat.

If you want more than one color on an accent, color the underside of white vellum with brush-tipped markers. If you opt for colored vellum, you'll have to glue each piece to your design, which may take more time and accuracy.

—*Heidi Schueller, Waukesha, WI*

Figure 12. Add a stained-glass accent to your layout for visual variety. *Page by Heidi Schueller.* **Supplies** *Patterned paper:* Cock-A-Doodle Design and Cherished Memories; *Vellum:* Paper Adventures; *Paper wire:* Paperbilities; *Buttons:* Theresa's Hand Dyed Buttons; *Computer font:* CK Handprint, "The Best of Creative Lettering" CD Combo, *Creating Keepsakes; Other:* Hemp.

5 Wrinkles Are Good

Add texture and dimension to your vellum by crinkling it. Add ink or embossing powder for more depth.

Figure 13. Ink and heat-emboss torn edges on your vellum tags for an offbeat look. *Page by Jennifer Ditz.* **Supplies** *Vellum:* Autumn Leaves; *Computer font:* 2Peas Fairy Princess, downloaded from *www.twopeasinabucket.com; Tags:* Making Memories; *Conchos:* Scrapworks; *Fiber:* Rubba Dub Dub, Art Sanctum; *Stamping ink:* VersaMark, Tsukineko; *Embossing powder:* PSX Design; *Other:* Nailheads.

Wrinkled and Embossed Accents

For the big heart accent, I crumpled the vellum and gently rubbed a VersaMark inkpad over the wrinkles. Next, I sprinkled the vellum with embossing powder, then heat-embossed it.

I used a craft knife to cut the center from the lower right metal-rimmed tags and replaced it with the crinkled and

→

Figure 4. Add a hanging heart to a special poem. *Example by Mary Larson.* **Supplies** *Patterned paper:* Karen Foster Design; *Punches:* Family Treasures (large hand), All Night Media (small hand); *Fibers:* Rubba Dub Dub, Art Sanctum; *Eyelets:* Dritz; *Other:* Heart locket.

A daddy and his daughters,
Walking hand in hand;
Though he isn't always with them,
They say they understand.

When he's away at work or play,
The memory of him lingers;
The two girls smile, because they know,
He's wrapped around their fingers.

A slight tilt of their sweet heads,
A smile, a lowered glance;
A hug and kiss and, "Daddy please?"
He doesn't stand a chance!

In later years he will recall,
With tenderness and love;
Two charming girls, with hands in his,
Two blessings from above.

one small different shape, such as a leaf.

As shown in Figure 2, lay the first small square over the leaf. Take the next largest square and lay that on top of the smaller one. Continue until all the shapes are used up, always going from smallest to largest.

Variation: Use a negative shape to frame a positive shape (Figure 3).

Simple Illustration. Use your punches to showcase words in your journaling or poems (Figures 4 and 6). Punch through the cardstock the poem is printed on and back it with paper. This is both easy and effective!

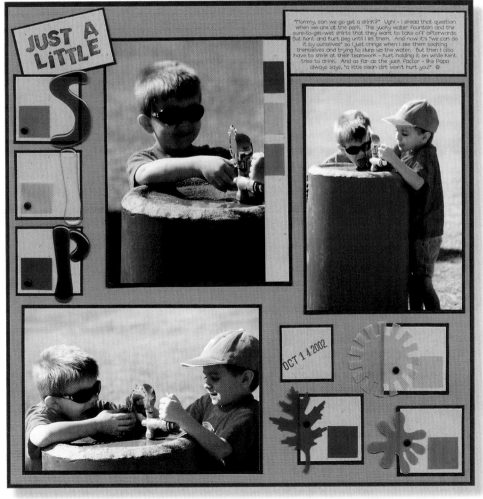

Figure 5. Offset bright colors with black for a striking layout. *Page by Mary Larson.* **Supplies** *Punches:* EK Success (sun), Emagination Crafts (water splat), Family Treasures (squares) and McGill (leaf); *Alphabet stamps:* Plaid; *Letters:* Squigglebets, Creative Imaginations; *Computer font:* CK Primary, "The Best of Creative Lettering" CD Combo, *Creating Keepsakes;* *Brads:* American Tag Company.

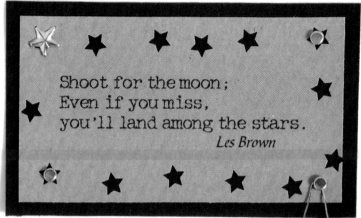

Figure 6. Punch a small shape around a quote or poem for an instant border. *Example by Mary Larson.* **Supplies** *Punches:* Oriental Trading Company; *Craft wire:* Making Memories; *Other:* Nailheads.

Positives

Now that you've got new ideas for negative punches, here are four fresh looks—mixed shapes, torn frame, outlined frame and fold and stitch—to try with positive punches.

Mixed Shapes. You don't have to do anything difficult or fancy to give a punched shape strong impact on your page. Simply take any shape, back it with a geometric shape, and you automatically give it more flair. Note how in

Figure 5 I offset the shape punches with squares in matching colors, then backed each set with a larger square.

Outlined Frame. Negatives or positives? It's hard to tell which was used on the frame in Figure 7. I simply added black punches on top of squares (so they'd look like they'd been intricately cut out) and placed them around the photograph. When duplicating this look, be sure the punch touches the outside of the square so the black area all looks connected. Try to choose relevant punches to complement your photograph.

Torn Frames. For the rustic look in Figure 8, scrapbooker Denise Pauley took star punches and ripped out the middle. To create this look, snip in the center of each star with microtip scissors. Cut off a bit of the paper, then fold back the edges. Decorate the

Common Punch Questions

Face a punch predicament now and then? Following are answers to common punch questions:

Q. Is there any rhyme or reason for using a positive versus a negative punch shape?
A. Yes and no. Sometimes it's just a matter of preference because they look the same. However, if you're punching lots of small shapes (like those in Figure 8), it's much easier to use the negatives so you don't have to glue tiny shapes on top of your paper.

Q. My punch keeps getting stuck and won't let go of the paper. What now?
A. I'm sure you're frustrated, but avoid throwing the punch on the floor (the

punch could break). Try punching through waxed paper to lubricate it.

If the punch is large, use your eyelet hammer (or something similar) to gently tap on the back where the metal is stuck. That usually does the trick. If it doesn't, tap the punch on the table, too.

Q. Why does my punched shape have ragged edges?
A. You probably need to sharpen the edges of the punch. Try punching through aluminum foil or fine-grade sandpaper several times until the rough edges are gone.

Q. Why is it so hard to punch through cardstock?
A. The thicker the cardstock or paper, the more difficult it is to punch through it. To make it easier, punch through wax paper

several times to lubricate the punch. Or stick the punch in the freezer for a half hour or so. The metal will constrict a bit and punch a little easier.

Q. My hands get so tired of punching. Is there anything I can do?
A. If you love punches and want to use them a lot, consider investing in a punch tool. Tapestry in Time makes a Power Punch (personal and professional size) that's great for punching large quantities. Or, consider using a punch designed for easier use, such as the new Gargantuan punches offered by Emagination Crafts (*www.emaginationcrafts.com*).

Also, many scrapbookers punch standing up to alleviate extra stress on their hands and wrists. Try it!

Companies That Manufacture Punches

Punches are a popular craft item, and it's easy to find them in hundreds of shapes, sizes and styles. Check the following:

- All Night Media
  www.allnightmedia.com
- American Pin & Fastener
  www.hyglocrafts.com
- A.W. Cute Stickers n' Stuff
  www.awcute.com
- CARL Mfg.
  www.carl-products.com
- eA-Zy Punch
  www.ezScrapBooks.com
- EK Success
  www.eksuccess.com
- Emagination Crafts
  www.emaginationcrafts.com
- Family Treasures
  www.familytreasures.com
- Fiskars
  www.fiskars.com
- Marvy Uchida
  www.uchida.com
- McGill
  www.mcgillinc.com
- Nankong Enterprises
  www.nankong.com
- Oriental Trading Company
  www.oriental.com
- Presto Craft (WonderPress)
  www.prestocraft.com
- Provo Craft
  www.creativexpress.com
- Scrapbook Sally
  www.scrapbooksally.com
- ScrapSakes
  www.scrapsakes.com
- The Punch Bunch
  www.thepunchbunch.com
- Westrim Crafts
  www.westrimcrafts.com

Note: Remember that die-cut systems (such as QuicKutz and Sizzix) produce accents that are similar in scale to punches.

Figure 7. Black punched shapes make a unique frame. *Example by Mary Larson.* **Supplies** *Punches:* American Pin & Fastener (bear), CARL Mfg. (foot), eA-Zy Punch (letter), Emagination Crafts (frog, tree and heart), McGill (leaf), Family Treasures (swirl, leaf, hand and square).

star punches with metallic rub-ons if desired, then place them on pop dots for added dimension.

Fold and Stitch. This is an easy one! Using a large or jumbo-sized punch, punch out several shapes in different colors. Fold each shape in half and line it up along the border (Figure 9). Poke two holes along the fold in the middle. Using a needle threaded with fiber or floss, stitch the shapes to the background. To keep the shapes from flattening, place pop dots under each side.

Other Ideas

Now that you're "rolling with the punches," try these ideas as well:
- Decorate photo corners with punches (see Figure 2).
- Create custom backgrounds. Try using tone-on-tone colors for a subtle look.
- Put together a punch packet.
- Place punches in a shaker box. Remember all those hand-held punches you haven't emptied for a while? Open them up and you'll have instant punch confetti!
- Use the negatives as temporary templates and fill the inside portion

with beads, glitter or other media. You can throw them away when you're finished!

◆ Create embossed texture. Adhere positive or negative punches to your paper, then ink and heat-emboss them.

◆ Make a fake charm. Punch it from metallic paper or color it with metallic pens, then hang it with a jump ring.

See how much fun positive and negative punches can be? Use them to spice up your layouts! ❤

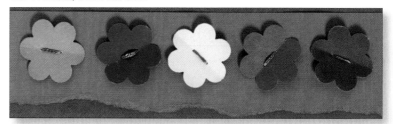

Figure 8. Create a cool star border with punches and fun extras. *Example by Denise Pauley.* **Supplies** *Punch:* Marvy Uchida, *Corrugated cardstock:* DMD, Inc.; *Handmade papers:* Maruyama, Magenta; Books by Hand, *Metal mesh:* American Art Clay; *Spiral clip:* 7 Gypsies; *Craft wire:* Making Memories; *Pop dots:* All Night Media; *Metallic rub-ons:* Craf-T Products; *Other:* Star brad.

Figure 9. A stitched fiber for the center of a flower lends a homemade touch. *Example by Mary Larson.* **Supplies** *Punches:* Nankong Enterprises; *Fibers:* On the Surface.

2 HOT NEW PUNCHING TOOLS

Enjoy punching your own creations? Here are two products you won't want to miss!

Punch-a-Petal. With the innovative Punch-a-Petal punch from Scrapbook Sally, you can punch six fun shapes (rose, daisy, tulip, poppy, sunflower and lily) and use them to build beautiful flowers like the rose shown below. Or, create a playful butterfly or bug!

Constructed of lightweight plastic, the Punch-a-Petal is designed for ease of use. For additional ideas, don't miss *Punch-a-Petal Step By Step*, a full-color, 22-page idea book that's packed with possibilities. Short on time? Watch for pre-punched petals coming soon.

Suggested retail price for the punch is $9.95, while the idea book retails for $9.95. For more information, visit *www.scrapbooksally.com.*

WonderPress Punch and Emboss System. Do you ever get frustrated when a punch doesn't reach as far as you need?

The WonderPress Punch and Emboss System offered by The Presto Craft Company can help.

The punch extends 6" into a page and accepts the interchangeable patterns in four different orientations. This means you can place your image in any direction you want, anywhere you want, on a 12" x 12" page.

The system includes 12 punch and six emboss patterns, with more on the way. It also provides added benefits such as embossing and a built-in ruler. Suggested retail price for the system is $21.95, with individual patterns selling for $5.95–$6.50. For more product details, visit *www.prestocraft.com.*

"slide" into action

10 cool looks you can create today

Figure 1.
Slide holders
come in a wide
selection of colors,
styles and sizes.

DURING THE PAST FEW YEARS, I've enjoyed seeing scrapbookers discover and use non-traditional items—metals, fibers, game pieces and more—on their scrapbook pages. One of the hottest trends today? Slide mounts, also known as slide holders. The first time I saw the mounts (a staple in the photography market), I couldn't wait to jump right in and play with ideas for both scrapbook pages and cards. I'll share many of my favorite discoveries here.

A Few Basics

You may have seen white slide mounts in photography stores, but did you realize the mounts also come in a wide spectrum of colors, styles and sizes? (See Figure 1.) You can find them in paper, plastic and metal.

And, while some have glass covers, most have empty frames just waiting to be used as is or embellished.

Where can you find slide mounts? Try your local scrapbook store, photography store, or the Internet. You'll find more options than you might have dreamed existed!

Are slide holders safe? Yes. Since the products are made for use with photographs, they're acid free. When considering a holder with a glass cover, be aware that it could break in your scrapbook. Determine if this is a risk you want to take or not.

BY ERICA PIEROVICH

Now The Fun Stuff

I like to consider my slide holders mini-canvases just waiting to be decorated. Here are some of the fun looks I've come up with, plus instructions on how to create them:

Tiny Picture Frames

Slide holders have traditionally been used to frame small pictures or portions of pictures. You can use the slide holder to "crop" and frame a certain section as a focal point, or you can frame small images entirely within the holder.

Sports scenes lend themselves nicely to the "picture frame" approach since they're often taken at a distance and contain small images (see example at right). Consider using more than one slide holder to help frame a picture series or create an interesting group of images. You can present the slides in a linear fashion or position them more randomly.

To create this look:

Use a hole punch to punch a hole in the corner of the slide holder. Apply a wet adhesive to the back of the ball, then insert the metal soccer ball accent into the hole.

Next, crop the picture to fit in the frame space. Attach the picture to the back of the slide with a strong adhesive. (I like Wonder Tape by Suze Weinberg.)

Other ideas? Use bits of flowers, trees or leaves to frame outdoor pictures. Or, position your slide holder on top of a 4" x 6" photo to draw attention to a certain area.

Want a larger-scale accent for a 12" x 12" page? Consider a larger mount like that used for the photo of my son in Figure 1. I simply cropped the picture and attached it to the back of the slide holder.

Titles

It's common for page layouts to contain distinctive titles, and slide holders are a fun way to jazz them up. Note how

Figure 2. House individual letters in slide frames for a look that's "superhero" cool. *Pages by Erica Pierovich.* **Supplies** *Slide holders:* Pakon; *Patterned paper:* Mustard Moon; *Vellum:* Provo Craft; *Mesh:* Magic Mesh, Avant Card; *Embroidery floss:* DMC; *Metal words and letters:* Making Memories; *Nailheads:* Chatterbox; *Spiral paper clips:* Target; *Chalk:* Craf-T Products; *Photo corners:* Fiskars; *Tag:* From Batman costume packaging (treated with Archival Mist to deacidify it); *Other:* Black embossed grid paper and tiny eyelets.

I used them to frame individual letters for my layout in Figure 2. The letters can be created from Scrabble squares, metal accents, stickers, computer fonts and more.

To create the Batman title slides:

Cut and attach black mesh to the back of the slide holder. Next, loop the jump ring through the metal letter and then through the mesh. Use wire cutters to close the ring firmly.

Mat the slides with gray squares attached to the back. Position the slides in a linear fashion to complete your title chain.

You can also use slide mounts to house individual words in a title. Use poetry beads to enclose the words (see example below). Or, write your title by hand, then frame portions with slide holders to add flair.

To create this look:

Apply pop dots to the bottom slides. Attach upper slides. Thread

the wire through the first slide, then thread the first bead through the wire. Repeat the threading for all of the slides and remaining beads.

Curl the ends of the wire. Finally, attach patterned paper to the back of the slides. Secure the beads to the patterned paper with adhesive.

Tags

A slide holder makes a great frame for a shaker on a tag (see example below). Or, use it to house key words or elements that are part of the tag. Fibers wrapped around the slide holder can be matched with the fibers on a tag for a coordinated look.

To create this look:

Cover tag with black mesh paper, then insert metal eyelet through tag. Cut and loop fibers through the tag hole. Push star brad through the metal eyelet. Punch holes and attach metal words with adhesive.

Punch a hole in the bottom of the slide holder with a hole punch. Apply a wet adhesive to the back of the metal word and insert the word in the hole.

Next, create an enclosed square from a page protector. Close three sides with adhesive. Fill the pocket with star confetti, then adhere the final side closed. Attach the pocket to the slide holder. Attach the shaker to the tag. Using one piece of wire, attach a flag pin to the bottom of the tag.

Another fun option? Use a 2" slide holder to house a tag. These slide holders come in red, blue, yellow, white, gray and black. You can also find them in green plastic and metal.

To create this look:

Wrap fiber around a slide holder that's covered with adhesive. (I used Wonder Tape.) Work the fiber all the way around the slide.

Cut your tag to the desired size, then punch a hole in it and insert an eyelet. Thread matching fibers through it, then attach the picture to the back of the slide holder. Attach the slide holder to the tag.

Next, create the words with rubber stamps and attach a smaller picture to the tag. Apply chalk to the edges for a more rustic look.

Chains

Slide holders can even be chained together. Simply place them snugly next to each other, or link them with ribbon or thread, wire and eyelets.

To create this look:
Attach satin ribbon to slides with adhesive tape. Apply die cuts to frame edges, then thread beads on embroidery floss and attach it to the back of the slide.

Apply fiber to the outer edges of your slides with adhesive. Crop and attach pictures to the back of the slides, or print the words, position them in the centers of the frames, and attach them.

Shadow Boxes

My favorite use of slide holders? Little shadow boxes! You simply place pop dots between two of the holders to provide some depth. This comes in extra handy when your embellishments are a bit lumpy or delicate and need added protection.

To create this look:
Apply spray adhesive to the front of the slide, then sprinkle it with sand. Repeat the procedure a few more times until you have the desired coverage of sand.

Apply water-design paper to the back of the slide to create a background scene. Join the two slide holders together with pop dots. Add shells for a sophisticated touch, then slip net over the completed slides.

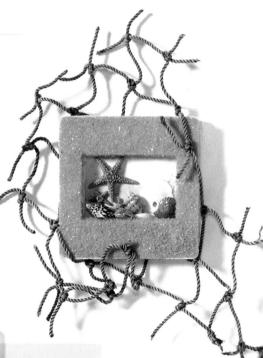

Where to Find Slide Holders

You can purchase slide holders at many scrapbook and photography stores. Can't find what you need? Check out the offerings online at:

◆ www.impressrubberstamps.com

◆ www.inkjetart.com/sp/67.html

◆ www.makingmemories.com

◆ www.scrapworks.com

Want to create a custom slide holder that looks like this? It's easy with the new KrystalKraft embellishments from Sunday International.

Other Embellishments

Slide holders can also provide a surface to stamp or chalk on. For best results with chalks or watercolors, be sure to place a piece of cardstock over the plastic side. Paper slides work best with this application, but are a bit more difficult to find.

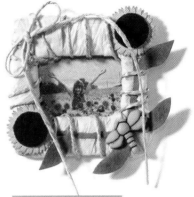

To create this look:

Stamp your slide holder with a swirl stamp and two colors of stamping ink. Apply pop dots to the back of the slide.

Next, position the slide over the area of your photo that you'd like to be a focal point. This is a fun way to highlight a subject within a picture with lots of background water.

Sand crystals, tiny marbles and flock also make great additions to slide holders. They're easy to apply and create lovely frames.

To create this look:

Apply spray adhesive to the slide holder and sprinkle with flock. Allow the adhesive to dry for a few minutes, then repeat the application until you've achieved the desired thickness.

Apply snowflake stickers. Print title on vellum, then attach it to the back of the slide holder.

Don't forget the power of other embellishments as well. Raffia, twine and fibers can easily be wound around slide holders for artistic flair. Or, use metal accents, buttons, stickers and punches to decorate the frame or interior area of a slide holder.

To create this look:

Apply adhesive strips to the sides of your slide mount. Wrap raffia around the frame. Attach sunflower stickers, followed by a dragonfly button.

Wrap twine around your slide-holder frame, then attach a twine bow. Attach a cropped picture to the back of the slide holder.

The ideas above are just a start. Whenever you need a "framed" accent, consider using a slide holder. Open your mind, let your imagination go wild, and "slide" into action! ❤

Whenever you need a "framed" accent, consider using a slide holder. Open your mind, let your imagination go wild, and "slide" into action!

eyelets revisited

Learn to set and use them in style

Figure 1. Tags with custom eyelet designs add a distinctive touch. *Page by Mary Larson.* **Supplies** *Patterned paper:* Scrap-Ease; *Ink pads:* Tsukineko; *Alphabet stamps:* PSX Design; *Eyelets:* Creative Impressions and Making Memories; *Paper piercer:* Making Memories; *Square metal rings:* 7 Gypsies, Mumbay Collection; *Computer font:* CK Constitution, "Fresh Fonts" CD, *Creating Keepsakes; Other:* Ribbon and walnut ink.

DO YOU REMEMBER the first time you saw eyelets on a layout? I do. It was two years ago, and while I loved the look, I couldn't find much in the way of eyelet choices. I remember scouring the sewing notions aisle at a fabric store, hoping to find eyelets in different sizes and colors.

Today, you can find eyelets in almost every color, size and shape. They're offered by several scrapbook companies, and they've quickly become scrapbooking staples. You may be using them successfully and often—or you may need a little help setting your first eyelet.

BY MARY LARSON

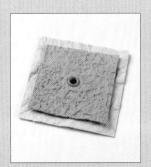

Step 1. Make a hole the size of the eyelet. Place the eyelet in the hole.

Step 2. Flip the eyelet and paper upside-down on a firm work surface. Insert the eyelet setter into the back of the eyelet, then hammer the top of the eyelet setter.

Step 3. Flip the paper over and admire your finished eyelet.

Read on, and I'll share the basics of setting an eyelet. You'll also find tips and shortcuts from those who've already set several eyelets. We can all learn a thing or two!

The Tools You'll Need

Before you begin, gather a few basic tools. Here's a quick rundown, plus a few recommendations.

♦ **Eyelets.** Choose from today's huge assortment of sizes, shapes and colors.

♦ **Hole punch.** Select a regular, hand-held hole punch for attaching eyelets near the edge of your paper. Use an anywhere hole punch to make holes closer to the center of the paper.

♦ **Hammer.** Use a hammer that's large enough and heavy enough to flatten metal.

♦ **Setting mat.** You can buy a "self-healing" mat made just for eyelets. Or, use another surface. Be aware that the wrong kind of material will likely become damaged from all the pounding and punching. And don't use a brick, which will just dull your hole punch and make it useless (don't ask me how I know that).

♦ **Eyelet setter.** Pick from several different sizes, with either a pointed or rounded end. *Note:* Dritz

makes eyelet pliers (see the sewing section of your craft store or a fabric store) that can be used for setting larger eyelets. Their big advantage? You don't need anything but the eyelets. Their disadvantage? The pliers won't reach in further than an inch, which means you're limited to using them along the edges of paper.

How to Set an Eyelet

After you've determined what size of eyelet to use:

❶ Decide where you want to place your eyelet. Use a hole punch or an anywhere hole punch to make a hole the size of the eyelet. *Tip:* I sometimes use a hand-held flower or square punch to hold the eyelet in place better.

❷ Place the eyelet in the hole, then flip the eyelet and paper *upside-down* on a firm work surface. *Tip:* I like to place the mat on top of my eyelets, holding it firmly in place, then flip the whole thing over. This keeps eyelets from falling out of the holes.

❸ Insert the eyelet setter into the back of the eyelet.

❹ With a hammer, make a couple of sharp taps on the top of the eyelet setter. Continue until the eyelet has been squished down on

the backside and firmly attached to the paper.

❺ Flip the paper right side up. If needed, tap on the front of the eyelet to flatten it a bit. *Tip:* To protect the eyelet, place a piece of cardstock over it before hammering.

Fun Looks with Eyelets

Once you've got the basics down, consider the following eyelet ideas. They range from simple to advanced.

Outlining

Outline a simple clip-art or drawn shape with eyelets. Here's how:

❶ Choose a shape to outline. *Tip:* You can find simple shapes in clip art, dingbats or templates. You can also draw your own sketch.

❷ Place the picture on the paper that will eventually contain eyelets.

❸ With a paper piercer, make small holes approximately ¼" apart. Follow the outline of the shape.

❹ Remove the picture of the shape. Punch holes where the pierced holes are positioned.

❺ Follow the basic eyelet-setting steps above. Don't worry if the eyelets aren't spaced perfectly—this will simply add a homemade touch like that in Figure 1.

Figure 2. Subtle fibers and eyelets highlight a special quote. *Page by Marpy Hayse.* **Supplies** *Patterned paper:* Mustard Moon, Magenta; *Vellum:* Over the Moon Press, EK Success; *Eyelets:* Emagination Crafts; *Fibers:* Adornaments, EK Success; *Computer font:* Garamouche, Impress Rubber Stamps, *Rubber stamp:* Impress Rubber Stamps; *Chalk:* Craf-T Products.

Connect the Dots

Just like the numbered dots in your child's activity books, you can connect eyelets to create a shape or line. In Figure 2, for example, Marpy Hayse used eyelets to emphasize the lines of a quote. In Figure 3, Delores Frantz used eyelets and cord to lace up a die-cut football. *Editor's note:* For additional ideas—for everything from baseballs to mitts to ice skates—see *Eyelets for Scrapbooks* by Design Originals.

For more intricate shapes, such as the flower in Figure 4, consider drawing the lines first, then punching the holes. If you'll be threading more than two ribbons or fibers through one hole (such as that in the stem of the flower), be sure to use a larger eyelet.

Figure 3. "Lace" up a football for a fun sports accent. *Page by Delores Frantz.* **Supplies** *Page:* Used with permission from *Eyelets by Scrapbooks* (Design Originals); *Marbled vellum:* CTI USA; *Eyelets and brads:* Making Memories; *Circle punch:* McGill; *Pen:* Zig Writer, EK Success; *Other:* White cord.

Figure 4. Fashion a festive flower accent with colorful eyelets and ribbon. *Example by Mary Larson.* **Supplies** *Eyelets:* Making Memories and Doodlebug Design; *Ribbon:* C.M. Offray & Son; *Other:* Brad.

Movement

With eyelets, you can stack photos or journaling to get more on a page (Figure 5). To accomplish this, punch holes through several layers of cardstock, then place an eyelet through all the holes.

When hammering the eyelet, avoid flattening it completely. Hammer just enough that the eyelet catches the back of the paper. Note how the layers swing away from each other so each photo or journaling note can be seen. In Figure 6, Denise Pauley turned decorative circles into "bubbles" to hide her journaling.

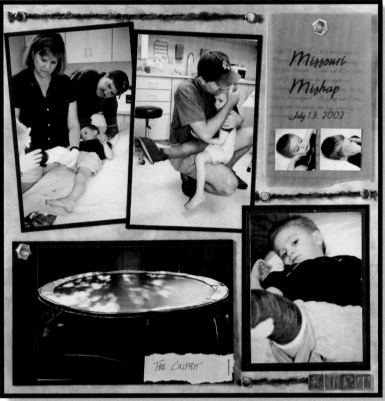

Figure 5. Attach several layers of cardstock together with large eyelets. *Page by Mary Larson.* **Supplies** *Patterned paper:* Sonnets, Creative Imaginations; *Eyelets:* Creative Imaginations; *Vellum:* Paper Adventures; *Computer fonts:* CAC Leslie, "Creatacard" CD, American Greetings; *Fibers:* Rubba Dub Dub, Art Sanctum; *Square punch:* Family Treasures; *Other:* Pewter letters, hexagon nailheads and colored staples.

Figure 6. Create textured bubbles with crinkled paper and eyelets for a clever journaling trick. *Example by Denise Pauley.* **Supplies** *Patterned paper and stickers:* Karen Foster Design; *Computer fonts:* CK Indigo, "Fresh Fonts" CD, *Creating Keepsakes; Eyelets:* Making Memories; *Metallic rub-ons:* Craf-T Products.

Closures

Eyelets are a strong, classy way to create closures for hand-made envelopes or anything else that opens up. Lori Houk uses eyelets and string in Figure 7 to make an old-fashioned closure.

To create a closure like Lori's:

❶ Punch a circle larger than the eyelet.

❷ Punch another, smaller hole in the middle of the circle punch-out.

❸ Thread the string through the hole, then place the eyelet in the hole next to the string and flatten. Make sure the string does not slip out.

❹ Wrap the string around the corresponding eyelet circle on the other side of the opening. Or just attach eyelets to a simple folded note and thread with string (Figure 8).

Figure 7. An eyelet and a circle make a cool, easy closure. *Example by Lori Houk.* **Supplies** *Eyelets:* Making Memories; *Rubber stamps:* PSX Design and Hero Arts; *Ink pad:* Stampa Rosa; *Label holder:* From *www.two-peasinabucket.com*; *Other:* Twine and tag.

Figure 8. Hide a personal note by folding it and tying it up. *Example by Mary Larson.* **Supplies** *Eyelets:* Making Memories, *Corrugated paper:* Current, Inc.; *Other:* Cotton string and glass pony beads.

Shapes

It's easy to create cute shapes with eyelets (Figure 9). Want to come up with your own designs? Look around and you'll see many items that can be duplicated with eyelets. Just use a simple approach like Sally Traidman did for the darling onesie in Figure 10!

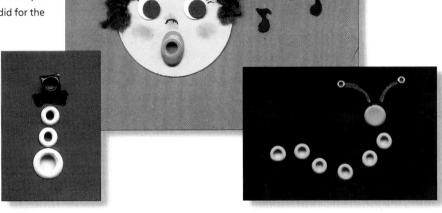

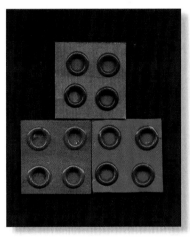

Figure 9. Colorful eyelets make simple yet snazzy shapes. *Bug, snowman and block examples by Mary Larson.* **Supplies** *Eyelets:* Doodlebug Design, Impress Rubber Stamps and Making Memories. *Singing example by Lee Anne Russell.* **Supplies** *Eyelets:* The Stamp Doctor; *Punches:* Family Treasures and McGill; *Chalk:* Craf-T Products; *Fiber:* On the Fringe; *Pen:* Zig Writer, EK Success.

Figure 10. Create a sweet onesie with flannel paper and eyelets for "snaps." *Card by Sally Traidman.* **Supplies** *Card:* Used with permission from *Eyelets for Cards & More* (Design Originals); *Eyelets:* Making Memories; *Patterned paper:* Source unknown; *Punches:* Family Treasures (bow) and Marvy Uchida (circles).

Companies That Make Eyelets

You can find eyelets in a wide variety of shapes, sizes and colors.
Check out the offerings from the following companies.
They're just a sampling of the many companies that offer eyelets!

Dolphin Enterprises

Emagination Crafts

Close To My Heart

Eyelet Queen

Making Memories

Nested

You can "nest" a smaller eyelet on a larger one. Expand the concept with different size and shape combinations. Try small squares inside large squares, triangles and circles together, or frame a small heart eyelet with a large square (Figure 11).

Here's another idea: Place the smaller eyelet inside a larger one, then set as normal, making sure you catch the smaller eyelet's shank as you flatten them both. *Tip:* Before setting your eyelets, add a tiny drop of liquid glue between the eyelets to keep them together and in place. *Variation:* Nest a small brad inside an eyelet instead.

Other Ideas

Over the past year, we've seen eyelets used several ways. Don't forget these possibilities as well:

- In the centers of letters
- To reinforce tag holes
- To attach vellum to cardstock
- To provide holes for lacing with ribbon or fiber
- For accents on punches or paper piecings

Now that you've got a good foundation and new ideas for eyelets, experiment. They're going to be around for a long, long time! ❤

Figure 11. Mix and match eyelet shapes for a fun layered look. *Example by Mary Larson.* **Supplies** *Star eyelets:* GoneScrappin.com (large) and unknown (small).

Eyelet Q & A

Following are a few of the questions commonly asked about eyelets, plus answers to help guide you.

Q. What are eyelets made of?
A. Eyelets are made from a variety of metals, including brass and aluminum. While brass eyelets take more pounding with a hammer, aluminum eyelets are softer and more easily set.

Q. Are eyelets safe?
A. It depends on their finishes. If safety is a concern, avoid placing eyelets near your photos. Or, use eyelets that are CK OK certified for safety, such as those by Baby Eyelets and Eyelet Factory.

Q. What kind of finish do eyelets have?
A. Some are painted, some are enameled, and others have a metal finish. Be extra careful when setting the painted eyelets or the paint can chip off. To avoid or minimize this, place a piece of cardstock against the eyelet during the setting process.

Q. What will the back of the eyelet look like after it's set?
A. As you pound on the back of the eyelet with a hammer, the eyelet will split, roll or burst. Sometimes it looks nice and sometimes it's unattractive. The most important thing is to ensure the eyelet is attached. As long as it's bigger than the hole it's in, the eyelet won't fall out.

Q. How do I set fancy shapes?
A. Shaped eyelets are set the same way as round ones. However, go slowly with larger eyelets to prevent the hole from buckling and becoming misshapen.

Q. Can I color eyelets myself?
A. You can change some finishes with Krylon leafing pens or embossing powder. Most of the time, however, you'll be able to find the color you need without modifying your eyelet.

Q. How do I remove an eyelet if it gets ruined during setting?
A. Very carefully! Despite your best efforts, at times you'll rip the paper or cardstock while removing an eyelet. Try to pry up the back of the eyelet with needle-nose pliers and slip the eyelet back out of the hole.

Always do your best to place eyelets carefully so you don't have to remove them. Or attach them to something (such as a photo mat) that can be replaced easily should the eyelet and its surrounding area end up damaged.

cork, fiber and copper

See what five scrapbookers did with three products

REMEMBER THE SKIT on "I Love Lucy" where Lucy and Ethel bought dresses that looked the same? They both expected the other to return the "duplicate" dress, but neither woman did. Eventually Lucy and Ethel destroyed both dresses while singing a song about friendship.

One of the things I love most about scrapbooking is that even if you and a friend use the same products, your pages will look unique. We put this theory to the test by giving five scrapbookers three products and asking each scrapbooker to create a layout with them. Note how they came up with completely different looks. Now, take the challenge yourself. What will you create?

3 Featured Products

- **"VEGETABLE GARDEN" FIBERS**
  Art Sanctum
  www.artsanctum.com

- **COPPER TILES AND STRIPS**
  Global Solutions
  800/769-3210

- **CORK PAPER**
  Magic Scraps
  www.magicscraps.com

BY LORI FAIRBANKS

"Simple, Ordinary Things"

by Amy Williams
Old Town, ME

◆ Quick color-wheel trivia: Why did Amy choose these colors and why do they work? Purple, orange and green are split-complementary colors.

◆ Amy crumpled her cardstock to add dimension and texture.

◆ She doubled up foam squares to pop her photo up over the fiber border.

Supplies *Cork paper:* Magic Scraps; *Copper tiles and strips:* Global Solutions; *Fibers:* Rubba Dub Dub, Art Sanctum; *Patterned paper:* The Paper Patch; *Computer font:* CK Newsprint, "Fresh Fonts" CD, *Creating Keepsakes; Chalk:* Craf-T Products; *Foam squares:* Therm O Web.

"Believe in Yourself Always"

by Renee Camacho
Nashville, TN

◆ Renee accentuated her photo mat by backing it with torn cork paper and tying it with fiber.

◆ Layer and overlap elements to create a collage look. Note how Renee placed her picture and photo mat straight to communicate a sense of order.

Supplies *Cork paper:* Magic Scraps; *Copper tiles and strips:* Global Solutions; *Fibers:* Rubba Dub Dub, Art Sanctum; *Patterned paper:* Design Originals; *Eyelets and oval page pebble:* Making Memories; *Alphabet stamps:* PSX Design; *Stamping ink:* Ranger Industries; *Other:* Fabric, photo mat and dictionary definition.

"Self-Confidence"

by Pam Kopka
New Galilee, PA

Supplies *Cork paper:* Magic Scraps; *Copper tiles and strips:* Global Solutions; *Fibers:* Rubba Dub Dub, Art Sanctum; *Computer fonts:* Aardvark, downloaded from the Internet; Times New Roman, Microsoft Word; *Embossing enamel:* Suze Weinberg.

◆ Pam cut out the circle designs on the copper strips, then used them as rivet-like accents on her layout.

◆ Note how Pam made small slits in her cardstock squares to anchor the fiber as she wrapped it.

◆ Pam embedded the copper tiles in molten embossing enamel.

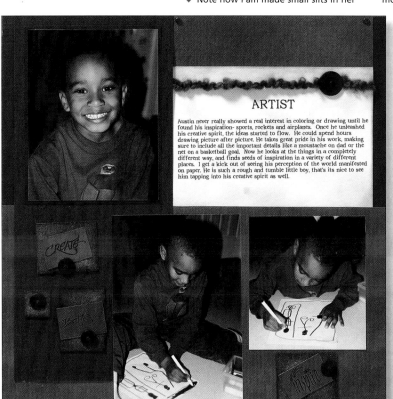

"Artist"

by Taunya Dismond
Lee's Summit, NC

◆ Notes Taunya, "Cork paper is very fragile, so be careful when cutting it. Also, remember that it's hard to move once the paper's been glued down. A nice characteristic? Cork paper is very forgiving. If you make a mistake while chalking or inking the edges, you can remove any excess ink with a cosmetic sponge."

◆ Taunya used buttons to anchor the tags and fiber and create a visual triangle.

Supplies *Cork paper:* Magic Scraps; *Copper tiles and strips:* Global Solutions; *Fibers:* Rubba Dub Dub, Art Sanctum; *Patterned paper:* Karen Foster Design; *Computer font:* CK Newsprint, "Fresh Fonts" CD, *Creating Keepsakes; Stamping ink:* Adirondack, Ranger Industries; *Buttons:* Making Memories; *Embroidery floss:* DMC; *Chalk:* Stampin' Up!

Idea to note: Taunya inked the edges of the cork paper to match her color scheme.

"Marty and Keith"

**by Lynne Montgomery
Gilbert, AZ**

◆ To help tie her layout together visually, Lynne framed her photos with copper and threaded fiber through copper eyelets. Note how she cut the diamond shapes from the copper strips and used them to accentuate her focal-point photo.

◆ Lynne used walnut ink to add rich color to her background paper.

Supplies *Cork paper:* Magic Scraps; *Copper tiles and strips:* Global Solutions; *Fibers:* Rubba Dub Dub, Art Sanctum; *Walnut ink:* Postmodern Design; *Copper sheeting:* St. Louis Crafts, Inc.; *Eyelets and magnetic date stamp:* Making Memories; *Letter stamps:* PSX Design; *Stamping ink:* Ranger Industries; *Sequin pins:* Fibre-Craft Materials Corp.; *Computer font:* CK Italic, "The Art of Creative Lettering" CD, *Creating Keepsakes.*

PHOTOS BY ANITA MATEJKA

You likely have thousands of pictures of your son or daughter smiling brightly at the camera. These shots are priceless, but what about the flip side? That's right—why not take some pictures from behind? It's a great way to capture a special moment in time or the bond between two subjects without interrupting a precious exchange. Try catching these moments from behind:

◆ Little friends holding hands
◆ A child playing with an animal
◆ Your child clinging tightly to the hand of a loved one
◆ A dad giving his child a piggyback ride
◆ Kids walking down a path covered with leaves, or along the beach at sunset

When taking photos from behind your subject, pay attention to the placement of the sun. If it's a bright day, you may need to use a fill flash to avoid shadows on your subject. Or, use the sun to your advantage to create an emotional silhouette photograph. Position yourself and your subject so you're both facing the sun (the sun will be farthest away from you). If the sun is too far down in the sky, avoid flares by using a lens hood or your hand to shade the top of your lens.

Every once in a while, don't forget to change perspectives and photograph your children from behind. You'll be surprised at the special moments lurking there!

—by Anita Matejka

sticker savvy

Give stickers proper placement

Figure 1. Fabric-print border stickers can add warmth to your layout. *Page by Mary Larson.* **Supplies** *Patterned paper:* Carolee's Creations; *Border stickers:* Mrs. Grossman's; *Title sticker:* Phrase Café, Sticko by EK Success; *Epoxy letters:* Bits & Baubles, Creative Imaginations; *Computer fonts:* CK Muddy, "The Best of Creative Lettering" Super Combo CD, *Creating Keepsakes; Other:* Textured paper.

WANT TO CREATE a fast page? An easy page? A classy page? Use stickers! In February, we showed you techniques to customize your stickers. If you're like me, you can always use more sticker ideas! This month we'll look at where to place stickers for maximum impact.

You've got all kinds of stickers to choose from: vellum stickers, clear word and quote stickers, realistic photo stickers, pewter stickers, fabric stickers and more. You can find stickers that are specifically designed as titles, borders and accents. Regardless of the sticker type, the trick is to place it effectively on your page without overwhelming your photos. Consider the following ideas:

BY MARY LARSON

Border Stickers

Don't confine your border stickers to just the border of your page. Try these ideas:

◆ Wrap your sticker randomly around a frame. Cut out the middle of the frame, then wrap the border sticker around the edges. *Tip:* Don't wrap the sticker all the way around. Instead, trim it off just over the edge, then fold the sticker under.

◆ Place sticker strips on your photo mat, then snip them off at the edges (Figure 1).

◆ Put shortened strips around a matted photo for a fast frame (Figure 2).

◆ Cut short strips of a border sticker and place them horizontally for quick impact (Figure 3).

Realistic Photo Stickers

Get a 3-D look without the bulk or hassle! Realistic stickers are photographic images of bulky items such as buttons, flowers, wire, leaves and more. It's hard to distinguish them from the real thing without touching them (Figures 4 and 5).

Figure 2. Frame your photo with a border sticker. *Sample by Mary Larson.* **Supplies** *Border stickers:* Karen Foster Design; *Other:* Nailheads.

Figure 3. Clip your border stickers for a change of pace. *Sample by Mary Larson.* **Supplies** *Border stickers:* Doodlebug Design; *Brads:* American Tag Company.

Figure 4. Button stickers add a homey look without the bulk. *Sample by Mary Larson.* **Supplies** *Patterned paper:* K & Company; *Stickers:* Sharon Ann Collection, The C-Thru Ruler Co.; Snip-Its, Pebbles, Inc. *Title sticker:* SewWhats, Sticko.

Figure 5. Accentuate a black-and-white border with cheery flower stickers. *Sample by Mary Larson.* **Supplies** *Stickers:* Sticky Pix, Paper House Productions; *Other:* Slide holders.

THEY TUG AT OUR HEARTSTRINGS. OUR SWEET LITTLE GIRLS.

THE dolls, THE dress UP, THE dances, THE TWIRLS,

Sweet girl

Metallic Stickers

Metallic stickers (some paper, some actual metal) are a charming way to add today's popular metallic look to scrapbook pages.

◆ Cluster metallic stickers in a corner of a page (Figure 6).

◆ Adhere metallic stickers over a fiber-wrapped border (Figure 7).

Figure 6. Flower stickers embellish a sweet picture. *Page by Mary Larson.* **Supplies** *Patterned paper:* Chatterbox; *Stickers:* Class A' Peels, Stampendous!; *Quote sticker:* Shotz Thoughtz, Creative Imaginations; *Title sticker:* Phrase Café, Sticko by EK Success; *Brads:* Karen Foster Design.

Figure 7. Create a sophisticated border with pewter stickers. *Sample by Mary Larson.* **Supplies** *Patterned paper:* K & Company; *Pewter stickers:* Magenta; *Fibers:* Magic Scraps and Rubba Dub Dub, Art Sanctum.

Word and Quote Stickers

Word and quote stickers (some of my favorites!) speed up page creation by providing you with ready-made titles and sentiments. Cut them apart if desired to create the perfect saying for your page.

More Sticker Ideas

Don't stop yet—try these other sticker ideas as well:

◆ "Ground" stickers (keep them from looking like they're floating randomly) by placing them on cardstock. Center your photos on the page, then place your matted stickers around them. For variety, make the blocks different sizes (Figure 8).

◆ Highlight one special sticker by centering it over four squares of cardstock or patterned paper. This will feature the sticker without taking the focus away from the photos (Figure 9).

◆ Create a checkerboard design with cardstock or pat-terned paper, then place small stickers in the middle of each block. Use this concept for borders, frames or accents (Figure 10).

A Few Pointers

Keep the following pointers in mind whenever you use stickers:

❶ Instead of spreading them out on your page, group different-sized yet similar stickers. Avoid the "sticker sneeze" look.

❷ Less is more. It may sound cliché, but it's true. Just because a sticker sheet comes with 10 stickers doesn't mean you have to use all (or even half) of them on a layout. One sticker, strategically placed, is often enough.

❸ Make sure your stickers don't compete with your photos. Your focal points should be your photo and journaling, not the accents.

Figure 8. Rustic colors and stickers give pages an autumnal feel. *Page by Mary Larson.* **Supplies** *Patterned vellum:* Shotz, Creative Imaginations; *Stickers:* Karen Foster Design; *Phrase stickers:* Shotz Thoughtz, Creative Imaginations; *Mesh:* Maruyama, Magenta; *Brads:* American Tag Company; *Computer font:* CK Twilight, "Fresh Fonts" CD, *Creating Keepsakes*; *Other:* Fibers.

❹ Still having trouble placing stickers? Keep the "visual triangle" approach in mind. Place your stickers where they help create a visual triangle with other page elements.

Now that you've got some quick and fun tips for sticker placement, pull out that stash. Give the ideas above a try! ❤

Figure 10. Use a checkerboard design for a fast and easy accent. *Sample by Mary Larson.* **Supplies** *Stickers:* Sticko by EK Success; *Textured paper:* Artistic Scrapper, Creative Imaginations.

Figure 9. Silhouette stickers look great on textured paper. *Page by Mary Larson.* **Supplies** *Patterned paper:* Freckle Press; *Metallic paper:* Magenta; *Stickers:* The Okie-Dokie Press; *Title sticker:* Shotz Thoughtz, Creative Imaginations; *Computer font:* CK Typewriter, "Fresh Fonts" CD, *Creating Keepsakes*.

tantalizing lettering templates

The basics, plus ways to liven up your titles and journaling

Figure 1. Layered templates take the guesswork out of matting letters. *Page by Mary Larson.* **Supplies** *Patterned paper and vellum:* K & Company; *Lettering template:* Frances Meyer; *Stickers:* Magenta (border) and Shotz Thoughtz, Creative Imaginations; *Small brads:* Magic Scraps; *Tag:* Making Memories, *Rub-ons:* Bradwear, Creative Imaginations, *Computer font:* AmerTypeCnd, downloaded from the Internet; *Metallic rub-ons:* Craf-T Products; *Other:* Name plaques and brads.

"HOW MANY LETTERING TEMPLATES do *you* have?" my scrapbooking buddies frequently ask each other. After counting, some of us sheepishly reply that we have 30, 40 or more— we're addicted! And, with so many cool new templates available, these numbers are sure to increase. Let's look at some basic and not-so-basic ways to use them!

BY MARY LARSON

The Basics

If you're new to lettering templates, let's talk about the basics:

❶ After choosing your template, lay it upside down on your cardstock. If you're using patterned paper, make sure the pattern is reversed.

❷ Holding the template steady, trace the first letter with a sharp pencil. If I'm using a letter with an inside cutout (like the letter "A"), I usually trace the inside piece first, then center the letter on it. Repeat this process for each letter.

❸ Cut out the center of the letter first; you'll have more paper to hold as you work. I prefer using a craft knife and a glass mat, but you can also use pointed scissors. Just punch the tip through the paper and carefully cut along the lines.

❹ Cut the outer lines. Scissors or a craft knife work well here.

Tip: For a clean cut with no tearing, cut *into* the corners instead of *away* from them.

Figure 2. Emphasize dry embossed letters with metallic rub-ons. *Sample by Mary Larson.* **Supplies** *Lettering template:* Frances Meyer; *Metallic rub-ons:* Craf-T Products; *Pen:* Doodle Dotter, Tombow.

Add Pressure

The trick to dry embossing an entire word is to line up the template on the right side of your cardstock and tape it down with low-tack tape. Flip it over and apply pressure with your stylus. In Figure 1, I used a template set that includes letters and shadow letters. I chose to emboss the shadows and cut out the letters. Here are more ideas for layered templates:

◆ Trace the shadow and dry emboss the letter.
◆ Dry emboss both the shadow and the letter.
◆ Dry emboss the shadow, then trace and color in the letter.

Add extra dimension to the dry embossing by lightly applying metallic rub-ons (Figure 2). Get another great look with these techniques by dry embossing the letters on vellum.

Figure 3. Heat emboss your title for a raised look. *Sample by Mary Larson.* **Supplies** *Lettering templates:* Typewriter, ScrapPagerz.com ("My 4"); Casual Caps, Wordsworth ("Sons"); *Rub-ons:* Bradwear, Creative Imaginations; *Stamping ink:* ColorBox, Clearsnap; *Embossing powder:* Stamp-n-Stuff; *Other:* Brads.

Apply Heat

Add extra dimension or detail to your letters with three noteworthy techniques:

❶ Apply stamping ink in the letter openings. Sprinkle embossing powder over the inked areas, then melt the powder with a heat gun (Figure 3).

❷ Trace the letters with a marker, then stamp small, random images inside the letters. Sprinkle the stamped images with embossing powder, then heat and cut out the letters.

❸ Trace the letters with a marker, then apply splotches of ink. Sprinkle the inked areas with embossing powder and heat before cutting each letter.

Decorate with Embellishments

I love embellishing my cut-out letters (Figures 4 and 5). In Figure 6, I cut out the letters, then embellished them with 3-D letters. Consider using these accents:

- Beads
- Fiber, ribbon and embroidery floss
- Buttons
- Eyelets and brads
- Punches
- Craft wire

Figure 4. Small embossed stars give dimension to a plain title. *Sample by Mary Larson.* **Supplies** *Lettering templates:* Big Fat Font, ScrapPagerz.com; *Stamping ink:* ColorBox, Clearsnap; *Embossing powder:* PSX Design; *Fibers:* On The Surface.

Figure 5. Splotchy ink gives a rough texture to a boyish title. *Sample by Mary Larson.* **Supplies** *Lettering template:* Spunky Better Letters, Déjà Views; *Rub-ons:* Bradwear, Creative Imaginations; *Stamping ink:* Brilliance, Tsukineko; *Embossing powder:* Stamp-n-Stuff; *Sticker:* Shotz Thoughtz, Creative Imaginations; *Tag:* Making Memories.

Figure 6. Double up on letters for an interesting way to accent a page. *Page by Mary Larson.* **Supplies** *Patterned paper:* SEI; *Lettering templates:* Lindzey ("Messy") and Script ("swim"), ScrapPagerz.com; *Water accents and letters:* Creative Imaginations; *Computer font:* CK Sassy, "Fresh Fonts" CD, *Creating Keepsakes*; *Eyelets:* Doodlebug Design; *Pen:* Zig Writer, EK Success; *Other:* Fibers.

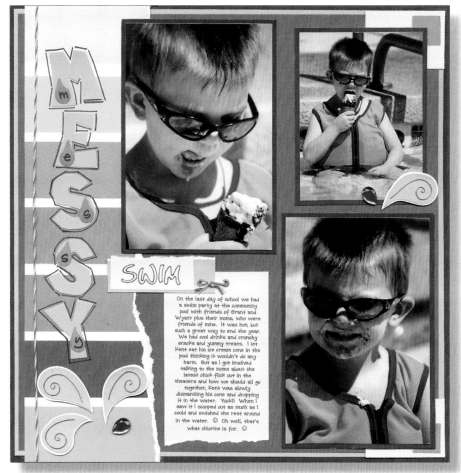

On the last day of school we had a swim party at the community pool with friends of Grant and Wyatt plus their moms, who were friends of mine. It was hot, but such a great way to end the year. We had cool drinks and crunchy snacks and yummy treats. I let Kent eat his ice cream cone in the pool thinking it wouldn't do any harm. But as I got involved talking to the moms about the latest chick flick out in the theaters and how we should all go together, Kent was slowly dismantling his cone and dropping it in the water. Yuck!! When I saw it I scooped out as much as I could and swished the rest around in the water. ☺ Oh well, that's what chlorine is for. ☺

Adorn with Texture

Cut your letters from textured paper. In Figure 7, I crumpled a piece of cardstock, smoothed it out and lightly applied metallic rub-ons. Next, I traced the letters on the reverse side of the cardstock, then cut them out.

Figure 7. Create a stone look with crumpled cardstock and metallic rub-ons. *Sample by Mary Larson.* **Supplies** *Lettering templates:* ABC Tracers, EK Success; *Metallic rub-ons:* Craf-T Products; *Brads:* American Tag Company.

Fill in the Blanks

A quick way to use lettering templates is to color inside the letters. In Figure 8, I dabbed ink inside the lettering template for a fun look. Before inking letters with centers, trace and cut out the inside piece, then adhere it temporarily before dabbing on the ink. You can also try the following:

◆ Draw plaids, stripes, dots or random scribbles with markers or colored pencils.
◆ Get a soft look with chalk.
◆ Add a metallic sheen to your letters with metallic rub-ons.

Alter Your Medium

In addition to cardstock and patterned paper, try cutting letters out of the following:

◆ Fabric, felt or foam
◆ Cork
◆ Duplicate photos
◆ Thin metal
◆ Specialty and handmade papers

Figure 8. Create a typewriter look by randomly applying stamping ink to a standard-font lettering template. *Sample by Mary Larson.* **Supplies** *Lettering template:* Typewriter, ScrapPagerz.com; *Stamping ink:* Fiskars; *Computer font:* 1942, downloaded from the Internet; *Circle accents:* Rollabind; *Metallic rub-ons:* Craf-T Products; *Other:* Ribbon.

Position Them

Place your letters on tags, punches or inside frames. I dropped letters into a slide protector sheet to create my title in Figure 9.

The Sky's the Limit

◆ Mix fonts from different templates for a whimsical look.
◆ Don't use the same template font or size for your entire title. Instead, use a small template for your secondary words and a larger size for the primary ones.
◆ If possible, match your journaling font with your template title font.

I've just covered a few of the many ways you can use lettering templates. Use these ideas as a springboard to create your own unique look!

Figure 9. Tuck letters and mesh into a slide sheet protector. *Page by Mary Larson.* **Supplies** *Patterned paper:* Sandylion; *Lettering template:* Smarty Better Letters, Déjà Views, The C-Thru Ruler Co.; *Mesh:* Magenta; *Eyelets:* Making Memories; *Computer fonts:* 2Peas Evergreen and 2Peas Gift, downloaded from *www.twopeasinabucket.com*; *Punch label:* Dymo; *Chalk:* Craf-T Products; *Other:* Slide protector.

Raised Letters

For a unique raised title, use embossing paste with your lettering template. This white paste adds a subtle, elegant look on white cardstock, or a dramatic look when used on dark paper. For variety, mix colored pigment powder in the paste. Or, you can wait until the paste dries and apply chalk, stamping ink or metallic rub-ons.

To apply the paste, follow these simple steps:

❶ Tape your lettering template in place with low-tack tape.

❷ Apply the paste with a metal palette knife (or a cake frosting spatula).

❸ Pull the knife flat across the surface of the template to scrape off the excess paste.

❹ Remove the tape and pull the lettering template straight up. Allow the paste to dry for an hour. Repeat these steps with each letter.

—*Lori Fairbanks, Creating Keepsakes*

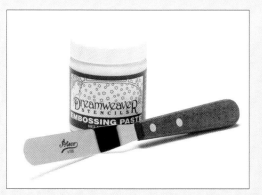

Create raised letters with embossing paste. *Samples by Lori Fairbanks.* **Supplies** *Lettering template:* Brush, Wordsworth; *Embossing paste:* Dreamweaver.

Etched Letters

To create an etched look with a lettering template, follow these easy steps:

1 Cover a large area of cardstock with embossing ink. Sprinkle the ink with embossing powder and heat it. Before the powder cools, add a second layer of powder and heat it. Let the powder cool completely.

2 Lay your template over the embossed area. Use a sharp tool in a pulling motion to etch the area within the letter.

3 Carefully crack the embossing powder.

Note: This technique doesn't work with smooth cardstock because it etches off in chunks. The cardstock needs to be a little porous for this to work.

—*Darcee Thompson, Preston, ID* ❤

Use the lettering template as a guide to carve letters from a heat-embossed title block. *Page by Darcee Thompson.* **Supplies** *Embossing powder:* Stampendous!; *Embossing ink:* Top Boss, Clearsnap; *Square rings:* 7 Gypsies; *Computer font:* CK Artisan, Becky Higgins' "Creative Clips and Fonts" CD, *Creating Keepsakes; Lettering template:* Cursive, Wordsworth; *Fibers:* Rubba Dub Dub, Art Sanctum.

LETTERING TEMPLATE MANUFACTURERS

Looking for lettering templates? Check out the offerings from the following companies:

◆ Chatterbox
   www.chatterboxinc.com

◆ Close To My Heart
   www.closetomyheart.com

◆ Club Scrap
   www.clubscrap.com

◆ Cock-A-Doodle Design
   www.cockadoodledesign.com

◆ The Crafter's Workshop
   www.thecraftersworkshop.com

◆ Cut-It-Up
   www.cut-it-up.com

◆ D. J. Inkers
   www.djinkers.com

◆ Déjà Views, The C-Thru Ruler Co.
   www.cthruruler.com

◆ EK Success
   www.eksuccess.com

◆ EZ2Cut, Accu-Cut Systems
   www.ez2cutshapemakers.com

◆ Fiskars
   www.fiskars.com

◆ Frances Meyer
   www.francesmeyer.com

◆ Provo Craft
   www.creativexpress.com

◆ Puzzle Mates
   www.puzzlemates.com

◆ ScrapPagerz.com
   www.scrappagerz.com

◆ Wordsworth
   www.wordsworthstamps.com

ILLUSTRATION BY CAROL NORBY

50 Favorite Quotes

by Lisa Bearnson

Express your feelings with another's help

"A quotation at the right moment is like bread in a famine."
— *The Talmud*

Call me crazy, but rather than borrow novels from the local library, I check out quote books. I read page after page and copy my favorite sayings into a spiral-bound quote book.

When did my love of quotes begin? Years ago, when I was a child. While growing up, I collected hundreds of quotes and hung my favorites on my bedroom walls. Even now you'll find quotes in my house—they're written directly on the wall in an artistic style. (See "Quotes, Home Style" on page 268.)

I also love to include quotes on my scrapbook pages. While the quotes don't take the place of my journaling, they help me express what I feel about life and the people around me. Read on for a sampling of my favorite quotes, plus a handy list of places to find memorable sayings. I've also included inspirational pages that incorporate quotes as well. →

THERE WAS NEVER
A CHILD SO LOVELY
BUT

HER
MOTHER WAS GLAD TO
GET HER ASLEEP

TAMI AND DELANEY

FEBRUARY 1999

From the first time that I saw this picture, I loved it. It was taken at our "Baby's First St. Valentine's Day Party" held at Pauline's house. With eight babies and eight mums and assorted other friends and relatives attending, it was quite the scene. When I saw TAMI sitting there, with DELANEY asleep in her arms, I thought it was the picture of serenity. Of course, much later when I showed the picture to TAMI, she had something quite different to say about the photograph. She just saw relief.

TAMI and I met at Rolling Strollers, an exercise group for mums with babies. DELANEY was only six weeks old at the time and Katja was six months. We became friends quickly and spent lots of time together, with our babes. We endured many of the firsts and the anxieties of new mums together; first teeth, breastfeeding experiences and the dreaded returning to work. Like all mums, I thought my Katja was the most beautiful baby ever, but when I saw DELANEY, I thought she was just mesmerising with her startling blue eyes and her porcelain complexion.

When this picture was taken, we both had just started back to work. I had decided to continue to breastfeed in spite of my pregnancy with Quinn. TAMI was in the process of weaning DELANEY. DELANEY was not accepting this transition a very well and TAMI was frazzled from the stress and fatigue of a fussy baby. When I came across a quote from RALPH WALDO EMERSON, I thought, nothing could describe this scene better.

While the page at left shares a universal message with just a photo and quote, the facing page adds meaning by sharing the mom's thoughts about weaning and returning to work. *Pages by LauraLinda Rudy.* **Supplies** *Red vellum:* The Paper Company; *Stickers:* Mrs. Grossman's; *Computer font for title:* Lemon Chicken (title), downloaded from the Internet and traced onto the page; Adorable (journaling), package unknown; *Ink pad:* Memories; *Pen:* Pigma Micron, Sakura. *Idea to note:* LauraLinda colored the white stickers black with an inkpad. *Quote:* "There was never a child so lovely but her mother was glad to get her asleep." — Adapted from Ralph Waldo Emerson

"Life itself is the proper binge."
— Julia Childs

"Children are the living messages we send to a time we will not see."
— John H. Whitehead

"No day is so bad it can't be fixed with a nap."
— Carrie Snow

"Where is home? Home is where the heart can laugh without shyness. Home is where the heart's tears can dry at their own pace."
— Vernon G. Baker

"God has given us our memories that we might have roses in December."
— J.M. Barrie

"Love the moment, and the energy of that moment will spread beyond all boundaries."
— Corita Kent

"A mother's arms are made of tenderness and children sleep soundly in them."
— Victor Hugo

"There is more to life than increasing its speed."
— Gandhi

"A friend is someone who knows the song in your heart and can sing it back to you when you have forgotten the words."
— Unknown

"Earth's crammed with heaven and every common bush afire with God."
— Elizabeth Barrett Browning

"Whatever you can do or dream you can, begin it. Boldness has power, genius, and magic in it. Begin it now."
— Goethe

Some feelings are so broad, they're hard to put into words. A photo and quote can help convey your message. *Page by Krista Boivie.* **Supplies** *Page software:* QuarkXPress; *Computer fonts:* AGaramond and Carpenter ITC, downloaded from the Internet. *Idea to note:* Krista manipulated the picture in Adobe Photoshop 7.0 with a variety of filters. *Quote:* "If I could tell you what I mean, there would be no point in dancing." — Isadora Duncan

"Love the moment, and the energy of that moment will spread beyond all boundaries."

— Corita Kent

Combine a lovely quote with equally lovely accents and journaling on your layout. *Page by Caroline Davis.* **Supplies** *Computer fonts:* 2Peas Crumbly Gingersnap, 2Peas Distorted, 2Peas Distressed and 2Peas Think Small, downloaded from *www.twopeasinabucket.com; Tags:* Avery Dennison and Impress Rubber Stamps; *Circle punches:* EK Success (small, for top of tag) and Family Treasures (large, for cutting out word "Molly"); *Buttons:* Hillcreek Designs; *Embroidery floss:* DMC. *Quote:* "Youth is, after all, just a moment . . . but it is the moment, the spark that you always carry in your heart." — Raisa Gorbachev

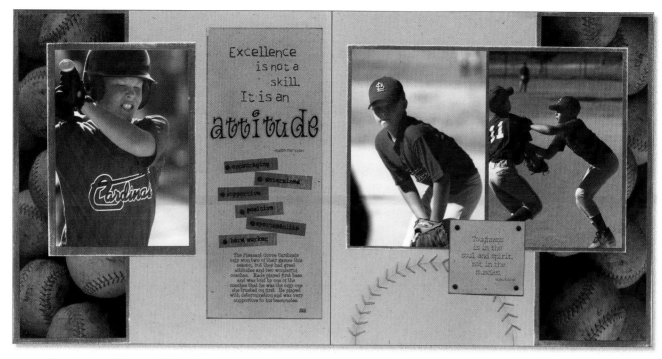

Use quotes to reinforce positive traits in a loved one. *Pages by Kristy Banks.* **Supplies** *Baseball photo strips:* Shotz, Creative Imaginations; *Letter stickers:* Provo Craft; *Stamping ink (around baseball stitches):* Tsukineko; *"2002" date stamp:* OfficeMax; *Computer fonts:* CK Carbon Copy ("Excellence is . . ."), CK Gutenberg ("Toughness is . . ."), CK Typewriter ("encouraging," "determined," etc.) and CK Stenographer (journaling), "Fresh Fonts" CD, *Creating Keepsakes; Other:* Linen jute and brads. *Ideas to note:* To create a baseball look, Kristy placed a half-circle of paper at the bottom of her page, then stitched and chalked it. She created a weathered look on her photo frames with sandpaper. *Quotes:* "Excellence is not a skill. It is an attitude." — Ralph Marston. "Toughness is in the soul and spirit, not in the muscles." — Alex Karras

"Once in a lifetime one should be allowed to have as much sweetness as one can possibly want and hold."
— Judith Obrey

"Where there is great love, there are always miracles."
— Willa Cather

"Faith is the bird that feels the light and sings when the dawn is still dark."
— Rabindnanath Tagore

"Alone we can do so little, together we can do so much."
— Helen Keller

"Seek not outside yourself—heaven is within."
— Mary Lou Cook

"A baby is God's opinion the world should go on."
— Carl Sandburg

Quote Sites and Quote Books

Looking for the perfect quote for a page? Consider the following:

QUOTE SITES

- *www.curiousquotes.com*
- *www.quotegarden.com*
- *www.quotablequotes.com*
- *www.inspirationpeak.com*
- *www.twopeasinabucket.com*

QUOTE BOOKS

- *Up Words for Down Days* (Allen Klein)
- *Leaves of Gold* (Leaves of Gold gift books)
- Susan Branch books (Little, Brown & Company)
- *Timeless Wisdom* (Gary W. Fenchuk)
- *The Scrapbooker's Best Friend, Volumes 1–3* (Chatterbox, EK Success)

Make an inspiring picture and quote more personal by including names, dates and ages in your photo mat. *Page by Lisa Russo.* **Supplies** *Toile fabric:* Jo-Ann Fabrics; *Computer font:* Rodin, P22 Type Foundry; *Embroidery floss:* Making Memories; *Other:* Mini brad. *Idea to note:* To adhere the toile, Lisa ran it through her Xyron machine. *Quote:* "Children are the hands by which we take hold of heaven." — Henry Ward Beecher

"Where there is great love, there are always miracles."

— Willa Cather

Liven your quote with fun decorative accents. *Page by Wendy Anderson.* **Supplies** *Patterned papers:* Colors By Design (green) and Mustard Moon (gray); *Eyelets, metal eyelet tags, snap, button and craft wire:* Making Memories; *Beads:* Treasure Beadz, Art Accents; *Letter stickers:* me & my BIG ideas; *Pen:* Zig Writer, EK Success; *Glue dots:* Glue Dots International. *Idea to note:* The rectangular metal eyelet tags were longer than Wendy wanted, so she snipped off the end with scissors. *Quote:* "There is only one way to lead a child down the right path . . . that is to go that way yourself." — Unknown

On Using Quotes
by Jana Lillie

Decide what works best for you

Some people have a way with words. Others, struggle. Enter the quote. The ready-made solution is touching, profound, and—best of all—complete. You can tap the power of a "perfect" thought that poetically mirrors your own.

When creating a quote page, determine what will meet your needs. If you want to convey a simple message fast (or wish to set a general tone), use a photo/quote combination. If you want to add factual value, include names and dates. If you want to boost emotional value (and this is my favorite), make the extra effort to include personal journaling as well. Help the quote come to life by sharing what it means for you and your memories.

Compare the effectiveness of the approaches in Figures 1a and 1b and 2a and 2b. Create the type of quote page that's best for your particular memory.

Figure 1a. Great photo, great quote, great accents—no wonder this page was selected for the *2003 Scrapbook Idea Book. Page by Cindy Schow.* **Supplies** *Patterned paper:* SEI; *Vellum:* Provo Craft; *Punches:* Darice (mini sun), EK Success (snowflake) and Marvy Uchida (large square); *Computer font:* TwizotHmk, "Hallmark Card Studio 2" CD, Sierra Home. *Quote:* "Friendship isn't a big thing; it's a million little things." — Author unknown

Figure 2a. Okay, not a quote, but a whimsical mix of words conveying a child's personality. *Page by Carol Banks, photo by Val Joyce.* **Supplies** *Patterned paper and vellum stickers:* Provo Craft; *Vellum:* Paper Reflections, DMD Industries; *Mini letter stickers:* Provo Craft; *Chalk:* Craf-T Products; *Pen:* Zig Writer, EK Success.

"Family faces are magic mirrors. Looking at people who belong to us, we see the past, present and future."
— Gail Lumet Buckley

"Imagination is more important than knowledge."
— Albert Einstein

"The only way to have a friend is to be one."
— Ralph Waldo Emerson

"A mother's love for her child is like nothing else in the world. It knows no law, no pity, it dares all things and crushes down remorselessly all that stands in its path."
— Agatha Christie

"Life's truest happiness is in the friendships we make along the way."
— Anonymous

"Babies are such a nice way to start people."
— Don Herold

"Life isn't a matter of milestones, but of moments."
— Rose Kennedy

"Seek the wisdom of the ages, but look at the world through the eyes of a child."
— Ron Wild

"We've had bad luck with our kids—they've all grown up."
— Christopher Morley

"A heart in love with beauty never grows old."
— Turkish proverb

"Life is a paradise for those who love many things with a passion."
— Leo Buscaglia

"I am beginning to learn that it is the sweet, simple things of life which are the real ones after all."

— Laura Ingalls Wilder

"Your only obligation in any lifetime is to be true to yourself."

— Richard Bach

"Think big thoughts but relish small pleasures."

— H. Jackson Brown Jr.

"A true friend is one soul in two bodies."

— Aristotle

"Enjoy the little things in life, for one day you may look back and realize they were the big things."

— Anonymous

"If there is anything better than to be loved it is loving."

— Anonymous

"There are only two ways to live your life. One is as though nothing is a miracle. The other is as if everything is."

— Albert Einstein

"The only thing worth stealing is a kiss from a sleeping child."

— Joe Houldsworth

"When you love someone all your saved-up wishes start coming out."

— Elizabeth Bowen

"Just living is not enough. One must have sunshine, freedom and a little flower."

— Hans Christian Anderson

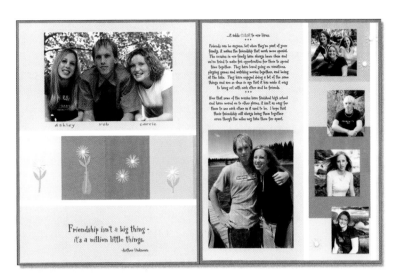

Figure 1b. This expanded version of the page at left includes more pictures. It also tells how the friends are cousins who are close in age and have a history of going on vacations, playing games and watching movies together. *Pages by Cindy Schow.*

Figure 2b. Including a letter on a facing page provides a date, personal words of affection, and insight into the personalities of mother and daughter. *Pages by Carol Banks.*

Idea to note: For the edge of the large journaling block, Carol ripped a piece of paper, then heavily chalked the ripped edge with various colors. She laid this paper down on the journaling block and with her finger rubbed the chalk off the ripped paper onto the journaling block, creating an uneven but clearly delineated border. Carol repeated this on all sides, re-chalking the edge and dragging it from there to her cardstock with her finger.

Journaling to note: "Caitlin Joy, this picture seems to capture your essence at two years old. You blew into our lives on a fair spring wind and quickly took root in our hearts. What a joy—and sometimes a challenge—to see your personality take shape! Your nature is not prim and cultivated like a rose; not flamboyant and exotic like a lily; definitely not shy and demure like a violet. You are fresh, vibrant and fun-loving. . . . Your nature is to celebrate life. You are our wildflower!"

Explain below a quote how it applies to you and your loved ones. *Page by Kerri Bradford.* **Supplies** *Patterned papers:* Carolee's Creations (dark purple) and Colors By Design (light purple); *Flower accent:* Jolee's Boutique, Stickopotamus; *Computer fonts:* Vivaldi ("I know . . ."), DTC; CAC Leslie (journaling), downloaded from the Internet. *Quote:* "I know well that happiness is in the little things." — John Ruskin

"Home is a place where the small are great and the great are small."

— Anonymous

"Children are the keys of paradise."
— Richard Stoddard

"If you obey all the rules, you miss all the fun."
— Katharine Hepburn

"And forget not that the earth delights to feel your bare feet and the winds long to play with your hair."
— Kahlil Gibran

"There is no such thing in anyone's life as an unimportant day."
— Alexander Woollcott

"Be glad of life, because it gives you the chance to love and to work and to play and to look up at the stars."
— Henry Van Dyke

"One of the secrets of a happy life is continuous small treats."
— Iris Murdoch

"Some people, no matter how old they get, never lose their beauty— they merely move it from their faces into their hearts."
— Anonymous

"A dream is a wish your heart makes—when you're fast asleep."
— Cinderella

"The art of being happy lies in the power of extracting happiness from common things."
— Henry Ward Beecher

"Love every day. Each one is so short and they are so few."
— Norman Vincent Peale

"Home is a place where the small are great and the great are small."
— Anonymous

"Where there is love, there are always miracles."
— Willa Cather ♥

Quotes, Home Style

Enter Lisa Bearnson's home, and you'll find these inspiring quotes on the walls:

FRONT ENTRY:
"Where we love is home—home that our feet may leave, but not our hearts."
— Oliver Wendell Holmes
(This quote is painted directly on the wall.)

KITCHEN:
"The beauty of family brings us cherished memories we wish to hold forever; for it is through our memories that our hearts find their way home." — Flavia

MUD ROOM:
"Happiness must grow in one's own garden." — Mary Engelbreit

TOY ROOM:
"Sweet childish days that were as long as twenty days are now." — Unknown

organizing your thoughts, part 1

Figure 1. Coming up with the perfect journaling was easy, thanks to a note previously written and stored in an index box. *Page by Rebecca Sower.* **Supplies** *Letter stickers:* Liz King, EK Success; *Punches:* Family Treasures (corner rounder and filmstrip) and The Punch Bunch (square); *Eyelets:* Making Memories; *Fibers:* The Card Ladies; *Pen:* Zig Writer, EK Success; *Other:* Paper clip. *Idea to note:* Rebecca punched small rectangles along the edge of the journaling cardstock, then tore the edges to imitate a page torn from a notepad.

Be prepared and create a gathering place

SOME PEOPLE are born organized. They keep immaculate homes. When they need an item, they know exactly where to find it. Their recipes are categorized and filed alphabetically. You know the type.

Then there are the rest of us—the organizational wannabes. I call myself "creatively chaotic," but we all know that's just a fancy name for *disorganized*. True, I do feel more creative in a slightly scattered setting, but I'm not sure it's worth it. Few things frustrate me more than sitting down to journal

ARTICLE BY REBECCA SOWER

on a layout and not being able to remember what I once *knew* I would never forget. Can you relate?

I resolved a while ago that—no matter what—I wouldn't assume my memory would serve me well. I began a primitive system of jotting down notes about the events, thoughts and feelings that I wanted to record in my scrapbooks for future generations. I wrote down *anything* I wanted to hold onto—something cute my child said, how a news story affected me, how a certain quotation fit how I felt at the time.

I soon had a big, scattered collection of paper scraps and scribbled thoughts to include *somewhere* within the pages of my scrapbooks. I fretted about where to store them. I couldn't risk heartfelt words or important thoughts getting lost because I wasn't *organized*. What I needed was a system!

REBECCA'S SYSTEM

After a lot of thought, I came up with a four-step system that's been working wonders for me. I figured out how to move my snippets of journaling from scattered piles to a finished layout (Figure 1).

The first two steps of my system, "Be Prepared" and "Create a Gathering Place," are covered here.

Next month, I'll share my other two steps, "Play the Matching Game" and "See It Through."

❶ Be Prepared

You never know when a moment of journaling inspiration might hit. When it does, be ready! I invested in a dozen small notepads (Figure 2) that are strategically placed in areas where I spend a lot of time—the car, my purse, the kitchen, my studio and even by the shower. For long road trips, I carry a hand-held voice recorder.

If you're like me, your best journaling ideas don't come when you sit down to work on a page layout.

Figure 2. Keep small notepads in accessible places around the house and office. Capturing your important thoughts will be much more convenient.

Figure 3. It was easy to recall the events from our zoo trip. Since I jotted down notes on my pre-printed "trigger" cards, I didn't have to rely on my memory for the day's highlights. *Pages by Rebecca Sower.* **Supplies** *Specialty paper:* Books by Hand; *Mesh ribbon:* Loose Ends; *Pen:* Tombow; *Fiber:* Adornaments, EK Success; *Punch:* EK Success; *Embossing powder:* PSX Design; *Other:* Wire, fasteners, buttons, copper washer and eyelet.

Too often, that kind of journaling comes across as half-hearted, space-filling, "did it 'cause I had to" writing. That doesn't do justice to your photos.

The best time to capture journaling for a great shot is usually during or right after the event that inspired the photo (see Figure 3). And the best thoughts seem to surface when we're carrying out rote actions such as cooking, driving or folding laundry. That's when we need to write. Trust me, *you can't trust your memory.*

I've included specific examples (in colored text) of when I grabbed my pen and pad (yes, right in the middle of what I was doing) and scribbled down my thoughts. This same process can work for you.

One night, I was cooking dinner and realized I was fixing a dish that had become a family favorite. The thought came to me that I wanted →

Figure 4. Create a gathering place, such as an index card box, for your journaling notes. You'll have a ready reference when you sit down to scrapbook them.

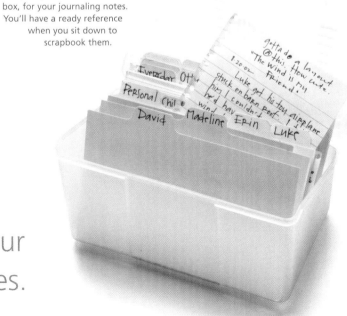

Start recording and capturing your priceless memories.

my daughters to have the recipe and someday cook the dish for their own families. I picked up my handy pen and pad, jotted down the date, then wrote: *"Mexican Casserole. Pass recipe down to girls. Tell how they liked to help me spread the layers of tortillas, cheese, etc. One of Daddy's favorites."* This process took about 30 seconds. Will I include the recipe in my daughters' scrapbooks or a family recipe book? I don't know yet. But that scrap of paper means I've written down the idea so I won't forget it later on.

My daughter had just started sixth grade when she popped the "Mom, may I start wearing make-up?" question. Here's what I scribbled down at the red light after the conversation ended: *"Madeline (so I'll know where to file the note later). Thursday, August 15, 2002. In car on way home from school, you ask if you can start wearing make-up. On the inside I screamed, "Nooo!" but on the outside I said, "Well, I think my mom let me start wearing lip gloss when I was in sixth grade, so let me think about it and we'll talk." (Groan!) I'm not ready for this—why are you growing up so fast?!"* Again, what I jotted down during the length of one red light pins down a new chapter in my daughter's life. Now, it's there on paper, not just floating around in that unreliable space in my head.

One of my children came home from my mom's house one day with a storybook I recognized from my childhood. I wrote: *"My Childhood (for filing purposes). November 12, 2001. Mom sent home a book with my kids that was mine as a child. One of my favorites. A Gift-Bear for the King. Scan cover and include in my scrapbook. Keep book in family to pass down. Fond feelings—Karen (my older sister) reading the book to me and eventually learning to read it myself. Even more special—reading that same book to my children."*

When it comes to writing, you can include just about anything in your scrapbooks and journals. The key is this: If it's important to you, it's important!

❷ Create a Gathering Place

Now that you have little notes and scraps of life scattered here and there, what's next? Pull them all together in one place! An index card holder or accordion file works well. While some people may choose to type the text into a computer once a week, I file my snips of paper and journaling reminders in an index box. I can then pull out what I need whenever I'm ready to scrapbook it.

I've broken my filing system down into the following cate-

gories. Use those that apply to your own situation (see Figure 5).

- **Family Members** (I include a section for each member, including myself)
- **My Childhood** (I share what I remember from my younger years)
- **Quotes, Poems, Sayings, Etc.** (I include only quotes that speak to *me* and reflect *my* feelings)
- **Spiritual Matters** (I share moments of inspiration, reverence and reflection)
- **Family Pets** (I record memories of these important members of the family)
- **Everyday** (I include the snips of today that I want to remember)
- **Events** (I include notes on the events and occasions that are specific to my life)
- **Holiday** (I record ideas for holiday journaling)
- **Other** (This is my catch-all for everything else and a must-have!)

Consider these other category ideas: Marriage (I put all my lovey-dovey thoughts in my "David" category), Extended Family, Family History, Hobbies and Interests, Home and Garden, School and Career.

You might also include a monthly section, a place to file the play-by-play aspects of your family's life. Then, you can refer to the appropriate month and incorporate that

You never know when a moment of journaling inspiration might hit. When it does, be ready!

Figure 5. What do you want to remember about your activities? Pre-print general topics (and allow extra writing space) on cards sized for your file box. After the event, write down the important points and any design ideas you want to include in your layout.

date-specific journaling into your layouts.

Stick with It

As time passes, you'll find yourself tweaking the system to suit your needs. The important thing is to get started and stick with it. Here are a few extra pointers as you get organized:

• Date *everything*! That means you should include the event date and the date you write the journaling.

• Mention photo ideas. When a complementary photo comes to mind, make a note of it.

• Write down design or title ideas. If inspiration hits and you come up with a great layout idea or title, record it.

• Pre-print fill-in-the blank cards that act as a trigger for what you want to record (see Figure 5). Believe me, if you take a few minutes immediately after an event to jot down your thoughts, it's easier to scrapbook that event later.

• Don't worry about whether you have photos to go with what you're writing down. If that worries you, you're missing the whole point. If you must have photos (and it's not a requirement—really!), use "extra" photos or take photos to support your notes.

Are you motivated to get started? I hope so. Remember, we'll cover the other two steps next month. In the meantime, try the above. They'll help you capture and record those priceless and irreplaceable memories. ❤

Any surprises?

Weather:

What did we do?

My personal feelings about the event:

When it was time to go...

Other notes:

Any surprises? *We had a hilarious Blue Ice accident. Blue ice, juice splattered everywhere. Oops!*

Weather: *very hot for June*

What did we do? *animals of course. I was glad kids didn't beg to play on huge playground. Saw a animal shows; baby tigers*

My personal feelings about the event: *Reminder to Rebecca: Having fun w/ kids is so much more important than work!!*

When it was time to go... *we were all hot and sticky. The girls hugged good-bye. Said we need to get them together more*

Other notes: *often*
Stood in line forever to buy rubber snake for Lulu that I probably could've picked up at Walmart.

Event:

Date & Time:

Why:

Who came:

Where:

What we ate & drank:

What I'd most like to remember:

Anything unusual happen?

organizing your thoughts, part 2

Play the matching game and see it through

Figure 1. Once you organize your thoughts, use creative boxes and lettering to draw attention to important journaling. *Page by Rebecca Sower.* **Supplies** *Page accents:* Cut-It-Up; *Embossed cardstock:* Lasting Impressions for Paper; *Square punch:* Marvy Uchida; *Patterned vellum:* Over The Moon, EK Success; *Pen:* Zig Writer, EK Success.

"The written word remains. The spoken word takes wing and cannot be recalled." — *Horace*

Wow! What a powerful thought. Imagine if we actually recorded all the thoughts and events we wanted to share with people in the future (see Figure 1). It's much simpler to incorporate meaningful journaling in your scrapbooks if you have a system for organizing your thoughts.

Last month, I shared two of four steps to organizing your journaling thoughts. Here's a quick overview:

❶ **Be prepared.** Keep small notepads in the places where you spend a lot of time. Jot down journaling thoughts and ideas as they come to mind.

❷ **Create a gathering place.** Use an index card file or your computer to keep those scattered-yet-worthy journaling thoughts in one convenient location.

ARTICLE BY REBECCA SOWER

Figure 2. If you write and organize your journaling thoughts before you begin a layout, the scrapbooking process will flow more smoothly. *Pages by Rebecca Sower.* **Supplies** *Computer font:* Antique Type, downloaded from the Internet; *Star eyelets:* Doodlebug Designs; *Pen:* Zig Writer, EK Success; *Star punch:* EK Success; *Word plaques:* Details, Making Memories; *Bandana accent:* Jolee's Boutique, Stickopotamus; *Other:* Jute.

The next two steps, covered in depth here, are:

❸ **Play the matching game.** This step is fairly self-explanatory, but I take a few unique approaches to make sure the photos work well with my words. Here's what I do.

First, I decide what type of journaling to use: event or non-event.

♦ **Event journaling** is tied to a certain occasion or event. When I scrapbook an event, it's easy to find the journaling for that event in my index box and match those words to the photos.

Sometimes I want to journal beyond one particular event. For instance, when I was ready to scrapbook my son's first birthday, I matched the journaling to the photos from the event. (That was the easy part.) Next, I referenced some thoughts and feelings I wrote down as he approached the end of his first year. I wove some of those impressions into the design of the layout (see Figure 2). The layout was easy to put together because I had already penned specific thoughts. I didn't have to strain my memory trying to recall how I felt about my son's first year of life.

In an ideal world, we could work on our layouts as soon as we got our photos from the developer. But we all know the reality—we have no idea how much time will pass before we sit down to scrapbook an occasion. This gives us all the more reason to write the details down while they're still fresh on our minds.

♦ **Non-event journaling** is not tied to a specific event. With it, I often use photos as visual "props." They portray the thoughts and feelings captured on my snippets of paper—the ones I've gathered and filed in my handy index box. I flip through the notes to find journaling thoughts waiting to be transformed into a layout.

Picture this: One day, I was thumbing through my file box and ran across the notes I'd jotted down shortly after my son started preschool. The words begged for a photo of my son with that mischievous, "watch out for me" look on his face. (It's not difficult to find one of those photos!) And there I had it (see Figure 3a)—the photos *and* the journaling I needed for a great layout (see Figure 3b).

As I pointed out last issue, I often remember specific photos while writing a journaling thought.

So Many Pictures, So Little Time

If you're like many scrapbookers, you're facing "truckloads" of photos. You wonder how you can possibly muster volumes of words for each photograph you own. Relax! Often, a few simple words are all you need for a set of photos. The important thing to remember is this: Make sure the things you want to say are included somewhere in the pages of your scrapbooks!

A quick photo reference in my notes gives me the foundation for a great layout. Many times as I flip through new photos at the photo lab, I'll say, "Oh, that's perfect!" for a journaling thought I've already written. When the journaling is written before the photos are developed, the scrapbooking process is much simpler.

4 See it through. Since you've already completed the journaling and gathered all the photos, this final step should be a snap. This is when I simply sit down (actually, I scrapbook standing up) and put everything in its place. Here's my typical putting-it-together process:

First, I spread out the photographs and journaling for the layout. I don't concentrate on anything other than the photos that best represent my journaling. I might see one or two photos or several to group together. I don't worry about leftover photos—I know I'll eventually use them somewhere else.

Next, I remove anything I'm not using on the layout. For me, it's best to remove all distractions from my work area.

Finally, I think about the design elements and journaling approach. Does the layout warrant a fun or creative approach? Should the journaling be something out of the ordinary?

If I work several photos into a one-page layout, I usually don't go for an over-the-top journaling approach. I just write my sentences by hand. (If I'm desperate for time, I sometimes revert to computer-generated type.) These are the layouts where I want the photographs to take center stage.

If my journaling is in paragraph format, such as a letter, it won't be read frequently by anyone other than the person for whom it was

Figure 3a. Pair your journaling thoughts with just the right photos to express your message. *Page by Rebecca Sower.* **Supplies** *Tag accent:* Rebecca Sower Designs, EK Success; *Computer font:* CK Constitution, "Fresh Fonts" CD, *Creating Keepsakes; Pens:* Zig Writer and Dotta-Riffic, EK Success; *Other:* Date stamp, thread and buttons.

intended. Sometimes the words are more powerful than the photos. In those cases, I take an "I want the world to know" approach in how I present my words. I do my best to capture the attention of the average reader (see Figure 1).

The Design Stage

Now it's time to work on the part that got me hooked on scrapbooking in the first place—the *design* stage! Here's where I leave you to work on your own. You're already a design expert, right? Enjoy yourself! Use design symbolism, create a mood with the decorative elements you choose—the sky's the limit!

With the forethought and

Figure 3b. If you jot down journaling thoughts as they come to mind, scrapbooking your memories will be much easier.

preparation I put into my journaling, I avoid wondering, "What in the world should I journal on this layout?" It's all about getting a system, paying more attention to your journaling, and capturing your thoughts as they occur. Your family and future generations will thank you for your efforts! ♥

say it with a song

Record your favorite lyrics on a layout

Page by Debbie Rose.
Supplies *Rubber stamps*: Junque; *Eyelet letters*: Making Memories; *Letter template*: Wordsworth; *Computer font*: Goudy Old Style, downloaded from the Internet; *Embossing powder*: Stampendous!; *Pen*: Uni-ball Gel Impact, Sanford; *Fibers*: Fibers By The Yard. *Idea to note*: Debbie heat embossed the "N" and "Y" with gold embossing powder.

In A New York MINUTE

"*...everything can change.*" The Eagles could not have known the irony these lyrics would one day carry, but just ask any New Yorker or American how true these words are after 9/11. Here we are in Central Park in 1998. How blissfully ignorant we were to what would some day happen in our beloved city. But the photo also reminds us of the excitement and joys that we experience in any given "New York minute". It captures how we spent one New York minute in our favorite Central Park spot - Sheep Meadow. As residents of the greatest city in the world, in a New York minute we have passed through Times Square at night under the neon lights, sipped Frappuccinos by the fountain at Lincoln Center, passed by Yitzhak Pearlman or Lauren Bacall as they strolled down our block. We would rather savor the pleasures of one New York minute than an hour in any other city in the world.

JUST THE OTHER DAY, I had to smile as I listened to my daughter, Jaeme, sing, "Baby, baby, I'm taken with the notion, to love you with the sweetest of devotion." Jaeme has been taken with singer Amy Grant ever since Jaeme was a baby, and I used to sing (admittedly off-key) the song "Baby, Baby" to her.

Now that Jaeme's a five year old with plans to become the next "American Idol," she belts out her own version of the song, complete with all the right dance moves. As Jaeme has gone from pacifier to pop star, from cute to cool, this song has played in the background of our lives.

Besides wanting to be a star, Jaeme also writes her own songs. My favorite? "Nobody Has a Key to My Office Door!" She inherited this talent from her great-grandfather (who played seven instruments), her grandfather (a guitar player who just recorded an album), and her Uncle Bud (a singer, songwriter and recording artist). I'm excited to create a lyrics layout that tells the story behind my daughter's musical heritage.

Paired with personal journaling on a layout, song lyrics are a wonderful way to tell a story. Here are seven layouts that use lyrics to help tell a story. →

ARTICLE BY RACHEL THOMAE

Layout on page 277

Page creator: Debbie Rose, New York, NY
Song title: "In a New York Minute"
Artist: The Eagles
Album: *Hell Freezes Over*

Debbie selected this song to reflect on the changes in New York City after 9/11. Her journaling tells us why she loves living in New York.

Journaling Spotlight: "In a New York Minute, . . . everything can change. The Eagles could not have known the irony these lyrics would one day carry, but just ask any New Yorker or American how true these words are after 9/11. Here we are in Central Park in 1998. How blissfully ignorant we were to what would someday happen in our beloved city. But the photo also reminds us of the excitement and joys that we experience in any given 'New York Minute.' "

Song Starter: Do you have a song that reminds you of a special connection to a certain place or time in your life? Include the lyrics on your page, along with an explanation of why the song triggers those memories.

Page creator: Melanie Howard, Oka, QC, Canada
Song title: "If You're Not the One"
Artist: Daniel Bedingfield
Album: *Gotta Get Thru This*

Melanie chose a heart-touching song to chronicle her heartbreak after the end of a romantic relationship. Notes Melanie, "This page is very personal, but part of what I call my scrapbook therapy."

Journaling Spotlight: "Why would I set something like this in a memory book? Because people, for all their hopes and dreams, get disappointed in life. I have suffered some serious heartbreak in my time, and I suffer through it now once again. Perhaps years from now, the way I feel will seem trivial, given the perspective that life and time can place on events. But today, I mourn the loss of yet another dream. I deal with the setback that hope diminished can place on a person. . . ."

Song Starters: Did a certain song help you get through a tough time in your life? What lyrics helped you make a difficult transition?

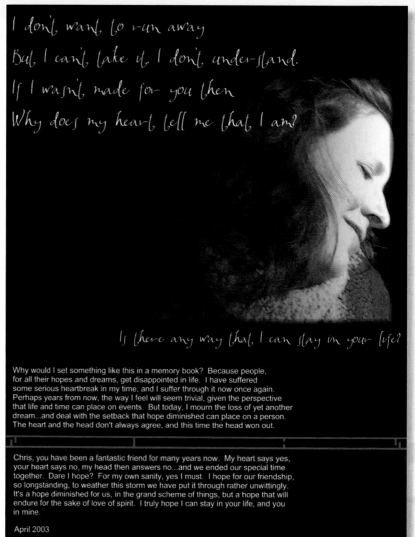

I don't want to run away
But I can't take it, I don't understand.
If I wasn't made for you then
Why does my heart tell me that I am?

Is there any way that I can stay in your life?

Why would I set something like this in a memory book? Because people, for all their hopes and dreams, get disappointed in life. I have suffered some serious heartbreak in my time, and I suffer through it now once again. Perhaps years from now, the way I feel will seem trivial, given the perspective that life and time can place on events. But today, I mourn the loss of yet another dream...and deal with the setback that hope diminished can place on a person. The heart and the head don't always agree, and this time the head won out.

Chris, you have been a fantastic friend for many years now. My heart says yes, your heart says no, my head then answers no...and we ended our special time together. Dare I hope? For my own sanity, yes I must. I hope for our friendship, so longstanding, to weather this storm we have put it through rather unwittingly. It's a hope diminished for us, in the grand scheme of things, but a hope that will endure for the sake of love of spirit. I truly hope I can stay in your life, and you in mine.

April 2003

Page by Melanie Howard. **Supplies** *Computer program*: MsPhotoDraw; *Computer fonts*: Dragonfly, downloaded from *twopeasinabucket.com*; Arial, Microsoft Word. *Idea to note*: Melanie's layout is entirely computer generated. She changed the words in the song to reflect how she "mis-sings" the song's lyrics and make them applicable to her page.

I took my love, I took it down

Climbed a mountain and I turned around

I saw my reflection in the snow covered hills

'Till the landslide brought me down

Oh, mirror in the sky

What is love?

Can the child within my heart rise above

Can I sail through the changing ocean tides

Can I handle the seasons of my life

Well, I've been afraid of changing

'Cause I've built my life around you

But time makes you get bolder

Even children get older

And I'm getting older too

Oh, take my love, take it down

Climb a mountain and turn around

If you see my reflection in the snow covered hills

Well, the landslide will bring it down

If you see my reflection in the snow covered hills

Well, the landslide will bring it down

Her landslide

It's track No. 2 on the new Dixie Chicks CD and the one Mom's declared to be her theme song. The lyrics and mood reflect the place she is at in her life and I often think it gives Mom strength each time she listens to it.

For the first time in 26 years, Mom will be living in an empty nest. No longer having to focus on the task of raising a family, she can now turn the focus inward on herself and Dad. But it's a difficult thing, because although they deeply love each other, she isn't sure if they have anything in common any more. Can they be a couple again? Can they regain that crazy love they once had for each other? Au if, heaven forbid, they can't...will she have the strength to move forward with hs life? It is Mom's moment of truth and her time to start living for herself...a terrifying proposition for such a caring and unselfish person. But Mom's strength is unfathomable...something she's exhibited with grace many a time before. She will take it through whatever outcome and be stronger for it. It's time for her to spread HR wings, now that she's finished helping the four of us kids spread ours, and find the person she is meant to be.

Pages by Erin Lincoln. **Supplies** *Eyelet charms, snaps and brads:* Making Memories; *Computer fonts:* 2Peas Flea Market, downloaded from *www.twopeasinabucket.com;* CK Constitution, "Fresh Fonts" CD, *Creating Keepsakes; Stickers and bradwear:* Creative Imaginations.

Page creator: Erin Lincoln, Frederick, MD
Song title: "Landslide"
Artist: Stevie Nicks (performed by the Dixie Chicks)
Album: *Home*

Erin created a layout around her mom's self-described theme song, "Landslide." The song's lyrics help Erin's mom have strength to get through the challenges of being an empty-nester now that her children have left home.

Journaling Spotlight: "It's track No. 2 on the new Dixie Chicks CD and one Mom's declared to be her theme song. The lyrics and mood reflect the place she is at in her life, and I often think it gives Mom strength each time she listens to it. . . . It's time for Mom to spread her wings, now that she's finished helping the four of us kids spread ours, and find the person she is meant to be."

Song Starters: What's your theme song? Have you had different theme songs through the years? Why does a particular song inspire or lift you?

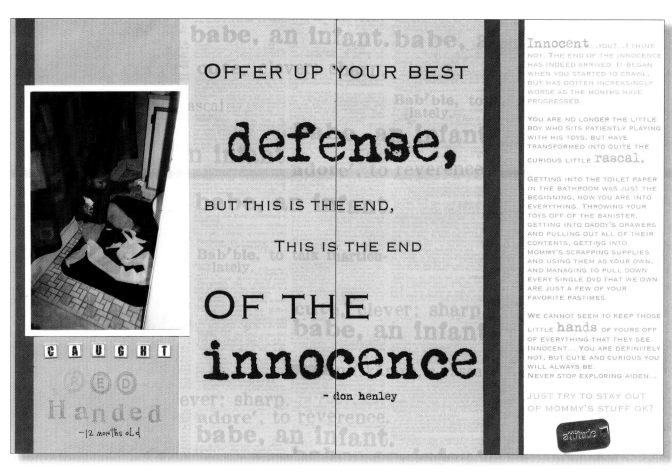

OFFER UP YOUR BEST

defense,

BUT THIS IS THE END,

THIS IS THE END

OF THE

innocence

– don henley

CAUGHT

RED Handed

–12 months old

Innocent...YOU?...I THINK NOT. THE END OF THE INNOCENCE HAS INDEED ARRIVED. IT BEGAN WHEN YOU STARTED TO CRAWL, BUT HAS GOTTEN INCREASINGLY WORSE AS THE MONTHS HAVE PROGRESSED.

YOU ARE NO LONGER THE LITTLE BOY WHO SITS PATIENTLY PLAYING WITH HIS TOYS, BUT HAVE TRANSFORMED INTO QUITE THE CURIOUS LITTLE rascal.

GETTING INTO THE TOILET PAPER IN THE BATHROOM WAS JUST THE BEGINNING, NOW YOU ARE INTO EVERYTHING. THROWING YOUR TOYS OFF OF THE BANISTER, GETTING INTO DADDY'S DRAWERS AND PULLING OUT ALL OF THEIR CONTENTS, GETTING INTO MOMMY'S SCRAPPING SUPPLIES AND USING THEM AS YOUR OWN, AND MANAGING TO PULL DOWN EVERY SINGLE DVD THAT WE OWN ARE JUST A FEW OF YOUR FAVORITE PASTIMES.

WE CANNOT SEEM TO KEEP THOSE LITTLE hands OF YOURS OFF OF EVERYTHING THAT THEY SEE. INNOCENT... YOU ARE DEFINITELY NOT, BUT CUTE AND CURIOUS YOU WILL ALWAYS BE. NEVER STOP EXPLORING AIDEN...

JUST TRY TO STAY OUT OF MOMMY'S STUFF OK?

attitude

Pages by Nia Reddy. **Supplies** *Patterned paper:* 7 Gypsies; *Poetry dog tag:* Chronicle Books; *Computer fonts:* Mom's Typewriter and Copperplate Light, downloaded from the Internet; *Rubber stamps:* Junque; *Stamping ink:* Colorbox, Clearsnap; *Transparency sheet:* Apollo. *Idea to note:* Nia printed her quote on a transparency sheet and overlaid it on patterned paper.

Page creator: Nia Reddy, Brooklyn, NY
Song title: "End of the Innocence"
Artist: Don Henley
Album: *The End of the Innocence*

Nia portrays her son's changing behavior—from innocent baby to adventurous toddler—on a scrapbook layout titled "The End of the Innocence."

Journaling Spotlight: "Innocent . . . You? . . . I think not. The end of the innocence has indeed arrived. It began when you started to crawl but has gotten increasingly worse as the months have progressed. You are no longer the little boy who sits patiently playing with his toys but have transformed into quite the curious little rascal. Never stop exploring, Aiden. . . . Just try to stay out of Mommy's stuff, OK?"

Song Starters: How can you use song lyrics to document your child's changing behaviors or developmental stages? Can you use song lyrics to take a humorous look at a frustrating or challenging time in your life?

Pages by Leah Yourstone. **Supplies** *Glossy cardstock:* Paper Zone; *Stamping ink and organdy ribbon:* Close To My Heart; *Paint:* Lumiere, Jacquard Products; *Rubber stamps:* Club Scrap (letters), Inkadinkadoo (clock and dress) and Hero Arts (script); *Paper ribbon:* Loose Ends; *Computer font:* Night Sky, Club Scrap; *Other:* Fabric and bead trim, library book pocket and paper clips. *Ideas to note:* Leah created unique background paper by painting glossy white cardstock with paint and dye ink. She added stamped images, beaded trim, and bits of hand-painted paper ribbon.

Page creator: Leah Yourstone, Issaquah, WA
Song title: "Little Miss Magic"
Artist: Jimmy Buffett
Album: *Coconut Telegraph*

Leah was inspired to create a page about her daughter's hopes and dreams after hearing the chorus to "Little Miss Magic." The lyrics tucked into the journaling pocket include the phrases "Little Miss Magic, what you gonna be? Little Miss Magic, just can't wait to see."

Journaling Spotlight: "Melanie, probably the best thing about being a parent is watching your child grow up. I am constantly wondering what you will be like when you grow up. What will you be? Perhaps a mother like I am? At this point in your life, you can be anything you want to. At six years old, you say that you want to be an archeologist, a dancer, a 'spy,' a scrapbooker, and a mother. . . . You also say you want to live with me forever. (I will always remember that!)"

Song Starters: Does your child have a favorite song that describes what the child wants to be when he or she is an adult? Do you have a favorite song that inspires you to fulfill a wish for yourself or someone else?

She's the daughter I never dreamed I would have. She is the spitting image of her Daddy. His eyes look right at me when I look at her. She's precious, she's spunky, she's beautiful and she's complicated.

Unconditional

She has seen more change in her young life than can be called fair. She wears it well and you would never know.

How do you tell a little girl to look forward to stability and home, to unconditional love and to forever? The answer is, you cannot. We can only lead by example.

I love her and I will always be around for her when she wants me there. My greatest hope for her is that she will one day understand the unconditional love I have for her. I will keep it right here until she is ready for it.

When you feel afraid .When you lose your way. I'll find you. Just try to smile and dry your eyes. I will bring back the moon in to your sky. Wherever you went remember darling. I'll be there to sing to you. I promise you. I promise to. Comfort you and sing to you.

There's so much to learn. When you want me there. I'll show you.

Though you grow away. No matter how you change. I'll know you. When you tire of life alone. There will always be one sure way back home.

Through the years you'll always be a lullaby in the heart of the child in me. Anytime anywhere I'll be there for you. I'll be there to sing to you. I promise you. I promise to.
                                                    Kenny Loggins

Pages by Cheryl Bahneman. **Supplies** *Mini brads*: Stampin' Up!; *Computer font*: MS Hei, downloaded from the Internet.

Page creator: Cheryl Bahneman, Acworth, GA
Song title: "Cody's Song"
Artist: Kenny Loggins
Album: *Leap of Faith*

Cheryl affirms her unconditional love for her stepdaughter in this layout.

Journaling Spotlight: "She's the daughter I never dreamed I would have. She is the spitting image of her daddy. His eyes look right at me when I look at her. She's precious, she's spunky, she's beautiful and she's complicated. She has seen more change in her young life than can be called fair. She wears it well and you would never know.

"How do you tell a little girl to look forward to stability and home, to unconditional love and to forever? The answer is, you cannot. We can only lead by example.

"I love her and I will always be around for her when she wants me there. My greatest hope for her is that she will one day understand the unconditional love I have for her. I will keep it right here until she is ready for it."

Song Starters: Does a certain song invoke feelings about a certain person in your life? Why does the song remind you of him or her?

Page by Cathy Zielske. **Supplies** Slide holders: ScrapWorks; Computer font: Cacaelia, Adobe Systems.

and where was I before the day

that I first saw your lovely face

the luckiest

From our earliest days, you've always had the magic touch for picking a song to play for me that would melt my heart. I still remember the first time I heard the Tom Waits' song "Blind Love," that you put on a mix for me, and I knew: he really likes me. I'll also never forget the time we were driving in the car, and had been going through some of our growing pains together, and you popped a tape into the cassette player and there was Van Morrison singing, "Have I told you lately that I love you?"

But of all the songs you have played for me over the years, none has touched me more than track number 19 on my 2003 Valentine's Day Love Mix that you made

for me. "The Luckiest" by Ben Folds, is one of those songs that grabs your heart and squeezes until you're almost certain it's going to burst. I was sitting at the computer working when the song came on. As I sat and listened, the tears filled my eyes upon hearing the words, especially the verse that said, "Next door, there's an old man, who lived to his nineties and one day, passed away, in his sleep, and his wife, she stayed for a couple of days and passed away. I'm sorry I know that's a strange way to tell you that I know, we belong."

That you didn't write the words was irrelevant. That you would echo the sentiment is a pure gift of your love to me. And I am, the luckiest.

Page creator: Cathy Zielske, St. Paul, MN
Song title: "The Luckiest"
Artist: Ben Folds
Album: *Rockin' the Suburbs*

Cathy professes her love for her husband in a layout inspired by a special song that he selected for her on Valentine's Day.

Journaling Spotlight: ". . . But of all the songs you have played for me over the years, none has touched me more than track number 19 on my 2003 Valentine's Day Love Mix that you made for me. 'The Luckiest' by Ben Folds is one of those songs that grabs your heart and squeezes until you're almost certain it's going to burst.

"I was sitting at the computer when the song came on. As I sat and listened, the tears filled my eyes upon hearing the words, especially the verse that said, 'Next door, there's an old man, who lived to his nineties and one day passed away in his sleep, and his wife, she stayed for a couple of days and passed away. I'm sorry, I know that's a strange way to tell

you that I know we belong.'

"That you didn't write the words was irrelevant. That you would echo the sentiment is a pure gift of your love to me. And I am the luckiest."

Song Starters: What special romantic songs have you shared with your significant other? What song was playing when you met for the first time? What song was playing on the night you got engaged? What's "your song" and why? ❤

try our scribble tags alphabet

LUCKY FOR US SCRAPBOOKERS, tags aren't just for packages anymore. Whether they're funky, classy, whimsical or elegant, tags are a charming addition to any scrapbook page (Figure 1).

The Scribble Tags Alphabet is a perfect way to incorporate the "tag craze" into your scrapbook (Figure 2). It offers the appearance of three-dimensional tags, without the bulk of store-bought tags. Even better? You can customize these tags to create any look you want. At first glance, you might think you need to be an artist to draw this alphabet, but by using easy-to-create templates or a ruler, you can draw perfect tags every time.

Creating Round Tags

Follow these simple steps to create round tags (see Figure 3):

❶ Use a template to draw two circles, one slightly smaller than the other. (*Tip:* Create templates by punching two circles from vellum, discarding the punched pieces, and using the "holes" as a tracing template. You'll be able to see through the vellum to line up the circles.)

❷ Draw a small circle in the tag and use another circle template to draw in the wire hanger.

❸ Use colored pencils, chalks or markers to color the tag.

❹ Use a colored pencil, sharpened to a fine point, to scribble text over the tag. You can use squiggly lines to simulate text, or you can write actual words (illegible is better).

Creating Rectangular Tags

To create rectangular tags, with or without cords, follow these steps (see Figure 4):

❶ Use a ruler, or freehand a rectangular tag. Leave a space along the top if you want to add cords. Next, draw a circle, leaving a section open at the top of the tag. (*Hint:* Trace a pre-made tag, cut it out and use the hole as a template.)

❷ Draw two small rectangles along the top of the tag.

❸ Add two small connecting rectangles between the hole and the top of the tag. Sketch in the two cords as shown.

❹ Draw a larger circle around the small hole and add a shadow to the right and bottom sides of the tag. Color and add scribbled text as shown in the instructions for round tags.

Figure 1. Utilize the versatility of tags to create custom looks for your scrapbook pages. *Page by Karen Burniston.* **Supplies** *Die cuts:* Deluxe Cuts; *Computer fonts:* Casmira and Pinnacle, downloaded from the Internet; *Pen:* Zig Writer, EK Success; *Colored pencils:* Prismacolor, Sanford.

ARTICLE BY KAREN BURNISTON

Figure 2. The Scribble Tags Alphabet can be funky, classy, whimsical or elegant, depending on the tag style, colors and letters you choose. *Alphabet by Karen Burniston.* **Supplies** *Pen:* Zig Writer, EK Success; *Colored pencils:* Prismacolor, Sanford; *Chalks:* Stampin' Up!.

STEP BY STEP

Figure 3. Follow these simple steps to create round tags.

Figure 4. Follow these simple steps to create rectangular tags.

Figure 5. Once you've drawn your tags, follow these steps to draw letters inside the tags.

Figure 6. Have fun with the Scribble Tags Alphabet. Use your imagination to come up with your own variations. *Samples by Karen Burniston.* **"OUR TRIP" Supplies** *Compass rubber stamp:* Above the Mark; *Stamping ink:* Adirondack, Ranger Industries; *Photo corners:* Canson; *Chalk:* Stampin' Up!; *Colored pencils:* Prismacolor, Sanford; *Black pen:* Zig Writer, EK Success. **"ART" Supplies** *Black pen:* Zig Writer, EK Success; *Metallic silver pen:* Zig Painty, EK Success; *Metallic blue eyelets:* Source unknown; *Rubber stamps (photo corners):* Moe Wubba; *Stamping ink:* Ancient Page, Tsukineko.

Creating the Lettering

After creating the shaped tags and filling in the scribble writing background, follow these steps to create the letters (see Figure 5):

❶ Lightly pencil lowercase letters, one per tag.

❷ Sketch in a fatter letter around the pencil lines, adding serifs.

❸ Outline with a black pen and erase your pencil lines.

❹ Fill in letters with a black pen.

Adding a Custom Touch

Once you've gotten the hang of the Scribble Tags Alphabet, let your creativity flow. Try using uppercase letters, stickers or a computer font. Design tags in different shapes, or create patterned backgrounds instead of scribbles. For additional ideas, check out the samples in Figure 6. The possibilities are endless!

Dig out those circle templates, punches or cutters. Dust off that ruler and pencil. Sharpen your colored pencils and put that creative spirit to work on some scribble tags. You'll be thrilled with the looks you can create! ❤

Learn fresh ways to create this popular vintage look

Get layout inspiration from an old manual typewriter. *Pages by Anita Matejka.* **Supplies** *Patterned paper:* Provo Craft; *Computer fonts:* Teletype (title) and Lydian BT (journaling), downloaded from the Internet; *Buttons:* Source unknown; *Silver leaf pen:* Formby's; *Other:* Royal Dimensional Magic, Plaid. *Ideas to note:* Anita scanned the yearbook and reduced it to fit her layout. She scanned and enlarged the year on the yearbook.

Faux Typewriter Keys

Typewriter-key accents are a great way to add vintage flair to your pages. From flat to lumpy, here are a few ways to create the look. Stylize your look by changing the color of the key face or border.

3-D TYPEWRITER KEYS

To create this look, gather several ridged buttons of the same size (color doesn't matter). Also gather a silver leaf or black paint pen, a computer printout of your letters (with space to cut around each letter), and Plaid Royal Coat Dimensional Magic or Crystal Lacquer. Next:

❶ Paint your buttons, making sure you cover the sides and ridges. Set the buttons aside to dry.

❷ Print the letters for the keys. In Microsoft Word, you can create white lettering on a black background. To do this, select the "Highlight" or "Shading" button on your toolbar and change the background to black. If you use the highlight button, change your words to white first. (*Note:* Let the printer ink dry for several minutes, so the ink won't run when the liquid is applied.)

❸ Cut or punch out each letter so it will cover the center of the button. Adhere each letter.

❹ Add Crystal Lacquer or Dimensional Magic to the top. Keep the liquid in the center of the button to create a raised effect.

❺ Dry thoroughly.

FLAT TYPEWRITER KEY

Layer two circles and add a small letter sticker to the top layer. Use chalks, metallic rubs, Pearl-Ex, metallic paper or metal to add dimension.

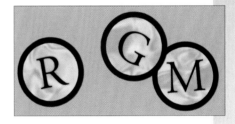

FONT FINDINGS

You can also purchase rubber stamps or sheets of photocopied typewriter keys from your favorite stamping store. Check out the die cuts featured at *www.foofala.com* and the stamps at *www.junque.net.*

For more examples of keys and interesting tidbits about antique typewriters, be sure to visit the following web sites: *www.typewriter.rydia.net,* *www.fontsnthings.com/themes/type-written.html* and *www.free-typewriter-fonts.com.*

—by Anita Matejka

A Lesson in Paper Acidity and Lignin

The up side to textured papers is that they're fun to work with, add dimension and can lend another layer of meaning to your layouts. The down side is that they aren't always acid and lignin free. So, how do you know if your textured paper is safe for your layouts? Test it!

Acid Free?

The easiest and most inexpensive way to test paper's acidity is with a pH pen. The higher the number, the less acidic your paper is. While a pH of 7.0 is considered chemically neutral, any number above 6.5 is considered acid free by national standards. The numbers range from 0 to 14.

But, enough with the science lesson. Let's test your paper. Here's how:

1. Using a pH pen, draw a thin line in a corner or scrap of your paper. If the paper has a coating, tear it, then draw a line in the paper's core.

2. Wait a few seconds.

3. Depending on the pen, if your paper turns yellow, it's acidic. If it turns purple or blue, it's alkaline (acid free). Green means it's a neutral paper.

Some pens come with a color chart to give you a better reading. Others do not.

For a more complex and thorough testing method, visit *www.librarypreservation.org/preservation/paper1.htm.*

Lignin Free?

But what about lignin? Found naturally in wood, lignin is the stuff that makes wood sturdy. However, when wood is ground for paper making, it loses its stability and will eventually darken and decompose with age. (Hence the problem with newspaper, which contains a high amount of lignin.) The grinding process also increases the amount of acid in the paper unless it's chemically treated.

Luckily, you can use a lignin pen. Like the pH pen, it turns color on your testing surface. Check the label for specific color indications.

For a more thorough (but time-intensive) testing method, complete the following steps:

1. Cover half of a piece of textured paper with an opaque cover, such as aluminum foil.

2. Expose the entire surface to strong light for several weeks (the stronger the light, the quicker the results). Natural window light will work.

3. Check the paper periodically. Carefully re-cover the hidden half each time.

4. If the exposed section becomes darker, the paper has a high lignin content. (Think of what newspaper does over time.)

When All Else Fails

What happens if your paper tests acidic? Spray it with an archival spray, such as Archival Mist (*www.preservationtechnologies.com*) or Wei T'o Deacidification Spray (*www.archivalsuppliers.com*). Both products provide an alkaline buffer to prevent acid decay.

At this time, we're unaware of a product that will remove or buffer a high lignin content.

Where to Find Testing Pens

Following is information on where to find testing pens, along with their prices.

Pens to test for acidity

• pH Testing Pen, $3.95, Light Impressions (*www.lightimpressionsdirect.com*)

• Abbey pH Pen, $5.95, Abbey Publications (*http://palimpsest.stanford.edu/byorg/abbey/*)

• Lithco Paper pH Test Pen, $10.85, Lithco, Inc. (*www.lithcoinc.com*)

Pen to test for lignin

• Lignin Indicating Pen, $8.20, University Products (*www.archivalsuppliers.com*)

Note: The chemicals in this pen are hazardous. Be sure to keep it out of reach of children.

Want more information on paper preservation, acidity and lignin? See the CK publication *SOS: Saving Our Scrapbooks* or visit the following web sites:

• *www.preservation.gc.ca*

• *http://aic.stanford.edu/treasure*

• *www.rit.edu/~661www1/*